A SUPERNATURAL WAR

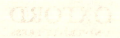

1

A WAR FULL OF WONDER

'Who has not paid his tribute to the superstitions of trench life?'
(Benito Mussolini, November 1915)[1]

Violent collective crises generate many extraordinary personal and national experiences that transcend both our sense of reason and our understanding of the boundaries of the possible. The First World War was no exception. It was considered at the time as a unique portal into the occult or hidden aspect of the human condition, a moment when the spiritual and the psychical fate of humanity was in the balance. Supernatural visions, such as the notorious appearances of ghostly medieval archers at the Battle of Mons in 1914, were reported and debated in a way never before experienced in national public life. Churches, occultists, and psychical researchers across the warring countries saw opportunities to extend their horizons and influence, while the public reached for traditional and novel ways of coping with the realities of warfare. Pursuing the supernatural threads across the combatant countries reveals that magic, religion, and science were comfortable companions in the crucible of modernity that was the First World War.

The First World War has been described as the first scientific conflict in terms of both the innovative, technological developments that were embraced by the military and the new advances in medicine, engineering, physics, and chemistry that were inspired by the war effort across the combatant countries. But the emergent social sciences in America and continental Europe also saw the war as a unique opportunity to further scholarly understanding of behavioural traits and beliefs, and, ultimately, to reveal the essence of what it meant to be human. The battlefields of France and Belgium were considered a unique laboratory for sociological, psychological, and anthropological research. What better environment to study the extremes of physical and mental endurance, to test the effects of stress and the symptoms of trauma as people faced mechanized mass warfare for the first time? The work on shell shock is the most well-known outcome of this academic interest. But there were other areas of social science research that have received much less attention.

Psychology was established as an academic subject in Germany in the 1870s. The First World War presented the youthful discipline with unprecedented opportunities to further cement itself in universities, to prove its value to national interests, and, more specifically, to the military-industrial complex. German psychologists were active, for example, in devising and employing aptitude tests for employees and the military, and for assessing combat motivation. Applied psychologist and frontline officer Paul Plaut used his observations in the field, as well as a questionnaire disseminated at the beginning of the war, to construct a theory of psychic crisis, which he saw as manifesting itself in a variety of ways, including 'superstitious' observances and rituals.[2] But, during the war, and in part thanks to it, America overtook Germany as the powerhouse of psychological research. During the 1920s, one third of all psychology papers in the world were written by American scholars and professionals.[3] Until America entered the war in April 1917, American psychologists could claim to be perfectly placed to make a dispassionate, unbiased assessment of the mental consequences of the conflict amongst military personnel and on the home fronts. In 1915, for instance, George Washington Crile wrote of how he jumped at the chance to take charge of a unit of the American Ambulance in France. He did it for compassionate reasons, but also to further his research on the physical consequences of combat 'when under the influence of the strongest emotional and physical stress', and specifically to study the effects of insomnia and extreme fatigue in soldiers.[4]

American psychologists had also pioneered the scientific study of contemporary superstition as an established academic field. In 1907, the educational psychologist Fletcher Bascom Dresslar published a huge survey of superstitious beliefs among 875 school students, with the purpose of peeping 'into that darkly veiled but interesting mental realm which holds the best preserved remnants of our psychic evolution, as well as those ethnic impulses which are responsible for much of our present behaviour'.[5] Others conducted similar studies during the war years, including a four-year survey of the superstitious beliefs of first-year psychology students at the University of Oregon between 1913 and 1917.[6] Although such research was not extended to the military in this period, American psychologists were alive to the stories of visions and spiritualist seances emanating from Britain and France, and they were intrigued by their significance. In 1916, the pioneering American child psychologist, eugenicist, and first president of the American Psychological Association, Granville Stanley Hall, wrote in his 'Psychological Notes on the War' that, as a striking instance of credulity, the Angels of Mons reports were of great interest to the psychologist as an expression of stress and anxiety in wartime. 'No war was ever so hard on the nerves,' he observed.[7] An editorial in the American *Journal of Educational Psychology* in May 1918 opined that due to the heightened religious feeling, general gloom, and bereavement, 'A particularly sinister form of the weakness of credulity seems to be on the increase among the intellectuals of England and France in the acceptance of evidence of spiritistic manifestations.' It suggested that the flood of literature on spiritualism and psychic phenomena would have a pernicious, lasting psychological effect on the 'uncritical masses' in both countries.[8]

The public build-up to war, and life under war conditions, were explored as an aspect of crowd behaviour by the British social psychologist Wilfred Trotter and others. In his successful book, *Instincts of the Herd in Peace and War* (1916), he described Germany as a 'perfect aggressive herd' characterized by the wolf, and Britain as a 'socialised' herd modelled on bee behaviour.[9] Psychologists and sociologists were also interested in the nature and influence of rumours and false news that disseminated across the combatant populations, and which exposed, like superstition, the same vein of what they considered mass credulity in wartime. What we call fake and viral news today were issues a century ago. There were numerous spy panics, false reports of German atrocities in Belgium, and rumours of Zeppelin raids along the American coast, to name but a few examples. Russians were said to have disembarked in their tens of thousands in Scottish ports. News of the Kaiser's death or suicide circulated periodically. Germans even heard stories of an earthquake in London.[10] From early on in the war, Lucien Graux, who served as a medical doctor at the front and behind the lines, decided to compile all the rumours and false news he could find, some directly from soldiers, but most collected second-hand from newspapers and other printed literature. His motivation was to explore the psychology of optimism and pessimism in wartime. This resulted in a huge multivolume publication of material published in 1918.[11] The same stories also fascinated fellow Frenchman Marc Bloch, who would go on to pioneer the history of mentalities. He enlisted as a sergeant in the infantry, rising to captain, and received the *Légion d'honneur* for his bravery in action. He had a more perceptive and sophisticated intellectual perspective than Graux, dismissing his volumes as 'a long anthology of bits and pieces, borrowed from this or that source'. For Bloch, the rumours he heard at first hand in the trenches were a fascinating insight into the psychology of eyewitness accounts and how legends, gossip, and rumour were born and how they propagated themselves. 'No question should fascinate anyone who loves to reflect on history more than these', he wrote in 1921.[12] He was convinced that military censorship and poor postal connections led to 'a wonderful renewal of oral tradition' in the trenches. Bloch felt his life at the front was like living the history of a preliterate age, and, as such, provided a unique opportunity to learn historical lessons about an otherwise lost world of popular culture. In reality, and with hindsight, the role of print was essential to the spread of rumour and tradition in the trenches, with soldiers' home-made newspapers acting as one medium for the spread of gossip, songs, legends, and humour.[13]

'The superstitious rites that came out of the war or were revived by it deserve a separate study,' said Bloch. 'Mr. Dauzat gives them an important place.' He was referring to the French linguist and folklorist Albert Dauzat, who, in 1918, published a social-psychological study of rumours, legends, prophecies, and superstitions generated by the war.[14] It was the first and, until recently, only comprehensive study of First World War supernatural beliefs, primarily among the French but also with reference to related material from British, Swiss, and German newspapers and research. For Dauzat, like the psychologists, visions, apparitions, prophecies, and the wearing of amulets were all on the same spectrum of credulity, and represented ancient fears and superstitions that were exhibited to a greater or lesser degree by stress on weak or emotive brains. But beyond the physiological and psychological, folklorists like Dauzat were also intrinsically interested in the beliefs expressed and their deeper cultural meaning.

Some European anthropologists and folklorists (the two disciplines intertwined at times) also saw the war as a unique laboratory. From the beginning of the folklore movement, which emerged across Europe in the mid-nineteenth century, the collection of superstitious ideas amongst the rural population had been one of the key activities of its practitioners. By 1914, there was no shortage of evidence for the continued widespread belief in magic, witchcraft, omens, and ghosts. While their interests in folklore, or *Volkskunde* in German, overlapped with the psychologists, and they could be no less condescending in their references to the supernatural at times, folklorists considered superstitions in different ways and contexts, and studied them for different purposes. Otto Mauser, the German director of the Bavarian dictionary archive, wrote enthusiastically in 1917, 'Among all the humanities, however, the task of personally observing and collecting the manifold manifestations of the war falls to *Volkskunde*.'[15] Superstitions were collected along with folk songs, legends, religious observances, slang, and material culture to explore the transmission and communication of ideas, beliefs, and expressions amongst men thrown together by war and forced to live in unusual intimacy under extraordinary conditions. Italian folklorists, for instance, were particularly interested in the cultural exchanges between soldiers from very different regions of Italy. Prisoner of war camps provided another laboratory for folklorists and physical anthropologists to examine European ethnic traits (little interest was paid, however, to the millions of non-European colonial soldiers).

At the time, there was a strong impulse in folklore and anthropological studies to recover and collect—like archaeologists of the intangible—beliefs, practices, and traditions that were considered survivals from the early stages of human society, mental fossils from a prehistoric age. Tribes across the globe were thought to be still stuck in this early phase of 'primitive' magic and totemic religious worship, while in Europe only fragments of this distant world remained among the uneducated poor, or lay long dormant in the wider population. The conditions created by the war were thought to have reawakened these 'primitive' tendencies or to have shaken them to the surface. Armchair scholars scoured the press for evidence, but some were out in the field apparently glimpsing the traits of this elementary past at first hand. The American anthropologist Ralph Linton, for instance, drew upon his own front-line experience in France, fighting with the 42nd 'Rainbow' Division of the American Expeditionary Force (AEF), in exploring the creation of primitive, totemistic behaviour in 'modern' societies. He noticed the way groups of soldiers generated their own unofficial insignia and set of observances, and also adopted mascots. In one instance, a 'subnormal hysteric' was considered to be gifted with prescience, and the enlisted men in his group relieved him of regular duties so long as he forecast the outcome of expected attacks. He compared this observed behaviour with recent studies of the totemism of Australian aborigines, Melanesians, and native North American tribal groups, concluding that the AEF complexes and 'primitive' totemism both resulted from 'the same social and supernaturalist tendencies'.[16]

Swiss folklorists were the pioneers in developing a new field of *Kriegsvolkskunde* or war folklore. Although the country was neutral, it mobilized its army at the time and set up POW camps. It was far from being detached from the concerns and imperatives of the warring French, Italians, Austrians, and Germans on its borders. In 1915 the Swiss Society for *Volkskunde*, founded in 1896 by Eduard Hoffmann-Krayer, gained the support of the Swiss military to distribute a German questionnaire via the venerable journal of military strategy and politics, the *Revue Militaire Suisse*, as well as in Swiss magazines. It was also disseminated in French periodicals and translated into Italian. It consisted of thirteen themes or questions addressed to Swiss soldiers who came from a mix of linguistic and ethnic backgrounds. The survey included questions about the ways in which they protected their lives. Did they possess medals, blessed items, amulets, magical objects, and the like? What popular remedies were employed by soldiers? What omens predicted war?[17] The project was devised principally by Hoffmann-Krayer and German-Swiss folklorist Hanns Bächtold-Stäubli, who was employed as a military censor during the war. The data gathered resulted in a series of small publications and fed into the monumental *Handwörterbuch des deutschen Aberglaubens (Handbook of German Superstitions)*, which was edited by Hoffmann-Krayer and Bächtold-Stäubli, and published after the war.[18]

The Swiss project acted as a research nexus across the warring countries. Bächtold-Stäubli kept up a personal correspondence with Dauzat about their findings, and the Swiss initiative motivated the latter to launch his own questionnaire on French soldiers' jargon. It also gave impetus to German and Austro-Hungarian folklorists, inspiring both individuals and the creation of numerous new local folklore clubs and associations. Most focused on folk song, music, folk art, and trench slang, rather than superstition.[19] These were popular topics for the enthusiastic Italian researchers of *folklore di guerra*, but several Italian folklorists also created important collections of lore and material culture regarding trench religion and popular magic.[20] The most influential was the psychologist and army chaplain Agostino Gemelli (1878–1959), who was as much motivated by clerical concerns as scholarly insight. For him, the superstitions and songs of the front provided the freshest insight into 'the simple soul of our soldier'. But his research exposed what he considered primitive and inferior beliefs that needed to be countered by 'true' faith. To this end, he instigated a religious revival campaign amongst the troops in hospitals and in the combat zone, distributing triangular pieces of cloth to be worn on the chest bearing the motto *In hoc signo vinces* ('In this sign you will conquer') and the words *protezione del soldato* ('protection of the soldier').[21]

One of Gemelli's arch-critics at the time was Raffaele Corso (1885–1965), who attacked both Gemelli's and Dauzat's social-psychological approaches, and, most significantly, the prevalent view that the theatre of war had created a unique stage for new and recrudescent superstitions. Corso's view was that the popular magic and protective traditions practised by the soldiers were merely an expression of the wider, pervasive superstitions of the Italian peasantry at the time, 'transported by the wartime air, spread from life in the fields to that in the battlefields, where it seemed to seed and flower, almost as a rebirth'.[22] There was no unique laboratory. Corso saw popular magical beliefs as pervasive amongst the poor and uneducated, and an expression of primitive prejudice. This derogatory view of popular belief aside, Corso was one of the few scholars who put two and two together, weighing up the rich evidence for the pervasive popular adherence to popular magic across the country with the evidence being recorded in the trenches, and concluded, basically, that 'war folklore' was simply folklore.

From plentiful wells of wartime folklore we move to drought conditions. When Dauzat, writing in 1918, surveyed the contemporary scholarly literature on wartime beliefs, legends, and folklore, he referenced the Italians, Swiss, French, and Germans, but when it came to Britain all he had to say was, 'nothing to report'.[23] He was right. Scour the pages of the journal of the Folklore Society for the war years and there are very few references to the conflict. The annual addresses by its president, Robert Ranulph Marett, who had established a Department of Social

Anthropology at Oxford in 1914, included war themes without exploring the folkloristic aspects of wartime behaviour or belief. In his address 'War and Savagery', published in March 1915, he told his audience that they were 'hardly in a mood for any scientific occupation. Our thoughts are fixed upon the War,' before providing a global cross-cultural overview of the meaning of savagery.[24] Subsequent addresses only touched tangentially on war matters or did so in abstract philosophical terms. In his final address before the end of the war he referred briefly to those collecting 'the superstitions resuscitated among all classes by the war', before suggesting intriguingly that 'the nation can afford to recapture something of its primitive innocence'.[25] Turn to the main organs of academic anthropology at the time, such as the British Association for the Advancement of Science, and the Royal Anthropological Institute and its journals, and the war likewise appears a distant interest, with little scholarly potential. A few physical anthropologists applied their discipline to war matters in order to assess the ethnic basis for the conflict, and the racial differences between the British and the Teutonic foe.[26]

The only substantive war folklore going on in Britain was conducted by a City of London bank cashier, amulet collector, and amateur folklorist, Edward Lovett (1852–1933). His numerous collecting trips to the docks, markets, and back streets of east London during the war proved just as rich as his folklore collecting in the countryside around his home in Croydon and the southern counties. In December 1916, he gave a lecture at the Horniman Museum in south London entitled 'The Influence of the War on Superstition', in which he talked about some of the charms and mascots he had collected, describing their popularity in wartime as 'a retrograde movement of two hundred years'.[27] Later, in the only book dedicated to urban folklore at the time, *Magic in Modern London* (1925), Lovett wrote of his numerous casual encounters with soldiers on the home front during the war, which provided new insights and information. On a visit to the south coast, for instance, 'there were two convalescent soldiers sitting down, so I made an excuse by asking a question and then sat down near them offering each a cigarette'. He then began to ask them about charms and talismans. On another occasion, he was waiting for a train at East Croydon station when he spotted a friend who had been at the front and invalided home. They began to chat, and in his usual fashion, Lovett said, 'Oh, by the way, I am collecting notes on the amulets and mascots carried by our chaps. I wish you would give me one or two scraps of information if you can.' Then, one day, when he was on the London Underground going from Monument to Farringdon, he struck up a conversation with a 'Colonial soldier' who seemed lost. Another opportunity arose. Lovett helped him with directions, and then, seeing as he was going to the front, asked whether he carried a charm or mascot with him.[28] There were no systematic surveys, questionnaires, or psychological theorizing. But Lovett's casual and human approach to folklore collecting produced some of the most valuable glimpses into the personal meaning of mascots and charms that we have.

In Britain, the Society for Psychical Research (SPR) was the only organization of scholars and researchers conducting research into the supernatural aspects of the war. Similar bodies in France and Germany did likewise. Founded in 1882, the SPR members were described in *The Times* in 1920 as 'all sorts of scholarly men—some philosophers, some clergymen, some politicians, and men of science'.[29] While some of its high-profile members, such as the physicist Oliver Lodge, who was its president between 1901 and 1904, and Arthur Conan Doyle, became ardent advocates of spiritualism, other leading figures in the society, like Frank Podmore (1856–1910), remained deeply sceptical and considered most mediums to be downright frauds. Podmore and others, including Conan Doyle, expended much time and energy instead on investigating hauntings and people's telepathic hallucinations of the dead. Both agreed from their investigations that there was solid evidence that telepathy existed, and, as we shall see, further evidence was sought from soldiers and their relatives during 1914–18. Other aspects of the occult and the war were also examined by members of the society. In 1916, having just surveyed a range of prophecies published since the outbreak of the war, German-born Oxford University philosopher Ferdinand Canning Schiller observed, 'our Society exists for the express purpose of raking over the rubbish-heaps of orthodox science, and must not shrink from the search for truth in unlikely places'. He concluded there was none to be found in the war prophecies, though. 'As a matter of fact, it must be confessed that the evidence was so bad that it did not seem to warrant further investigation. The bulk of it is just irresponsible, unauthenticated, unverifiable, and often anonymous, hearsay.'[30] We will revisit this conclusion shortly.

In 1915 the celebrated French founder of sociology, Émile Durkheim (1858–1917), wrote a cheap tract analysing the German mental attitude towards the conflict. It was clear to him that the war was a result of German social pathology, a national 'will mania'. 'To justify her lust for sovereignty, she naturally claimed every kind of superiority; and then, to explain this universal superiority she sought for its causes in race, in history, and in legend.' 'Thus', he concluded, 'was born that multiform Pan-German mythology, now poetical and now scientific.'[31] Durkheim was one of numerous high-profile academics and writers who willingly turned their hand to writing such anti-German propaganda, solicited and endorsed by their respective governments. The new social sciences were well placed to provide such 'authoritative' opinion on the racial inferiority and the pathological egotism of the enemy, and the accusation of being 'superstitious' was bandied about by both sides in the conflict as a useful shorthand to characterize the national weakness and moral regression of their populations.

The newspapers sometimes took their lead from the academics, and the academics sometimes took their lead from the newspapers. The latter were full of stories about the foolish superstitions of the enemy. Numerous reports appeared in the Allied press early on in the war regaling readers with examples of the credulous nature of the Kaiser. So, in November 1914, a Belgian newspaper stated that the Kaiser 'believes in the evil eye, in the ill luck attached to the number thirteen, &c. Persons who have visited his study know that it contains a complete collection of works on chiromancy and the occult sciences. All the prophecies trouble him.'[32] The *Sunderland Daily Echo* reported in October 1914: 'Superstitions akin to those which have been obsolete among the British peasantry for nearly a century are at this day rife among the uniformed sons of "*Kultur*". There is hardly a German soldier in the ranks who does not carry some sort of charm.' The examples it related included Tyrolean Austrian soldiers who wore bats' wings sewn into their underclothing.[33] The German and Austro-Hungarian press contained similar propagandist reports.

While noting how the psychological strain of the war was bound to lead to a recrudescence of primitive beliefs, Ferdinand Schiller observed that it was 'just as natural that the allies should circulate stories of supernatural interventions on behalf of their just cause as that the Germans should revert to the magical practice of hammering nails into images'.[34] The word 'revert' was all important in this statement. He was referring to the evocative and provocative academic accusation that the German authorities were inspiring re-emergent heathenism, and promoting superstition, by creating *Nagelfiguren* or nail statues. Between 1915 and 1916, hundreds of wooden monuments representing great German heroes, such as Charlemagne, as well as eagles, lions, crosses, submarines, and the like, appeared in public places in towns and villages across the country. Citizens and soldiers were invited to purchase nails of iron, silver, and gold, each attracting a different price, which they hammered into the wooden objects. The practice was a public ritual of patriotic, collective support for the war, with the funds raised going to good causes such as war widows, orphans, disabled soldiers, and the Red Cross. The most spectacular of these *Nagelfigur* was a 12-metre-high wooden statue of General Paul von Hindenburg (1847–1934). It was erected in Berlin with a platform around it so that the public could hammer nails up the torso.[35]

In October 1915 the French newspaper *Le Temps* printed an article on the origin of the wooden Hindenburg, based on the views of Swedish ethnographer Nils Edvard Hammarstedt. He considered this vogue for nail statues a contemporary manifestation of the basic human urge to propitiate the gods by making offerings. Or perhaps it was a primal act of magic, the people purchasing and hammering the nails secretly wishing to gain supernatural favours. The newspaper believed that Hammarstedt had not truly grasped the sinister importance and gravity of the German *Nagelfiguren*, though: 'The erection of the wooden statue, the fixing of the nails, constitutes strange survivals of idolatry,' thought the paper.[36] The issue was taken up in the pages of the highly respected journal *L'Anthropologie* in 1916. In one article, the leading French anthropologist René Verneau (1852–1938) compared the wooden Hindenburg with the fetish practices of the Loango of what is now western Gabon. While it was easy to push the comparison too far, he acknowledged, he believed there were fundamental similarities with the African religious practice of driving nails into wooden fetish figurines. The German state was accused of cynically reinstituting ancient cultic practices amongst its population. He recognized that some of those who stuck nails in the fetishes saw their actions as nothing more than a patriotic amusement. But he was concerned that the 'naïve' who made pilgrimage to the statues were motived by more troubling appeals to supernatural aid as

Fig. 1.1. The 12-metre high *Nagelfigur* or wooden nail statue of General Paul von Hindenburg, erected in Berlin. The public purchased nails to hammer into it for charity.

they hammered in their nails, foolishly praying to the German idol in the hope of achieving their desires. 'Our enemies impede the triumph of civilization,' he concluded.[37] Swiss archaeologist and folklorist Walde-mar Deonna responded with a more nuanced perspective on the nailing of effigies and trees, noting similar recent folk rituals in the popular religious practices of all the warring countries. He concluded, neverthe-less, that the *Nagelfiguren* of 1915 and 1916 were an echo of ancient tree worship, and were 'the continuation in the twentieth century of very old superstitions, the renewal of which has been promoted by the war, reinforcing the mystical and credulous aspects of the warring parties'.[38]

This overview of how the war stimulated intellectual interest in the 'superstitious' highlights the challenges facing the historian in uncover-ing and interpreting the supernatural aspects of the conflict. How do we cut through the early academic assumptions, the propaganda, the myth-making, and the condescension towards the uneducated? To begin with, from this point onward, I will avoid the term 'superstition', which pervades the literature of the period, and continues to be used uncrit-ically by psychologists. When cited, it will be placed between inverted commas to mark that it is used in relation to the opinion of others. Historians of witchcraft and magic have been sensitive to this for a while, aware of how, in both the past and the present, 'superstition' has been widely applied to denote irrational, ignorant, or fallacious beliefs and practices. Following the Reformation, it was used by Protestant theologians to denounce Catholic rituals and theology.[39] Because it is such a loaded term, we need to place it in context, and be aware of how it was understood and used in the past. I do not hold the view that the beliefs and practices explored in this book are in any way symptomatic of backwardness or credulity. Indeed, as we shall see, those who carried charms for protection, performed rituals for good luck, went to fortune tellers, or claimed to see ghosts were often well-educated, thoughtful people who were self-analytical about what they did and experienced: they were anything but 'superstitious'.

There are a range of valuable sources, other than the scholarly studies of the era, that illuminate the wider cultures of belief in wartime. The newspapers were far from supine tools of propaganda, and they often cast a reflective and critical eye on the unorthodox beliefs and practices of their own countries, reporting apparent supernatural instances or the popular resort to magic which did not cast a patriotic light on national fortitude and confidence. Personal letters to and from the front can provide unique insights as well. But as historians of the First World War have long debated, they bring their own challenges, such as the influence of the military censors on what soldiers and sailors chose to write and how they expressed themselves. What did they conceal from their loved ones about their fears, imaginings, and rituals? There is also the matter of letters destroyed during and after the war for personal or family reasons.[40] Battlefield memoirs also came into their own as a literary genre. Some were written during the conflict, and many in the decades after. They were rich in personal reflection, and the visceral experience of trench and aerial warfare, and their authors were some-times remarkably open about their emotional lives. Some even pur-ported to be the memoirs of the spirits of the war dead communicated from the other world via spiritualist seances. But such personal sources that survive concern only a minuscule percentage of First World War combatants, of course, and we should not forget that many soldiers were unable to write. In Italy, literacy rates were around 65 per cent nationally in 1915, but significantly lower in rural southern parts of the country. In Russia, one third of the workforce lacked basic literacy. While literacy rates were high in Britain, they were much lower amongst the British Army's many colonial troops.[41] Although the trenches may not have been the sealed world of oral tradition depicted by Marc Bloch, it is important to be aware that what survives on the written or printed page does not necessarily capture the richness or complexity of battle-field folklore or the intensity of supernatural experiences.

Thousands of oral history interviews with veterans were recorded on both sides half a century or more after the end of the First World War. While some interviewers asked questions regarding soldiers' religious views, by and large they focused on combat and the physical side of battlefield life. The humour, boredom, and mundanities of trench exist-ence often come through, and unbidden but brief reminiscences about beliefs and traditions occasionally crop up. James Gough Cooper of the Royal Fusiliers, who was interviewed in 1973 about his experience of the Western Front, recalled, for instance, sitting on a patch of grass one day in a lull and finding a spider on his shoulder. He was about to swat it away when another soldier shouted at him gruffly, 'Don't knock that spider off you ****. That's lucky.' Gough brushed away the spider anyway, and, shortly after, a shell landed killing all the men around him, and the man who warned about the spider was among the casualties.[42] But, as with all oral histories, we need to be conscious of selective memory and what was considered more or less important to discuss so many decades after the event. Other sources bear silent witness to popular wartime mentalities. The material culture, in the form of charms, talismans, mascots, and lucky postcards, reminds us of the value of 'things', and how the sentimental attachment to personal items elided feelings of love and protection. Cheap, mass-produced trinkets were forged into talismans of great potency, while holy items accrued secular power in the furnace of battle.

Piecing together the myriad fragments of thoughts, experiences, reports, reminiscences, images, and objects gives us an impressionistic but illuminating picture of a war redolent with supernatural associations. The task now is to disentangle what they all mean, and why they are important to our understanding of life during the First World War.

2

PROPHETIC TIMES

A critical study of the prophecies which have either come into being or have taken up a new lease of interest and importance owing to the Great War is no improbable undertaking when the war itself shall be over, and it might provide a curious kind of instruction as well as some entertainment.

(Occultist Arthur Edward Waite, writing in 1916)[1]

The advent of the First World War was hardly a surprise. As the Belgian poet and essayist Maurice Maeterlinck observed in 1916, 'True, it was more or less foreseen by our reason; but our reason hardly believed in it.'[2] Numerous books and articles were written in Britain and France during the late nineteenth and early twentieth centuries debating the inevitability of a great war in Europe. There had also been periodic spy and invasion scares in Britain with regard to rumours of French, Russian, and German attacks. Popular fears were fed by the burgeoning genres of 'invasion lit' and futurist fiction, and, by the early years of the twentieth century, Germany had become the predominant threat in such stories, as the first tremors of the coming war were beginning to be felt.[3] Some had clear political undercurrents. Erskine Childers's spy novel *Riddle of the Sands* (1903), concerning the discovery and foiling of German plans for invading Britain, was credited with highlighting Britain's poor military presence in the North Sea, in contrast with Germany's growing naval power. William Le Queux's scaremongering novel *The Invasion of 1910* was commissioned for serialization in the *Daily Mail* in 1906 for the purpose of boosting the paper's campaign for greater military spending. With its account of German outrages in towns along the east coast, it went on to sell over a million copies.[4] Such war fiction also proved popular in France. In the late 1880s, the French officer and novelist Émile-Cyprien Driant (1855–1916) wrote *La Guerre de demain* (*The War of Tomorrow*), which described at length the brave derring-do adventures of French soldiers in a future war against Germany, including a story of balloon warfare. Driant was killed in action at the Battle of Verdun. Similar *Zukunftskrieg* (future-war fiction) proved popular in Germany as well. August Niemann's *Der Weltkrieg: Deutsche Träume* (*The World War: German Dreams*) (1904) was a story of high political intrigue and military prowess as an alliance of Germany, Russia, and France wages war against Britain. The British navy is crushed at the Battle of Flushing, and the invasion begins in Scotland.

Such nationalistic storytelling fostered a receptive public environment for the wave of prophetic literature that surged over the combatant countries during the early months of the war, inspired by rumour, evangelical optimism, astrological calculations, occult zealotry, and the utterances of rogues. When, in February 1918, Charles Oman, who for the first two years of the war worked as a censor in Whitehall, gave his presidential address to the Royal Historical Society on the subject of 'Rumour in Time of War', he described the prophetic literature of the war as a curious relic, the last survivor of 'a very ancient and prolific race'. As such, he noted that a dozen or so prophetic war pamphlets from different countries had been collected by the National War Museum (later the Imperial War Museum), which had been founded the previous year.[5] But as we shall now see, the dark years of the war were far from the end times for this venerable, divinatory tradition. Indeed, they were seen by some as the herald of a profound spiritual enlightenment, a prophetic intimation of a glorious new world order. Still, as the nineteenth-century American humourist James Russell Lowell advised, 'Don't never prophesy—unless you know.'

Prophecies Old and New

The compendious list of French war literature *La Littérature de la guerre*, published in 1918, listed eleven principal booklets of war prophecies published between 1914 and 1916, some of which contained dozens of different examples. The editor also referred to the thousands of handbills containing prophecies that circulated around the country.[6] Maurice Maeterlinck counted no fewer than eighty-three predictions and prophecies concerning the coming of the war.[7] In Italy, Giuseppe Ciuffa compiled a book of over a hundred war prophecies in 1915, many of which were the same as those in the French literature, but there were also some distinctly

Italian ones.[8] Old prophecies were recycled and given new meaning and popularity in Germany as well, particularly variations of a prophetic folktale that had first been recorded in 1701, known as *die Schlacht am Birkenbaum* or 'the Battle of the Birch Tree'. It concerned a time when the world would be godless. A frightful war would break out with Russia and the North on one side, and France, Spain, and Italy on the other. A prince dressed all in white would emerge as a saviour after a terrible bloody battle near a birch tree on the border of Westphalia. Was he the Kaiser?[9]

Prophecies also swirled around the conflict in the Near East. In November 1914, the spiritualist Wellesley Tudor Pole (1884–1968), who served during the war as a major in the Royal Marine Light Infantry, and then in the Directorate of Military Intelligence in the Middle East, surveyed what he knew of relevant prophecies circulating in relation to the Ottoman Empire. One was that when a European king called Constantine married a Sophie, then a new dawn of Christianity would begin in Constantinople. Constantine I ascended to the throne of Greece in 1913, and his wife was called Sophie. The Persian prophet Baha'u'llah (1817–92), the founder of the Baha'i movement who believed he was chosen as the 'promised one' of a universal faith, was reported to have predicted the rise of German hegemony and the downfall of the French and Ottoman empires. The Rhine would ultimately run red with German blood, he apparently foretold, and then there would come 'The Most Great Peace'. Tudor Pole was a promoter of the Baha'i movement in Britain, and believed the war would run as Baha'u'llah prophesied.[10] When, in September 1918, the Ottoman army was defeated at the ancient city of Megiddo, the leader of the Baha'i movement at the time, Abdu'l-Bahá, declared that this was the Armageddon of the New Testament and welcomed the beginning of the end times.[11] Such biblical prophecies will be discussed in more detail later, but for the moment let us survey the gallery of First World War prophets, ancient and recent, real and legendary, beginning with the most famous non-biblical prophet of them all, Nostradamus.

The prophecies of the French physician-astrologer Nostradamus (1503–66) were published in his own lifetime, and have been reprinted many times since. Consisting of hundreds of quatrains with odd word combinations, strange jargon, and obscure references to battles, disasters, and plagues, there is nothing obviously applicable to the First World War. But that did not stop what has been described as the 'Nostradamian battles of World War 1'.[12] Little attention was paid to

Nostradamus in Britain, though the British occultist Frederic Thurstan turned to the quatrains to see whether they prophesied anything about the Dardanelles campaign and the future rule of Constantinople. The results were less than clear. The Nostradamian battles were primarily between several French and German esotericists seeking to find patriotic cause in the abstruse phrases of the quatrains.

The main proponent on the French side was A. Demar-Latour, whose booklet *Nostradamus et les événements de 1914–1916*, sold for 1 franc 25 centimes in 1916. Demar-Latour translated the quatrains into modern French and then set about unlocking their secret meaning with regard to the war. One quatrain ran as follows:

> Sous l'opposite climat Babilonique,
> Grande sera de sang effusion;
> Que terre et mer, air, ciel sera inique
> Sectes, faim, regnes, pestes, confusions.

> Under the opposite climate of Babylon,
> There will be a great effusion of blood;
> So great indeed that the earth and the sea, the air and the sky will seem to be
> in revolt
> There will be disorders, famine, diseases, and overthrow of kingdoms.

According to Demar-Latour, the disorder was thought to refer to Germany and Ireland, and the famine also concerned Germany. His other revelations included apparent references to the German atrocities in Belgium, the outcome of the Battle of the Marne, the advent of German heavy artillery, the fate of Serbia, and the invention of the submarine—the latter was divined from a reference to 'the fish living under and above water'. As to the Kaiser's ultimate defeat, Demar-Latour found significance in this quatrain:

> The great camel will drink the waters of the Danube and of the Rhine,
> And he will not repent.
> But the soldiers of the Rhône and still more so those of the Loire will
> make him tremble.
> And near the Alps, the cock [France] will ruin him.[13]

On the German side, the astrologer Albert Kniepf unsurprisingly came to some very different conclusions. He deciphered one quatrain as prophesying that when the French passed beyond the Ligurian Sea, between Italy and Corsica, they would be beaten by the followers of Mohammed and the countries of the Adriatic.[14]

But this was not just some obscure battle of wits and imagination between a handful of occultists. Nostradamus aroused considerable public curiosity. So, in February 1915, the prominent German newspaper *Kölnische Zeitung* printed a heartening translation of one quatrain as:

> Albion, ruler of the sea,—
> When the air mountain comes?
> And the bell in the tube,
> And the ship in the bell,
> Thy last hour shall have come.

The newspaper told its readers that this evidently referred to Germany's invention of the Zeppelin and submarine. Another interpretation of one of Nostradamus's cryptic quatrains was deciphered as 'London would be destroyed by sails coming from the sky.'[15] The popular influence of such newspaper predictions is indicated by a report by an American correspondent in Berlin, and by others, that the Zeppelin crews had subsequently adopted Nostradamus as their patron saint.[16]

Throughout the war, there were periodic flurries of British press interest in the English prophetess Joanna Southcott (1715–1814). This farmer's daughter from Devon attracted a considerable following in her lifetime, declaring she was the Woman of the Apocalypse mentioned in the Book of Revelation, appearing as 'a great wonder in heaven; a woman clothed with the sun, and the moon under her feet, and upon her head a crown of twelve stars'. She also claimed, at the age of 64, to be pregnant with the new messiah. There was nothing in her prophetic utterances while alive that pertained to the Great War, but on her death she left a sealed wooden box of prophecies that her will dictated could only be opened in the presence of all twenty-four bishops of the Church of England, or their representatives, at a future moment of great national danger. So, with the outbreak of the First World War, there was a renewed interest in what Southcott's prophecies might have to say. Would the bishops agree to attend and so enable the opening of Joanna Southcott's box? No, of course not. Nevertheless, shortly after the outbreak of war rumours spread that Southcott had, in fact, predicted its advent, and, indeed, the end of the world in 1914, and also that

Fig. 2.1. Front cover of Ralph Shirley's *Prophecies and Omens of the Great War* (London, 1915). Shirley was editor of *The Occult Review*.

a king named George would be the last ruler of England and would give up the kingdom to God. A Southcottian disciple and historian of the movement, Alice Seymour, wrote letters to the press to scotch this rumour. She stated that there was no record of Southcott saying any such thing or, as according to another rumour, that she had ordered that the box be opened in 1914.[17]

When the hundredth anniversary of Southcott's death came around in December 1914, there was renewed media interest. A newly launched, populist London paper, the *Daily Call*, which promoted itself as 'a penny paper for a halfpenny' and consisted mostly of war news, stories, and patriotic calls for a strong army, launched an eyebrow-raising campaign for the box to be opened. It argued this was necessary 'if only to avert "the terrible calamities" which some of her followers aver will follow a refusal'.[18] The summer of 1917 saw a final flurry of war interest in the opening of the box of prophecies. The *Daily Express* reported a rumour that the Canon of Westminster had been tasked with gathering the necessary clergy.[19] *The People* devoted a whole column to Southcott, observing, 'should our clergy really have decided to look into these papers their action is likely to arouse as keen a controversy as did the writings of the woman herself'.[20]

Nostradamus and Southcott were real people who uttered prophecies and attracted followings. But many of the venerable prophets held up as predicting the war were less concrete historic figures, thereby providing excellent foci for the fabrication of new prophecies. One of the most widely known in France was Saint Odile. According to legend, she was born blind in the seventh century AD. Her father, the Duke of Alsace, sent her to a monastery at the age of 12. She prayed ceaselessly to be able to see, and on her thirteenth birthday the miracle happened. By the fourteenth century, her relics were being venerated, and she subsequently became known as the patron saint of Alsace and also of eye patients. In 1916, at the time of the Battle of Verdun in eastern France, a pamphlet entitled the *Prophecies of Saint Odile and the End of the War* (1916) circulated widely; it included a new legend that, at the age of 31, she had miraculously prophesied a great war between France and Germany.[21] The first of the prophecies began: 'The time is come when Germany shall be called the most bellicose nation on earth. From her bosom shall arise the terrible man who will make war on the world. The war he will undertake will be the most frightful war mankind has suffered.'

She then went on to say that Paris would be saved, 'though everyone will believe it doomed to destruction'. The war would be long, but finally 'the era of peace under iron' would lead to men adoring God and the sun would shine with unusual splendour.

The prophecy was quickly denounced as a fake by a leading Alsatian scholar, and the English occultist Arthur Edward Waite independently came to the same conclusion.[22] But few in France heard their criticisms, and, selling for just 1 franc, the *Prophecies of Saint Odile* went into a second edition before the end of the year. The prophecies it contained were, moreover, also reprinted in clerical magazines and newspapers, with a knowing absence of commentary as to their authenticity.[23] With the Battle of Verdun grinding on in the mud and destined to become one of the cruellest battles in history, there was a collective will to bolster French morale, particularly amongst the soldiers and their families in the Franco-German eastern region of the country. Stoffler's preface to the *Prophecies* ended with the rousing cry, 'Vive l'Alsace-Lorraine française!'[24] The booklet was banned by the German authorities as a consequence, but the Odile prophecies quickly became embedded in French folklore.

The Prophecy of Mayence was another widely reported document in France during the early years of the war. Supposedly found in an ancient convent in 1854, it consisted of eighteen verses that depicted the course of a great war on French soil. One of them ran as follows: 'In spite of the heroic resistance of France, a multitude of soldiers, blue, yellow, and black, shall scatter themselves over a great part of France.' It ended with the prediction that 'William, the second of that name, shall be the last King of Prussia.' It was undoubtedly a recent fake, first appearing in a newspaper on 23 August 1914, and it was actually a variant of the *Schlacht am Birkenbaum* prophecies. Germany also had its own industry of spurious prophecy-making. The 'Prophecy of Altstaetting', supposedly written by a monk in 1841, stated that war would break out in August 1914 and that Germany and Austria would be victorious by Christmas. The prophecy first appeared in November 1914.[25] In 1916 a pamphlet sanctioned by the German censors appeared that purported to be a prophecy that was written down by a Tyrolean monk in 1717 and rediscovered in 1821, which told of a world war won by a German prince.[26] When another new German prophecy was published in 1915, which again purported to be an eighteenth-century prediction of world war with Germany victorious, the mayor of Eschweiler, where the 'original' was said to reside, had to declare publicly that no such prophetic manuscript was kept by the town hall, and that no one knew anything about the author or the origin of the text.[27]

Although quite widely disseminated in England and France, the Prophecy of Pinsk was of particular interest elsewhere. It was supposedly uttered by the spirit of Andrew Bobola, a seventeenth-century Polish Jesuit martyr. One night in 1819, a monk named Korzeniecki was in his monastic cell in Vilnius dwelling on the fate of his beloved country and praying to Bobola, when the martyr appeared and told him to open the cell window and peer out of it. The view was normally over the enclosed monastery garden, but when Korzeniecki looked out this time, he saw a vast plain stretched out before him. The spirit of Bobola explained it was the plain of Pinsk in northern Poland where he had been martyred. He told the monk to look out of the window once more and he would see the destiny of Poland. This time the plain was covered in a vision of warring English, French, Prussian, Russian, Ottoman, and Austrian soldiers. Bobola explained that when such a future battle was over, Poland would be restored as a nation state, 'and I shall be recognized as its patron saint'. The earliest publication of this story was in an Italian devotional magazine *La Civiltà Cattolica* in 1864. From here it appeared in a book of Catholic predictions and 'impending general calamities' entitled *The Christian Trumpet* (1873). The Montreal newspaper *Le Devoir* printed the account from *La Civiltà Cattolica* in full in late August 1914, while the French Catholic papers also printed versions in August and September.[28] Over in Germany, several publications appeared assessing the Pinsk prophecy, and knowledge of it was described as widespread in German lands, including those parts of Poland that were then in the German and Austro-Hungarian empires.[29]

National politics and propaganda also lay behind one of the more unusual war prophecies—that which concerned the appearance of the Black Pig of Kiltrustan in Ireland. In April 1918, two small girls of Kiltrustan, Roscommon, claimed to have seen the apparition of a black pig. It was reported to the local clergyman, who went to the spot where the ghostly porker was said to have appeared, but he saw nothing. But word soon spread, crowds began to gather in vigil, the children of the parish were frightened to go out, and people attributed their illnesses to its appearance. Rumour had it that the pig would appear three times during the war and that there would be great trouble unless it was shot by a one-eyed marksman in the field behind Kilmore rectory. Excitement about the black pig was stoked by a poorly written tract entitled *Prophecies of St. Columcille of the remarkable events that will happen to England and Ireland before and after the war*, which had recently spread widely in the north of Ireland. Printed in Dublin, and purportedly compiled from original documents by an eminent divine of the Catholic Church, it was basically a crude piece of political propaganda that reworked an old prediction attributed to the sixth-century saint that the Irish would conquer the English. It had previously circulated during the Irish rebellion of the mid-seventeenth century and again during the 1798 uprising.[30] It foretold the massacre of Catholics by either the English or Orangemen in the Valley of the Black Pig, followed by the eventual vanquishing of the English: 'the Saxons will flee beyond the sea, and not remember to come back'.[31]

Maurice Maeterlinck dismissed such wartime prophecies as nonsense, but considered two of those current as 'more curious and worthy of a moment's attention'.[32] The more famous and influential of the two is known as the 'prophecy of the *curé d'Ars'*. The *curé* of Ars, Jean-Baptiste Vianney (1786–1859), had an international reputation in his own lifetime for his pastoral work, reforming what he saw as pervasive lax morality in the aftermath of the French Revolution. By the end of his life he was receiving thousands of pilgrims every year. Prophetic utterances attributed to him began to circulate soon after his death, and were first printed in 1872, as they were thought to have predicted the French defeat during the Franco-Prussian War the previous year. But they also referred to unfinished business: 'The enemy will not quit the country altogether. They will come back again, and they will destroy everything on their line of march.' But then, 'they will retire towards their own country, but we shall follow them up, and not many of them will ever reach home'.[33] Interest in the prophecy died down only to reignite in August 1914, at a moment when the first stage of the sanctification of Vianney stalled due to the war. The high profile of the *curé* would have ensured that 'his' prophecy would have risen to public attention more widely than others in France, but the fabrication of a striking new addition at the end of the old prophecy ensured it became something of a national sensation: 'much more terrible things will happen than have yet been seen. Paris will suffer, but a great triumph will be witnessed on the Feast of Our Lady.' The Feast day of the Virgin is 8 September, and so the creation of the new fake prophecy gave hope at a moment when French troops were being pushed back towards Paris by a rapid German advance.

The prophecy was reported by the English *Daily Chronicle* in early September 1914, and reprinted in the regional British press, with the observation that French confidence had been inspired by its dissemination. The publication of the prophecy in the French press was, however, criticized by Catholic organizations. In October 1914, the *Annales d'Ars*, the monthly magazine of the sanctuary dedicated to Vianney, complained that 'every day or nearly every day we are asked about the prophecy of the blessed *curé d'Ars* or information on the predictions that he had made concerning the current war'. It desired to state publicly, once and for all, that the prophecy published by the newspapers was false and that they knew of no authentic predictions made by the blessed *curé*. This statement was widely reprinted in diocesan magazines across France. It was also echoed on the other side of the world by the Catholic periodical the *New Zealand Tablet*, which told its readers, 'Catholics cannot defend a prophecy which is so unauthenticated as this one.'[34]

A Profusion of Modern Prophets

As well as the reinterpretation, reinvention, and faking of prophecies by dead or legendary figures, there were also hordes of living prophets who staked their claim to oracular greatness—though usually with the power of hindsight. They came in many guises and professed a variety of occult inspirations. At the modest end of the scale were the likes of the seaside fortune teller Clementina Norton, who proudly claimed during her prosecution in 1915 that at 'Southend on a public platform I prophesied the war'. Then there were the notorious boasters, such as the ritual magician Aleister Crowley. Under the name Frater Perturabo, he wrote to the *Occult Review* in September 1914 to state that on 8 May 1910 he, along with an acquaintance high up in the Admiralty and a well-known violinist, had conjured up the spirit of Mars, who was named Bartzabel. They asked him if there would be war in Europe, to which Bartzabel replied, yes, within five years, and that Germany and Turkey would be involved.[35]

There were numerous claims by mediums. Arthur Conan Doyle was impressed by the Sydney medium Mrs Foster Turner, who, in February 1914, before an audience of hundreds, apparently channelled the spirit of the well-known journalist and spiritualist W. T. Stead (1849–1912): 'I want to warn you that before this year 1914 has run its course, Europe will be deluged in blood.' The London-based 'Scottish seer', Miss McCreadie, apparently told friends that, during a trip to France several years before the war, she had felt a foreboding psychic sense of turmoil and treachery, of a great conflict triggered by Germany.[36] There was a stir in occult circles in 1918 when a series of mediumistic interviews with Julius Caesar, purportedly conducted in Teddington, Middlesex, in 1909 and 1912, were published that seemed to prophecy the war and its ending. The first communication in 1909 began with the question, 'What is impending?' The reply from the Roman dictator was, 'War—horrid war. Mars is king…The weak must suffer. The strong will die. Those who are neither will suffer and live.' There followed a stream of cryptic lyrical statements, including, 'Red Poppies in the graveyard. And then Red Poppies in the smiling cornfields in the sun. Read, learn, and fear not.' Caesar returned to his poppy theme in October 1912: 'The Poppies cometh to pass before the Day of Christ. Note what we have said. Poverty and Hunger and the War-lust in every land on which lieth the shadow of the Cross…when Europe is exhausted the reign of Asia will begin, for there the sun is rising. So say we.'[37]

In France today, Mme Fraya is sometimes cited as the prophetic grande dame of the Great War, due in large part to a biography published in the 1950s that contained highly dubious claims about her wartime prowess and political clients.[38] Fraya's real name was Marie-Valentine Dencausse (1871–1954). Born in the Landes region of south-west France, she made her name as a chiromancer and graphologist, but also professed clairvoyant powers. She became a well-known figure amongst psychical researchers, and in 1913 the doctor and psychical researcher Eugène Osty published a book on metapsychic cognition in which he explored Fraya's powers and her 'very advanced' brain.[39] Her consulting room in the rue d'Édimbourg, Paris was frequented by international high-society figures. Just before the war, the Paris journal of the Radical Ottoman Party liked to mention the visits of its political rivals to the clairvoyant's rooms. She received press interest in December 1914 for her analysis of the Kaiser's handwriting, which, she stated, exhibited the signs of a strongly unbalanced mind, and that he was vain, slow to comprehend, and would offer a sad spectacle when he was inevitably defeated.[40] But look through the international literature of the war period and one name stands out above all the rest: Madame de Thèbes. Indeed, after the war the French press referred to Mme Fraya variously as the 'new Mme de Thèbes' or her 'proclaimed heiress' in the public consciousness.[41]

Madame de Thèbes was born Annette Savary at 52 rue des Envierges in the hamlet of Ménilmontant, in the commune of Belleville, around 1844. Her father was a carpenter, and at the time of her birth Ménilmontant was a small village on the outskirts of Paris that would soon be swallowed up into the twentieth arrondissement of the expanding city. She began working as a cashier in a gentleman's outfitters near the Palais-Royal, then around 1877 as a private tutor for a bourgeois family.[42] From around 1882 she was drawn to the stage and appeared in small roles in provincial tours under the stage name of Mlle Dhalyle. Then, in 1884, she became a confidante of the actress and notorious courtesan Léonide Leblanc (1842–94), herself a former primary school teacher. Leblanc, who was nicknamed 'Madame Maximum' for her prodigious sexual appetite, had many high-profile lovers, including George Clémenceau, who would later lead France through the last two years of the First World War.

It was in 1890 that Savary took her first big step towards celebrity and power, when she adopted the name Madame de Sauval and established herself as a card reader or *cartomancienne* at 46 rue Laugier. She then learned the more 'scientific' art of chiromancy, influenced by the work and fame of the Parisian artist and chiromancer Adolphe Desbarrolles. He had published an influential manual on the subject in the 1850s, which went through numerous editions in several languages over the ensuing decades. Desbarrolles died in 1886, and a gap appeared in the firmament of high-society prognosticators. Still, prognostication was a crowded market in Paris. An ambitious young woman trying to make her way in the business required an influential patron, and he appeared in the form of Alexandre Dumas, son of the famous novelist, and a successful dramatist in his own right. Dumas *fils* had a long-standing interest in chiromancy, having learned the art from Desbarrolles. Savary and Dumas were introduced by a mutual acquaintance, the son of the popular painter of cats, Louis-Eugène Lambert. Savary was invited several times to Dumas's home in Paris and his country mansion at Marly. There is no evidence as to whether their relationship was sexual, however. Although a public critic of society-climbing courtesans, Dumas was not averse to sleeping around. The first public mention of

Fig. 2.2. Madame de Thèbes (c.1844–1916), the most famous living prophet of the First World War.

their relationship concerned a dinner party hosted by Dumas that included several eminent doctors and members of the Académie Française, and involved a discussion on and session of palm-reading. The nature of the dinner party and its guests was reported with a raised eyebrow by *Le Figaro* in March 1893.[43] A few days later, the conservative daily newspaper *Le Gaulois* mockingly compared Savary to the mussel and potato salad that had come into vogue in Paris salons after its description in Dumas's play *Francillon*, referring to 'this Madame de Thèbes, who Dumas has just thrown at us, as, not long ago, the indigestible *salade japonaise!*'[44] But Savary proved no flash in the pan.

It was Dumas who suggested to Savary that she adopt the professional name 'Madame de Thebes' in reference to a play he had been working for years called *La Route de Thèbes*, a psychological drama centred on a mysterious woman. He never finished the play but the creation of Madame de Thèbes was completed to great effect. By the time Dumas died in 1895, de Thèbes's business was well established, and for the next two decades the elite of Parisian society made their way to her consulting rooms at 29 avenue de Wagram. There were several clients from the literary world. Marcel Proust once went to consult her after feeling ill. She read his palm, gave him a worried look, and sensibly told him go 'far away for a rest'. There were international royal and political clients. A Serbian diplomat recalled in 1917 how in the early 1890s Queen Nathalie of Serbia had taken two female acquaintances to see Madame de Thèbes, one of them, Draga Mashin, who was to become her daughter-in-law. Mashin and her future husband Alexander, now the king of Serbia, were assassinated in a coup in 1903—an event Mme Fraya claimed to have predicted. Apparently de Thèbes had, likewise, informed Mashin 'that she [Mashin] cherished very high ambitions, that she would see the desire of her heart fulfilled, but that very fulfilment would lead to a catastrophe in which both she and her husband should perish'. Writing of his time in Haiti, the travel writer Harry Franck observed the influence of Madame de Thèbes amongst the Caribbean island's tumultuous political elite: 'If the stories which gradually leak out from the confidences of returning natives to their friends are trustworthy, she tells all Haitians that they are someday to become president of their country, not a bad guess under old conditions...More than one revolution has been started on the strength of her Prophecies.'[45]

Madame de Thèbes had a successful publishing career, with titles such as *L'Énigme de la main* (1901). The vehicle for her First World War prophecies, though, was her *Almanach de Mme de Thèbes*, the first volume of which appeared in 1903. It was released at Christmas and, unlike British predictive almanacs at the time, its contents were largely based around her divinatory investigations as a chiromancer, though numerological and astrological observations were included.[46] In her *Almanach* for 1913, de Thèbes had predicted, 'Germany menaces Europe in general and France in particular. When the war breaks out she will have willed it, but after it there will no longer be Hohenzollern or Prussian domination.' She was far from alone in her confidence. Several prominent French diviners and occultists also indicated war would break out in 1913, including the influential Gérard Encausse, otherwise known as Papus. In January 1913, he predicted in the occult magazine *Mystéria* that the year would be dark, bringing many tears, bloodshed, and cruel bereavements: 'never have the signs of war been so numerous'. 'I am no prophet', he declared, but 'the hour is dangerous and the future menacing'. This was certainly true for himself, as he died from tuberculosis in 1916 while working in the French army medical corps.[47] The French author J.-H. Lavaur had published a range of prophecies that collectively pointed to the end of the German empire in 1912 and 1913. In the preface to his 1914 edition, he accepted that 1913 ended without the predictions being realized, but he said his conclusions remained absolutely justified in that 1913 'was the beginning of a period of two years in the course of which the said events would infallibly occur!' This edition would go on to be published in Spanish and Romanian.[48] The supposed prophecy of Count Leo Tolstoy, which circulated in England and France, foretold that Europe would be consumed by a destructive calamity in 1913. In Germany, meanwhile, gloomy predictions were made about the number 13, as it was in 1813 that the bloody campaign with Napoleon was fought. The centenary heralded a new conflict.[49]

War obviously did not come that year, but deeply puzzled by the strength and number of the war predictions, several occultists suggested there was a crucial reason. Countess Zalinski, a compiler of prophecies of the Great War, wondered in 1917 whether 'some great occult force or power interposed in an effort to stay the calamity, but which was able only to postpone it for a single year'. The electrical engineer and 'thought power' advocate F. L. Rawson believed the delayed outbreak of war was due to the many prayers that had been said by 'mental workers' striving for peace.[50]

As 1914 loomed, several French diviners rolled back on the ominous predictions. Mme Andrée, who read coffee grounds, and the tarot reader Mme Lorenza assured readers that there was no reason to worry, and that 1914 might even be a prosperous period: 'I do not foresee any particularly serious events—such as war—for the year 1914', divined the latter.[51] But de Thèbes stuck to her claims, with her *Almanach* for 1914 warning:

> This year we shall pass through the gravest and most decisive hours. It will be a year especially happy for France, in spite of blood, in spite of tears, and in spite of uneasy omens, victory! Victory! We have nothing to fear from the trials of fate. France will emerge renewed in strength, reconstituted by war.

Regarding Germany: 'All is disquieting in her destiny. The person of the Emperor is most threatened by fate. It is not the eagle of victory he bears on his helmet.'

During the early months of the war these pronouncements were repeated in the international press from New Zealand to America, Britain to Germany.[52] The French press regularly reported on and criticized the activities of Madame de Thèbes. Her almanac for 1914 was a popular seller on the streets of Paris. 'Men lend an ear to prophecies', wrote one reporter from the capital, 'and books containing the predictions of Madame de Thèbes and the Prophecy of Mayence are for sale on the boulevards.'[53] There was also a trade in bogus prophecies under her name. She wrote to the newspapers several times during 1914 and 1915 to complain of the 'audacious jokers' who were peddling such street literature. The only predictions on the war she had published, spoken about, and authorized, she stated, were her *Almanachs* for 1913 and 1914.[54]

While one Austrian newspaper dismissed 'the famous Madame de Thèbes' as being a mere agitator for the 'Pan-Slavic' clique in Paris who sought to unify the Slavic nations of eastern Europe, she was widely feted as an extraordinary international figure.[55] Such was her fame due to her war prophecy that in 1915 the Finnish-Swedish film director Mauritz Stiller made a romantic drama about an ambitious politician who does not realize that he is the illegitimate son of none other than Madame de Thèbes, but this knowledge falls into the hands of a political rival. By this time, de Thèbes sought a degree of refuge from the media scrutiny and glare, and bought a farm in Meung-sur-Loire, south-west of Orleans, where she raised turkeys. The French press did not miss a trick in mocking her flight to the countryside. *Le Cri de Paris* observed that she 'who can announce the fall of empires and the death of kings, a dozen months in advance, cannot foresee from one week to another the rise or fall in the price of eggs'.[56] She died alone in her country home in December 1916, her adopted son having died of an illness sometime before—a fate she said she had read in his palm. Her demise was global news, reported in newspapers from Austria to Australia and America.[57] She left a bequest that the capital from the sale of her farm be used to provide a dowry for one of the poorest and most deserving girls born in Ménilmontant who agreed to marry that same year, the recipient to be chosen by the parish priest. As befitted the resting place of a global superstar, she was buried in the celebrity-laden Père Lachaise cemetery, not far from her birthplace.

Looking to the Stars

During the war, as at other times of conflict down the centuries, people pondered the portent of unusual astronomical occurrences in the sky. Italian and Serbian soldiers were keen interpreters of meteors, shooting stars, and halos. A total eclipse of the sun across the Baltic and Russia on 21 August 1914 was taken by some as a bad omen about the nascent war. And when the white dwarf Nova Aquilae was detected by telescope in June 1918, it led to speculation in the press as to whether it heralded anything for the conflict's end.[58] Then there were the planets: the brightness of Venus was the focus of particular attention in Italy as the 'star of peace'. One planet, above all, was thought to preside over the outcome on the battlefields—Mars. 'Was it the influence of Mars, the god of war, which drove the wind on the warpath?', pondered the *Whitby Gazette*, in its report of a lecture at the London Royal Institution entitled 'Wireless Messages from the Stars'. The lecturer observed how the position of Mars in relation to the constellation Leo was just the same as at the time of the Crimean and Boer wars. This was surely no coincidence. In France, the bellicose astrologer Raoul Larmier predicted the fall of the Hohenzollerns in 1913 or 1914 because of the conjunction of the malign planet Saturn with Mars in the House of Taurus.[59]

The scanning of the skies for portentous comets and shooting stars was an aspect of natural astrology, but most of the astrological rumin-ations about the war concerned the 'science' of natal and horary astrol-ogy. In simple terms, the former concerns the calculation of the position of the planets and constellations in the heavens at the exact moment of a person's birth. A horoscope or birth chart can then be constructed that indicates what the future holds based on the qualities of the most influential planets and constellations. Horary astrology involves calcu-lating the position of the planets at the moment a question is asked, such as 'When will the war end?'.

On the eve of war, there was little apparent public preoccupation with astrology in France and Germany, and there were only a handful of manuals and guidebooks compared to those explaining other occult sciences such as palmistry and cartomancy. Most of those who pub-lished on the astrology of the war, such as the Frenchman Albert Faucheux (F. C. Barlet), were theosophists who practised astrology more as an aspect of mystical occultism than a practical 'science'.[60] At the centre of the very small astrological fraternity in Germany was the Austrian actor and occultist Karl Brandler-Pracht, who set up astrological societies in Vienna, Munich, and Leipzig between 1907 and 1910. He and several others, such as Otto Pöllner, Wilhelm Becker, and Ernst Tiede, would be central to the popularizing of astrology in Germany during and after the war.[61] Britain was recognized as the superpower in the astrological world, and the renaissance of popular astrology in Germany was based, in part, on German translations by the likes of Brandler-Pracht and Becker of English astrological manuals. Before setting up his prof-essional astrological service in Berlin in 1910, for instance, Becker had gone to England to learn astrology from Alan Leo, a theosophist and the founding editor of *The Astrologer's Magazine*. While there, he acquired the German rights to several of Leo's numerous popular astrological books.

The vast majority of the population never consulted an astrologer in person, but many people read or heard about their war predictions, which were set out in numerous pamphlets, such as *The Great Devasta-tion: A Prophecy of the Times That Are Coming upon Europe, Astrologically Interpreted by Sepharial* (1914). While British newspapers only began to

Fig. 2.3. An Austrian satirical newspaper pokes fun at the British wartime interest in astrology.

produce the now very familiar horoscope columns from the 1930s, during the First World War they periodically reported on the latest astrological pronouncements, sometimes with a disapproving air, sometimes with tongue firmly in cheek, but often without comment. Astrologers also gave numerous public lectures. In February 1915, for instance, the press reported on a public talk at the Picture Palace in Wells, Somerset, in aid of the Red Cross by the president of the Cardiff Astrological Society, Mr T. Gould, entitled 'Astrology and the Great War', in which he observed that eclipses were the most potent causes of conflict. Later that year, Mr H. B. Hammond lectured at the Arthur Hall, Dover, on 'Astrology as a Guide to Life', and fascinated his audience by revealing the Kaiser's horoscope and what it meant for Germany's destiny.[62]

But it was Britain's venerable astrological almanacs that had the widest influence on wartime popular culture. The main titles were: *Zadkiel's Almanac*, named after the nom de plume of its founder Richard James Morrison (1795–1874); *Raphael's Almanac or the Prophetic Messenger*, which dated back to the 1820s; and the granddaddy of them all, *Moore's Almanac* or *Vox Stellarum* ('Voice of the Stars'), founded by the astrologer–physician Francis Moore in the 1690s. *Moore's Almanac* sold in its hundreds of thousands every year during the nineteenth century and became deeply rooted in folklore.[63] Its pronouncements for the coming year were a perennial fascination for the press. As to the war, *Moore's* certainly gains first prize for the most understated prediction of the coming conflict, with its advice for August 1914 reading: 'The vacation is likely to be disturbed by adverse events, in which the travelling public are involved.'[64] Out on the battlefield, one officer reminisced, in 1921, about his Cockney army driver, who called one of his horses Old Moore because "e knows every blinkin' fing like Old Moore's *Almanac*'. One evening they were warned of a gas attack, and the recently supplied nosebag gasmasks for horses were put into action. When the officer walked back to the rear of the column labouring in his own gas mask, he saw that his driver had taken his off already. When he asked why he was not wearing his, 'he leaned over the saddle and replied, in a confidential whisper, "Old Moore chucked his orf, so there ain't no blinkin' gas abaht—'e knows."'[65]

As the war clouds gathered, and during the early months of the conflict, the race was on to calculate and unpick the horoscopes of the European aristocracies and the leaders of the combatant countries to see what lay in store for their subjects. The German astrologer Ernst Tiede concluded from his examination of the horoscopes of Europe's statesmen that there was a two-to-one chance that the Central Powers would be victorious.[66] Not surprisingly, British astrologers read the same horoscopes very differently. In September 1914, E. H. Bailey gave his assessment in the periodical *Old Moore's Monthly Messenger*. The president of France had 'a fatalistic horoscope', concluded Bailey. The Sun was conjoined with the Moon, and in square to Mars and Venus, which were 'terrible influences, indicative not only of war but of personal violence'. The king of Italy was born with Mars and Saturn conjoined, however, which denoted that he was keeping out of conflict, though an impending solar eclipse could change things. As to the Kaiser, he had 'Mars in square to the radical Sun'—'another evil ray'. Bailey concluded with the stirring news that there was every indication from the stars that 'the greatest victory in the annals of the British Army and the ultimate crushing of the German Empire' were in prospect.[67]

As the war progressed, the almanac compilers applied their calculations to mapping out the twists and turns of the military campaigns. A digest of the war predictions in *Moore's Almanac* for 1916 is typical. The 'Voice of the Stars' predicted violence and further bloodshed in Italy in January, and that 'the legions of Germany will be rolled back to the borders of their own country'. For February, however, it appeared that 'our enemies will be active, and may gain temporary advantages'. The centre of Europe would be, by then, a scene of 'carnage and devastation'. In May, the position of Jupiter to Mars presaged a 'brilliant victory' for the British navy. In August, the new moon falling on the Kaiser's Saturn signified the beginning of Germany's downfall. Aviation would also make great strides. As for December, 'the end of the year does not, to my judgement, see the end of the war ... So far as our own country is concerned, continued progress and victory are assured.' Unsurprisingly, *Old Moore's* longstanding, though less popular, astrological competitor *Raphael's Prophetic Almanac* followed in a similar vein for 1916. There was no immediate end in sight to the bloodshed and sacrifice, but the stars assured a glorious victory whenever it would come.

In 1915, the Jesuit priest Herbert Thurston analysed the content of a range of astrological almanacs and their myriad war predictions up to that date, including *Old Moore* and *Zadkiel's Almanac*. His explanation of the 'system' used by almanac compilers was spot on. As he noted, they worked on the balance of probabilities: 'an immense number of shots are made—that many of them are mutually inconsistent matters little— and it is hoped that a fair proportion of these will go near enough to the mark to be claimed as successes'. He noticed how they made prognostications three times over in each issue. First, the headline predictions appeared in the general outlook for the year, then in the monthly calendar of events, and also in the horoscopes of important people. The forecasts in each could be quite divergent from one another and even contradictory, as a means of covering a range of prognosticatory possibilities. Statements were also phrased with 'judicious hedging'— 'we are not told positively that a war will take place, but that peace is seriously menaced; we are not informed that the Emperor of Austria, for example, will die, but that he ought to take care of his health'.[68] *Raphael* rather gave the game away when 'he' apologized as follows: 'My Almanac is published on the first day of August in each year, and the great war broke out in 1914 a few days afterwards, consequently I was unable to make special reference to it in the 1915 edition.'[69]

If the British almanacs were unanimous in their predictions of ultimate victory, they were remarkably coy about when that would happen. After giving a brief overview of *Old Moore's* predictions in 'his' almanac for 1918, one British newspaper grumbled humorously in August 1917 that '"Old Moore" does everything but tell us when the war will end.'[70] This was very true, but people also read what they wanted into astrological predictions. An Essex vicar noted in his diary for September 1917, 'many of the country people have absolute faith in the predictions of "Old Moore's" *Almanac*. Several have told Dr Smallwood how relieved they are to know that the war will be over in 1918; Old Moore says so.' This was actually because *Moore* predicted that in April 'the foe will be pressing at the gates', so villagers were quite sure that Germany would launch a failed invasion of Britain that month.[71] *Zadkiel's Almanac* for 1915—one of the few almanacs for that year to be printed *after* the outbreak of the war—thought that with Uranus setting, Russia would swiftly defeat Germany, and the war would probably end before 1915 arrived. It was less confident in subsequent years.

Writing in January 1915, Sepharial, the pen name of astrologer Walter Gorn Old (1864–1929), critiqued the astrological efforts to date, and announced that according to his own meticulous mathematical calculations the war would not end 'until Saturn comes to the opposition of the Sun in the Kaiser's horoscope', and that would happen in August 1917. This conflicted with the verdict of an Austrian astrologer, Karl Zanovsky, who after months of calculations reported to the Austrian press that the war would end on 17 August 1916, with three emperors and three kings being victorious. In March 1918, German occultist and astrologer Oskar Ganser had a dream: 'I was with my deceased father. He said to me, "my dear son, you have calculated carefully, but you have not considered various factors; the war will not be over on 2 May 1918, but on 19 August 1919. You will experience that."'[72] Then, in the autumn of 1918, a Bombay newspaper printed the latest calculations of the Calcutta astrologer Manmatha Bhattacherjee, who forecast that the Allies would enter Cologne by 1 July 1919 and the Germans would finally capitulate by 5 September 1919.[73] I have not come across any astrological predictions that accurately predicted either the armistice or the eventual end of the war.

Each time the stars failed, the astrologers would go back to their charts. It was questioned how the horoscope of one man could foretell the fate of a whole empire. But Alan Leo was bullish: 'To say that the horoscopes of monarchs have no national influence is to deny the truth of Astrology.'[74] They returned over and over again to see how past developments in the war had related to the horoscopes of the rulers and the position of the planets and constellations at the time. The successful astrological matches were taken as firm proof, while the many inconsistencies and failures were rarely discussed. Ralph Shirley stuck his neck out into deep astrological space in January 1917 by suggesting that, as well as employing horoscopes, the course of the war could even be mapped out by assessing the signs of the zodiac governing the different combatant countries. 'There have been some curious confirmations,' he observed, 'though we are still left in doubt with regard to very important points in this connection.'[75] 'Twice over have we had confirmation of the rule of Libra over Austria,' he concluded for example. The first proof was that Mars transited Libra at the time of the victories of the Russian general Brusilov against the Austrians in the spring of 1916. The successful German campaign against Rumania led by Field Marshal Mackensen was corroboration that Leo ruled over Rumania.

Armageddon and the New World Order

While much time and thought were expended in proving that the war had been predicted in old prophecies or by the application of occult sciences, as the horrific nature of the conflict unfolded, the war came to be seen as an omen, in itself, of a far more momentous transformation of the world to come, a metaphysical crisis of spiritual destiny. For Christian occultists such as the French mystical philosopher and electrical engineer Marcel Forhan, the war was a spiritual conflict in which Germany and Turkey would be defeated, because Jesus would finally bless those who he loved. Members of the British ritual occult organization the Golden Dawn talked expectantly of a war that would herald a magical new age.[76] Numerous authors reached for their Bibles to see what the Old and New Testaments had to say. One argued that the war was playing out the ancient biblical struggle between the Assyrians and the Israelites. The British were gifted a special providence by God, like the Israelites, and Germany harboured the poison of jealous hatred in their breasts, like the Assyrians. Their fate would be the same.[77]

The Apocalypse predicted in the Book of Revelation, with the antichrist descending to wreak catastrophic death and destruction on the battlefield of Armageddon, proved the most obvious analogy. It was depicted and described in numerous artistic and literary representations of the Western Front. The German painter Max Beckmann repeatedly dreamed of the destruction of the world. While serving as a hospital orderly, he came across a cemetery blown to pieces by grenade fire, and wrote home to his wife of the tombs ripped open and bones and skeletons hurled into the air and exposed, as if in some mocking pantomime of the Resurrection. The work of fellow German artist and machine gunner Otto Dix similarly borrowed from the biblical imagery of sixteenth-century art in portraying life in the trenches as a modern Armageddon.[78] A vision of the Apocalypse was also the creative key to the international best-selling novel by Blasco Ibáñez, *The Four Horsemen of the Apocalypse* (1916). This novel about an Argentinian family with German and French members who are drawn into the war on opposite sides also includes Tchernoff, a wild Russian mystical socialist living in Paris, who, on seeing the French troops heading for the front, prophesies that 'when the sun arises in a few hours, the world will see coursing through its fields the four horsemen, enemies of mankind'. He goes on

to describe a vision of the horsemen, the emissaries of German militarism, leading the Apocalypse: 'The blind forces of evil were about to be
let loose throughout the world.'[79]

For some, the Apocalypse was not a metaphor for the war: the war
was truly the end times of the Book of Revelation. While that meant
the near annihilation of humankind, it also heralded the return of Christ
on earth and a wonderful future—a new millennium. Only a small
percentage of humans, the elect, would survive to repopulate this
New Jerusalem or Kingdom of God on earth. While the Book of
Revelation had long been either ignored or quietly disputed in Christian
theology, over the centuries profound upheavals, such as the German
Reformation or the British Civil War, inspired episodes of millenarianism that gripped sections of the population. The First World War was
no exception, and it fuelled pre-existing millenarian strands in evangelical Christianity and Western occultism. In America, several popular
evangelists were vocal in their conviction that the war was the ultimate
sign of the Apocalypse. The Baptist minister G. R. Eads wrote in
the Arkansas newspaper *Baptist and Commoner*, 'the end of the age is
approaching with lightning speed'. The African-American Pentecostal
leader Charles Mason likewise explained, 'present events proved that
we are living in the last days and the end was near'.[80] While most
equated Germany with the forces of the antichrist, the Iowa pastor
D. W. Langelett produced a pamphlet in German and in English, published by the German Literary Board, in which he expressed 'not the
slightest doubt that the present European war is a manifestation of the
wrath of God', concluding that 'England is the Gog of Prophecy and is
Therefore Doomed to be Defeated.' The people or peoples referred to in
Revelation as Gog and Magog, the sworn enemies of God according to
the Old Testament, were the servants of Satan who the Messiah would
finally defeat to usher in the new millennium. Langelett wrote the
pamphlet with the 'object of warning the small remnant of God's people
in England of the approaching doom', but grumbled that not one of
his fellow ministers with whom he discussed the unfolding prophecy
was responsive to promoting his anti-British interpretation.[81]

Charles Taze Russell, the founder of the Watch Tower Society (Jehovah's
Witnesses), dedicated much time to calculating from biblical references
when the world would end and concluded it would be the year 1914. By
the time of the war, there were over a thousand Russellite communities

and millions of copies of his books and sermons had been printed. The advent of war gave a further boost to Russell's aura of prophetic wisdom. He confirmed to his followers that 'the present great war in Europe is the beginning of the Armageddon of the Scriptures'.[82] When the Apocalypse clearly failed to happen, he had to revise his predictions. Before his death in 1916 he declared that Christ had, indeed, returned in spirit, but that the Apocalypse would happen sometime later.

These American influences enflamed millennial tensions across the Atlantic in colonial Africa, where several African evangelical prophets, influenced by Baptist missionaries and the Watch Tower Society, prophesied that the German Army would come and destroy the hated colonial rulers, enabling Africans to control once more their own lands and destiny under a supreme African ruler. In the Witwatersrand, near Johannesburg, prophets preached that the war was a sign to reject Western customs in preparation for salvation in a new era.[83] In Malawi (Nyasaland), around 1908, Kenan Kamwana, a subscriber to the Watch Tower Society, echoed Charles Russell by publicly predicting that the Second Coming of Christ would happen in October 1914. The British would be driven out and Christ would end taxation in the country. Concerned that Kamwana's followers might rise up in preparation for this glorious millennium, the British authorities deported him to South Africa. With the advent of war in Europe, the authorities' fears were confirmed when, in January 1915, the American-trained Baptist missionary John Chilembwe led a messianic revolt against British conscription of Africans that was inspired by a blend of millennial expectation and colonial repression.[84]

Millenarian evangelism regarding the war was not as influential in Britain, but there was evidently considerable public interest in the issue. Pamphlets appeared with such titles as *The Great War—in the divine light of prophecy: Is it Armageddon?*[85] Similar questions were posed in local newspapers. It was observed in 1915 that 'the word "Armageddon" has now become a household word; it appears in the Press, and is used by the "man in the street"', and the French professor of literature Fernand Baldensperger confirmed from experience three years later that the British 'specially indulged' in such wartime literature.[86] Numerous clergymen gave sermons and talks on the subject. In November 1917 Pastor W. W. Foulston preached on the matter to an audience at the

Congregationalist church in Aylesbury. He was inspired to do so because he had received numerous enquiries about the Book of Revelation in relation to the war.[87] The Reverend Henry Charles Beeching, preaching in Norwich Cathedral in September 1914, was quite clear in his views that the country was engaged in 'a war of Christ against anti-Christ', and that 'the battle is not only ours, it is God's, it is indeed Armageddon. Ranged against us are the Dragon and the False Prophet.'[88] But it would appear that most clergy refrained from such dramatic prophetic judgements. The Reverend J. W. Genders, for instance, told a large audience at Ilfracombe, Devon, that with three grandsons in the forces and two granddaughters in army hospitals abroad, he took a special interest in this question. He concluded that as dreadful as the war was, it was not the Armageddon of Scripture.[89] Foulston quoted approvingly from the Irish biblical scholar Robert Henry Charles, who had written that, 'Never in the whole history of Christianity has the power of Anti-Christ asserted itself so triumphantly as in the last three years,' but Foulston was ultimately not convinced that the Apocalypse was imminent.[90] The war was, nevertheless, considered a profound intimation of the metaphorical Armageddon that *could* befall humanity. When Bishop D'Arcy preached on the subject in Belfast Cathedral in December 1915, he explained that the Book of Revelation was not concerned with the course of history: it was a warning from God, and as such it 'possessed for them here and now, a value beyond all estimation'.[91]

The most vocal expressions of wartime millenarianism in Europe issued from the burgeoning theosophical movement. The Theosophical Society was founded in 1875 by the mystic Helena Blavatsky (1831–91). She constructed a faith that blended Western occult traditions with Eastern religion, Buddhism and Hinduism in particular. She claimed to possess her wisdom and secret knowledge from mysterious spiritual masters known as the Mahatmas, who resided in Egypt and the Himalayas. The concepts of karma and reincarnation were central to the theosophical faith and how the movement would come to view the war. Although by 1914 global membership of the Theosophical Society only stood at around 25,000 (2,905 of them in Britain), its cultural influence was significant. A prodigious amount of theosophical literature was produced during the war, including the battlefield paper *Kurukshetra*. A 'Soldiers and Sailors Literature' fund was created. Staff at the society's offices reported receiving letters from the front line expressing gratitude for the courage and strength such literature gave them.[92]

Following Blavatsky's death, the leadership of the society adopted a more millenarian outlook, particularly as expressed by the former Anglican clergyman Charles Leadbeater. When he met an adolescent Indian boy named Jiddu Krishnamurti at the headquarters of the Theosophical Society in Madras, Leadbeater, who professed to have clairvoyant powers, received the revelation that the boy was destined to be the vehicle for the awaited World Teacher—Christ reborn, who would establish a new world religion on earth. Krishnamurti was brought from India to Britain in 1911 and on the outbreak of war he and his brother were removed to Cornwall for a year, and then he was looked after by the theosophist Gertrude Baillie-Weaver and her husband in a house in Wimbledon.[93] A new branch of the Theosophical Society called the Order of the Star in the East was set up to welcome the World Teacher, with Krishnamurti at its head. The cataclysm of the war indicated that the triumph of spirituality over materiality that would herald the arrival of the World Teacher was imminent: the new spiritual age would begin in England.

The war was interpreted as a great cosmic movement, an inevitable battle between the powers of Good and Evil—sometimes referred to as the White Lodge and the Black Lodge. The supernatural 'Intelligences' of each were believed to draw upon the thoughts and desires of men and women for spiritual sustenance. While many theosophists downplayed the role of supernatural or semi-divine beings other than the Mahatmas, others, such as Alfred Percy Sinnett (1840–1921), sought to delineate the nature, history, and purpose of the Black Lodge and its role in the war. For Sinnett, the crisis represented by the conflict lay beyond the national karma of the countries concerned. To understand the cosmic significance of the war it was necessary to understand the great age of Atlantis that began millions of years before the earliest civilizations recorded in history. The first people of Atlantis were guided by the semi-divine members of the great White Lodge. But some mere mortals began to foster covetous and selfish desires for power, and so these dark devotees generated a new lodge to serve their purposes. The human dark host may have been wiped out with the rest of Atlantis by the Great Flood, but the karmic restoration of their collective evil was destined to manifest itself one day. Humankind would avail itself of the Black Lodge again.

In Atlantian times, the dark magical forces had existed in the astral plane, but as now manifest in the Great War, they had descended to the mental plane, and were all the more destructive for it. Germany had drawn down this evil, of course. 'The fate of the world depends upon the final extermination of that enemy,' Sinnett warned, 'the banishment from this world finally and altogether of those mighty entities aiming at its ruin.'[94]

Considering such views, it is hardly surprising that the war fundamentally challenged the principle of 'a universal brotherhood of humanity, without distinction of race' espoused by theosophists. In 1915, the Theosophical Society convention in America discussed a resolution to be agreed across all national societies with regard to the war:

(a) The war is not of necessity a violation of Brotherhood, but may on the contrary become obligatory in obedience to the ideal of Brotherhood.

(b) That individual neutrality is wrong if it be believed that a principle of righteousness is at stake.

The Berlin theosophical bookseller Paul Raatz, Secretary of the Union of German Branches of the Theosophical Society, wrote to the Convention Committee expressing bitter criticism of the political nature of the resolution. He argued that it was still too early for the principle of Universal Brotherhood to be fully defined, and 'the Committee is not justified in passing resolutions which bind the whole Society to one view'. The 1916 convention considered Raatz's letter at length, but resolved that 'it is the conviction of the Convention that the powers of good are now ranged against the powers of evil: that, among the nations, France is leading the charge of the White Lodge against the attack of Germany supported and directed by the Black Lodge and all of the evil forces of the world'. Several German-American members spoke up in support of this resolution, but, considering the sensitivity, there was general agreement to postpone a vote indefinitely.[95]

A mystical revolution was in the making, and the conduct of the war would be decisive. As one contributor to the American *Theosophical Quarterly* wrote in 1916, 'tolerated evil in us now may mean sinister world events twenty centuries hence. Sacrifice and aspiration now will without doubt bring spiritual fruit for centuries to come.'[96] There was a common view amongst British and American theosophists, though, that the fight was against German militarism and materialism and not the German people per se, many of whom they recognized were privately against the war. Their good karma would ensure that Germany would prosper spiritually and culturally once the bad national karma had played its course. Germans, as much as any other peoples, would contribute spiritually to the new age of Universal Brotherhood that would come after.[97] It was also argued by some that, through its pursuance of war and supposed atrocities, the German state was actually making good karma by uniting the decency of the world against the country. German troops would not die in vain. 'We were content with material progress, and Germany, by showing us how vile a thing material progress can be, turned our minds and hearts to spiritual values and to everlasting truths,' wrote one Theosophist. As a karmic consequence, 'the powers of evil are foredoomed: their success will become their undoing'.[98]

Theosophy was a 'broad church', and despite the principle of Universal Brotherhood, nationalist and racist interpretations of theosophy became prominent during the war. The Russian Theosophical Society had been founded in 1908, and during its early years it produced a flurry of literature to cater for its few thousand members and the growing public interest in their message. The environment in Russia was receptive, with the country being described as 'a continuous battle-field of prophecies' since the war's outbreak.[99] The society was confident that its rapid growth was a sign of the spiritual renewal of the world in the depths of conflagration. The writings of Anna Kamenskaia, one of the leading contributors to the main theosophical journal *Vestnik Teosofii* (*Herald of Theosophy*), which ran from 1908 to 1917, pushed a popular predictive view that Russia was destined to play a superior occult role in the war. The nation's karma was linked to the wartime suffering it would endure by cleansing the cosmic soul of the world. Traditional Slavic spirituality was destined, through theosophy, to conquer and rescue the decaying, egotistical, and materialist West.[100] Wellesley Tudor Pole was one British spiritualist who was in agreement, stating in late 1914 that in the midst of the current Armageddon, 'the Slav child-soul is destined to bring illumination to us all'.[101] But three years later such millennial enthusiasm was smothered by the Russian Revolution: the materialists had struck back. Still, as an article in the *Theosophical*

Quarterly in January 1918 explained, the revolution was clearly a manifestation of German karmic evil. Most of the Petrograd Bolsheviks talked a dialect of German, it claimed, 'and they still think in that German dialect'.[102]

Germany had its Christian evangelical prophets, such as the spiritual healer and clairvoyant Joseph Weißenberg (1855–1941). The Berlin authorities, concerned by the destabilizing effect of his pronouncements and the growth of his following, temporarily incarcerated him during the war, claiming he was insane, and continually hampered his activities. After the war he made international headlines in May 1929 by prophesying that the Archangel Gabriel had told him that Britain was imminently doomed by an earthquake and would sink beneath the waves of the subsequent apocalyptic flood.[103] However, the most influential nationalist millenarian tendencies in Germany and Austria were fuelled by theosophy.[104] In the latter country, the war was enthusiastically embraced by its leading occultist Guido von List (1848–1919), whose ideas would go on to influence the ideology of the early Nazi Party. An ardent nationalist, von List had spent decades piecing together what he believed to be the true religion of the ancient Germans, and endeavoured to unlock the mystic powers of the runes. He sought the renewal of a pure Aryan race and its pre-Christian faith and believed such a momentous time would inevitably come. This notion followed a long tradition of predictions of an age of Teutonic hegemony that date back to the medieval period. For List and his followers, the First World War heralded this long-awaited prophetic moment. In April 1915 he delivered a speech to the organization he had recently founded, *der Hohe Armanen-Orden* or High Armanen Order (HAO), in which he welcomed the conflict as the beginning of a millenarian struggle, which after much apocalyptic woe, would herald a new, true German age wiped free of corrupted Christian religion. A 'Strong one from Above' would institute a totalitarian regime that would end the corrosive influence of inferior non-German peoples. Influenced by his theosophist views, he believed that karma would ensure that the hundreds of thousands of German and Austrian war dead would be reborn as the elite shock troops of this new world order. One of List's disciples, the fantasist and racist Jörg Lanz von Liebenfels, embellished the vision, seeing the war as heralding the beginning of a bloody chaotic period that would ultimately lead to an 'ario-christian' New Age. Inferior races would be wiped off the face of the earth and a mystical priesthood would govern a supranational Aryan state led by superhumans imbued with holy electronic power.[105]

Another leading figure in Austrian and German occultism, Rudolf Steiner (1861–1925), founder of the Steiner school movement, argued publicly and repeatedly that the war was 'a conspiracy against German spiritual life'.[106] Although not formally a member of the Theosophical Society, he was responsible for leading its first German section in 1902. The society flourished under Steiner's industrious leadership, but he was all the while reformulating and reinterpreting aspects of Blavatsky's teachings. He rejected Krishnamurti, and in 1912 he co-founded the Anthroposophical Society, which soon had some three thousand members. Its aim was 'to nurture the life of the soul, both in the individual and in human society, on the basis of a true knowledge of the spiritual world'. The Anthroposophical Society was run from a village in Switzerland, but Steiner spent much time in Austria and Germany during the war, spreading his message and views. These included the belief that the conflict was the earthly manifestation of a cosmic spiritual battle, 'a world of demons and spirits which works through humankind when nations battle one another'. The war was necessary for the salvation of mankind, and 'Germandom' must conquer the spiritually bankrupt nations of the West and the spiritually immature Slavic foe in the East. It would result, he affirmed in early 1916, with the German people leading 'the entire realm of human spiritual culture'.[107]

666: The Sign of the Kaiser

And there was given unto him a mouth speaking great things and blasphemies; and power was given unto him to continue forty and two months. (Revelation 13:5)

Here is wisdom. Let him that hath understanding count the number of the beast: for it is the number of a man; and his number is six hundred threescore and six (Revelation 13:18)

And I saw the beast, and the kings of the earth, and their armies, gathered together to make war against him that sat on the horse, and against his army. And the beast was taken, and with him the false prophet that wrought miracles before him...These both were cast alive into a lake of fire burning with brimstone (Revelation 19:20)

If the war truly heralded the imminence of the Apocalypse, then for allied evangelicals, Christian occultists, and prophets one did not have to look far to identify the personification of the Antichrist. Reviewing a book entitled *Ancient Babylon and Modern Germany*, a Scottish newspaper commented in May 1916, 'there is an epidemic of this sort of thing just now, and attempts to identify Germany with Babylon and the Kaiser with Anti-Christ form a prominent feature of the literature of the war'.[108]

In September 1914 the national French newspaper *Le Figaro* published the sensational revelations of a recently discovered prophecy attributed to an early seventeenth-century monk called Johannes. No other details of this mysterious personage were forthcoming, though one English medium reported receiving a psychic message that he was an Italian.[109] The prophecy was given to the paper by the well-known art critic, novelist, and occultist Joseph Péladan (1858–1918), who claimed to have found a translation of it amongst his father's manuscripts on his death in 1890. His father had been a journalist with a preoccupation with ancient prophecies who had apparently obtained it from a French clergyman. According to Johannes's prophecy, 'the veritable Antichrist will be one of the Monarchs of his time; a son of Luther; he will invoke God and call himself His messenger'. This was clearly none other than Kaiser Wilhelm. Thankfully, Johannes predicted that this Antichrist would 'lose his crown and...die demented and alone'.[110] The prophecy disseminated widely, and was published in pamphlet form in Switzerland and France, leading one critic to grumble in 1916 that 'it has sold for far too long on our boulevards'.[111] In England, translated extracts were printed in the press under the heading 'Is the Kaiser the Antichrist?'[112] The occultist Ralph Shirley published his own edition entitled *The End of the Kaiser* (1915), and a cheap penny tract also appeared with the title *Doom of the Kaiser 'Anti-Christ'* (1914), which was offered on credit to the first two hundred purchasers in London and the provinces.[113] Speculation, rumour, and lies gave the prophecy a more venerable history of dissemination than it had. A correspondent to *Light*, Alderman Ward of Harrogate, said he had seen a copy in the hands of a Belgian judge he met in a London hotel, who said he had been in possession of it for many years. A correspondent to the *Daily Call* said he knew the prophecy had circulated in Dublin in 1868.[114] The general reception was understandably negative and sceptical. The prophecy was widely dismissed as a fraud, though Ralph Shirley thought it so remarkable in its prophetic accuracy that even if Péladan was its author, 'its extraordinary character would hardly be diminished'.[115]

The occultist Arthur Trefusis took a different prophetic inspiration to reach the same conclusion about the Kaiser. He focused on the early Christian author Lactantius, who wrote in the early fourth century about a prediction, then in circulation, that the despotic emperor Nero (d. 68 AD) would return as 'a messenger and forerunner of the Evil One, coming for the devastation of the earth'. Trefusis drew parallels between the brutality and cruel acts of Nero and the purported German atrocities in Belgium. 'The order to sink the *Lusitania* is in strict accord with Nero's record,' he decided, and 'asphyxiating gases, flame projectors, and corrosive liquid all show the mind of Nero'.[116] There was only one conclusion to be drawn: the Kaiser was Nero reincarnated, who in turn was the Beast of Revelations. The prophecy had been fulfilled. But all the Kaiser's schemes would fail, the Hohenzollern dynasty would end, and a terrible revolution would plague the German nation.

In June and July 1915 a number of British newspapers reported that a Montreal student had discovered firm proof that the Kaiser was indeed the Beast of Revelations.[117] He had deciphered 'the number of the man' by giving a sequential number to the alphabet (A = 1 through to Z = 26), totting up the value of each letter in the word 'Kaiser', and adding a six to each number—six being the number of letters in 'Kaiser':

K: 11 + 6 = 116
A: 1 + 6 =   16
I: 9 + 6 =   96
S: 19 + 6 = 196
E: 5 + 6 =   56
R: 18 + 6 = 186
                  666

This revelation was also printed in the French press the following year, where it was attributed to an English researcher.[118] In December 1916 a new calculation promulgated in Moscow did the rounds. According to this, it was worked out from a formula involving the lunar and calendar months that the war would last three years, three months, and six days, or 1,193 days. If that number was subtracted from the number representing the Kaiser's birth year, 1859, the result was 666.[119]

The Kaiser calculations were given a full-blown national airing in the spring of 1916 by the jingoist and propagandist Horatio William Bottomley (1860–1933). He was the editor of the popular patriotic newspaper *John Bull*, and an attention-seeking politician and demagogue, similar to a couple of figures in Britain and North America today, who was finally brought low by a fraud conviction shortly after the war. Bottomley, who was critical of government propaganda efforts, used *John Bull* to spout a constant stream of crude xenophobic rhetoric against what the paper called the 'Germhuns'. The Kaiser was described as the 'Potty Potentate of Potsdam' and the paper printed spurious stories such as that the Kaiser had been certified insane. Bottomley went so far as to call for a vendetta against all Germans in Britain.[120] His old personal assistant Henry Houston recalled in 1923 how, in early 1916, he and his master had met an old acquaintance of the latter called Mr Pritchard who was somewhat obsessed with the 666 prophecy. As Pritchard wrote down the calculation and cited the relevant passages from Revelation, Bottomley gave Houston 'a look that plainly indicated he had found his subject for the next week's article. The Beast of Revelation, the mystery of the ages, had been solved.' After Pritchard had left, Bottomley turned to Houston and asked, 'This is all right for next Sunday, but what shall we make the title? "The Mystery of 666"?'[121] A three-quarter-page article by Bottomley duly appeared under that title in several national papers in April 1916. He told readers that the revelation had been revealed to him by an 'interesting acquaintance' while snowed up in a Midlands hotel the previous week without telephone or post. After explaining the references to the Antichrist in Revelation and the numerological prophecy, he remarked, 'A fascinating theme, isn't it? Upon my word, the more you study the Book, the more remarkable the vision becomes. I confess it haunts me.' He ended on a lighter note, though, exclaiming, 'Phew! I must never get snowed up again!'[122]

German occultists came to very different conclusions, of course, when applying similar numerical divinations. An article in the occult periodical *Zentralblatt für Okkultismus* in 1916 totted up the number of the Kaiser from relevant astral dates and came to the conclusion that the emperor was, in fact, the instrument of God and destined to destroy Germany's enemies, who obviously had very bad karma. The author concluded that Germany would win and 'the ancestors would look down proudly from the sky'.[123] Meanwhile, by no means all occultists and evangelists in Allied countries were convinced that the Kaiser was the Antichrist either. In 1915, Marr Murray explained in his *Bible Proph- ecies and the Plain Man* that although the Kaiser bore resemblance to the Antichrist, he was not the real deal. This was because, Murray reasoned, the Kaiser had shown he was no military genius: 'if we imagine a blend of Napoleon and Kaiser then we have an idea of what the real Antichrist will be like'.[124] Most American evangelists also concluded that the Kaiser was a herald of the Antichrist but not the prophetic man himself. They kept more of an eye on the Pope and an alliance between the Vatican and the Germans as the firmest sign of the coming Apocalypse.[125]

In the autumn of 1915 the vice-president of the *Societé Universelle d'Études Psychiques*, Edmond Duchatel, proposed to hold a conference after the war to subject to close scrutiny all the predictions and prophecies that had been published about the conflict, and to clarify the actual dates of their publication or references to them.[126] Come the end of the war, there was little appetite, however, for treating the raft of dubious and failed war prophecies to further scientific inquiry. They were largely discredited as a body of evidence for psychic, occult, and scientific insight. But there was academic interest in how the prophecies had impacted upon society. In his book *Propaganda Technique in the World War* (1927), the young American sociologist Harold Lasswell, who would go on to become a pioneer of communication theory, noted the value of prophetic announcements in bolstering morale and undermining that of the enemy nations. 'It was safe to predict that they would carry reassurance to the most superstitious and credulous strata of the popu- lation,' he observed, but that the sophisticated would contemptuously dismiss them. As a consequence, he thought it 'perfectly safe to launch the crude and sophisticated together, for the people capable of reacting to the latter will not be estranged by the former; they will merely remain indifferent and condescending'.[127] Lasswell noted, in particular, the morale-nourishing influence of the *Almanach de Madame de Thèbes* amongst the French public during the early years of the war. But how complicit were the prophets and astrologers in producing propaganda?

There is a long history of state-inspired employment of prophecy in wartime, and France, Germany, and Britain had sophisticated propaganda machines during the war.[128] But, despite the overwhelming biases of the wartime prophecies, there is very little indication that the authorities in any of the combatant countries were involved in producing or commissioning such literature. In Britain, for instance, the National War Aims Committee, set up in 1917, was assisted by clergymen who produced patriotic rhetoric about the spiritual superiority of the British and their divine destiny to defeat the foe.[129] But there is no evidence that prophecies and astrologers were similarly co-opted. Horatio Bottomley's piece of 666 propaganda was clearly his own initiative, for instance, and, in other respects, the government found his jingoistic mouthing and methods highly distasteful. Religious interests, if not church authorities, were clearly involved in using prophecy for propaganda purposes, though. Sometimes religious motives were wrapped up in national interests, but sometimes the prophecies were intended for purely confessional promotion and advantage.

Did the astrologers and almanac-makers shape their predictions for the greater good of their respective countries out of patriotic zeal? It is most likely; otherwise how else could astrological calculations so predictably follow the narratives of glorious victory? But there were also commercial forces at play. While governments and military authorities did not actively produce morale-boosting prophecies, they certainly were not going to allow the propagation of ominous predictions detrimental to public confidence. In short, there was little latitude for publishing troubling national forecasts—and no commercial incentive either. Good news sold in wartime, and for the compilers of almanacs and the authors of astrological literature, the astral science was their livelihood. As long as the commercial and national imperatives aligned, the *public* soothsayers were largely free to go about their business. But, as we shall see in Chapter 3, the *private* discourse around wartime divination, as well as the myriad conversations in fortune tellers' consulting rooms across the combatant countries, was much less bullish in tone, and more worrying for the authorities.

3

VISIONS, SPIRITS, AND PSYCHICS

Sport is more in my line than Spiritualism and that sort of thing, but when you have experiences brought under your very nose again and again, you cannot help thinking that there must be something in such things.

(An officer wounded at Mons in October 1914)[1]

Numerous strange visions and sensations experienced by soldiers and their loved ones were reported during the war, and were described variously at the time as 'the uncanny under fire' or 'war and the weird'. Wars have always generated stories of apparitions, ghostly encounters, and strange premonitions, but there had never before been such a keen interest in the supernatural or otherworldly experiences of the military as during and after the Great War. This was due, in large part, to the extraordinary early twentieth-century convergence of scientific and religious interest in metaphysics and the esoteric respectively, coupled with a general public ever receptive to proofs of a spiritual side to life. And the key to understanding much of this rapprochement with the supernatural, and to how it has been interpreted since, lies in our understanding of the spiritualist movement.

For all the passing interest in the influence of spiritualism during the First World War, it is remarkable how little has actually been written about its place in society during the period. Most studies of spiritualism end in 1914 or focus on the post-war era. This has led to a series of problematic assumptions about the nature and popularity of spiritualism and its relation to the broader category of the supernatural.[2] Little distinction has been made in the literature, for instance, between spiritualism as an organized religion with its own societies and membership, general interest in spiritualist phenomena as evident from the boom in pamphlets and books on the subject and the work of psychical researchers, and the practices of self-styled mediums or clairvoyants who were often not members of any spiritualist organization. A range of spiritual experiences and phenomena, some rooted in folklore, some in religion, some in psychical research, have also been conflated with the tenets of and interest in spiritualism. The influence of politics and propaganda, both religious and secular, is also part of the story. So, what we need to do now is unpick the tangle of personal experiences, traditions, beliefs, and phenomena to reassess some of the assumptions that have been made about death, grief, and the belief in supernatural interventions in wartime.

Heavenly Signs and Visitations

The iconography and experience of protective divine visitation was a powerful spiritual and propaganda tool on both the home and the battle fronts, particularly in Catholic and Orthodox areas and amongst their armies. Morale-boosting Italian postcards, for example, depicted Christ appearing in the sky above the battlefield, casting his divine shield over Italian soldiers.[3] In Britain, in June 1916, the press widely reprinted a letter from a sergeant of the Royal Sussex Regiment to his mother in Eastbourne in which he described how on the morning of 22 May he and his comrades 'saw a most beautiful white cross in the sky', which slowly sailed along until it reached the moon. 'I think everybody about here saw it,' said the sergeant, 'and for about ten or fifteen minutes there was not a shot fired.' One Private Davies, from a Welsh regiment, also witnessed it and wrote, 'We were in the firing-line. For a few minutes it was like peace, everything was quiet. It was wonderful.'[4] The incident was immortalized shortly afterwards in a painting produced for the *Illustrated London News* by the artist Arthur Cadwgan Michael entitled 'The Cross in the Heavens above the Trenches'. On 10 October 1918 the Irish mailboat RMS *Leinster* was torpedoed by a German U-boat just outside Dublin Bay. Over five hundred people died. A couple of weeks later, Canon Pim of Christ Church, Dún Laoghaire, from where the mailboat set off, wrote to the *Irish Times* to state that gazing up at a clear sky shortly after, he and other people looking out to sea saw on the horizon 'a great white cross of absolutely perfect shape'. As it formed, it seemed to be full of the faces of men and women. Pim concluded, 'one

Fig. 3.1. The Cover of *Interventions de Sr Thérèse de l'Enfant-Jésus pendant la guerre* (Bayeux, 1920). It contains hundreds of letters from military personnel thanking Thérèse for her miraculous interventions during the war.

presumes to offer no explanation, but it was certainly there, and at least it was a symbol of surpassing comfort'.[5]

An article in the *Theosophist* in 1916 raised the question of why such visions only seemed to appear to British soldiers and their allies. After all, German soldiers also faced grave peril. The answer was actually straightforward according to the author. Those that appeared were spirits of 'Light' reflecting the power of Good, while 'so long as the Germans continue to act as fiends they will continue to attract the power of fiends'.[6] But angels were said to be active on all sides of the conflict, for in Catholic countries the notion of guardian angels was strong in formal and popular theology. If they were ever-ministering to pious Catholics, it was self-evident that they were watching over the battle-fields. A German postcard from 1916, for instance, shows a female figure with angel wings looking over the shoulder of a rifleman ready to fire, and bears the title 'The Warrior's Guardian Angel'. An accom-panying verse explains that the angel was sent from heaven 'to look after you'. 'It is not the question whether anyone caught a glimpse of them with his eyes, or a sound, with his ears. It is above sense, greater than sense,' explained a British Catholic lecturer in August 1915.[7] Yet it is not surprising that such imagery and conviction inspired the occasional report of 'real' angelic appearances during the war.

While mainstream Protestant theology considered the notion of guardian angels as Catholic superstition, evangelical Protestant groups embraced it as an expression of God's immanence, and 'His' continued intervention in human affairs. Indeed, the country most preoccupied with angelic visitations on the battlefield was Britain, as a consequence of the Church of England's crisis of confidence due to the war. Several reports of angelic apparitions were printed in the British Pentecostal periodical *Confidence*, which was edited by Alexander Alfred Boddy (1854–1930), an Anglican vicar serving Monkwearmouth, Sunderland, and a leading figure in the evangelical revival of the late nineteenth and early twentieth centuries. He had been at the front as a chaplain with the British Expeditionary Force for a couple of months, and his views on the war were shaped by his conviction that the conflict was a sign of the coming Apocalypse and the Second Coming of Christ. He was constantly on the lookout for instances of miraculous healing, providential occurrences, and deliverance through prayer to print in *Confidence*. In March 1916, for instance, he included several examples

Fig. 3.2. Patriotic German postcard depicting a 'warrior's guardian angel' watching over and aiding a rifleman.

of prayers answered during German air raids. So a tradesman in north-eastern England called together his eleven shop assistants for two minutes' prayer that the Lord's good hand would protect them. That night a Zeppelin raid badly hit the district, but 'seven of the assistants living in different parts were wonderfully protected when homes nearby were wrecked, and not one of the eleven was harmed'.[8]

Examples of angelic visitations were gold dust. In January 1916, J. G. Davies of Rhondda, a stretcher-bearer in the King's Royal Rifles, wrote to Boddy stating that angels had been seen over the trenches near Ypres in October last:

> We were in a trench besides St. Jean (near Ypres), Belgium, and the shells showered on us. I as a stretcher bearer went down the trench to see if anyone was wounded, but stopped now and again to hear the men praying, so finding nothing to do, I prayed myself and the trench was one line of prayer. After the shelling no one was wounded, but we all saw a host of angels, and talked about them; and I told them that the Lord was on our side.

Boddy sent him a questionnaire to complete to obtain further details. In response, Davies said the vision occurred about 12.30 in the morning. It was a clear sky and the shelling had just ceased. The angels, including the faces of men and women, came from a very high distance, lowered themselves to be more visible, before ascending again until they were lost from sight. It lasted for a quarter of an hour. And this was not the only occasion Davies had witnessed a divine presence:

> Another time when in the trenches we heard a voice sounding through the air, about 9 o'clock at night, and the moon was clear, and I saw an angel flying with a trumpet in his mouth. Some were very much frightened, but I said, 'Cheer up! It is all for good to them that love the Lord.'

In response to the questionnaire, Davies reported that this occurred at 9 o'clock on 7 December 1915. 'The angel was about twenty yards away, and I heard the voice, which sounded like a rolling of the sea and it weakened away, then I heard the words were "Destruction!" "Destruction!" then he vanished.'[9] At the Battle of Passchendaele, in 1917, a Canadian soldier, William Breckenridge, of the 42nd Battalion, had a similar experience. As the shells poured down, he looked up at the night sky and 'in the heavens there was a vision. There appeared in the clouds, as they passed a sliver of moon light, a band of angels hovering to and fro.' He pointed them out to his mate, and said, 'They must be watching over us ... We will be alright.'[10]

Back on the home front, in August and September 1917 the *Daily News*, and many other papers, reported first the appearance of angels in the sky above the Thames near Grays, and then that, on the night of 17 September, several people saw two female angels appear over the town of Waltham Abbey, just north of London. They paused on the church tower and unfurled a scroll bearing the word 'Peace' in letters of fire, before disappearing. An angel was also reported a few months later appearing in the sky above Dundee.[11] The supposed eyewitness accounts of the 'Angels of Essex' were treated summarily and with casual scepticism by the press. *The Globe* pondered, tongue in cheek, 'How is "Angelitis" contracted? Is it contagious or hereditary?'[12] This was in considerable part due to a degree of wariness and weariness regarding the long-running public controversy over the Angels of Mons.[13]

In late August 1914 the British Expeditionary Force was forced to retreat rapidly at the Battle of Mons. It was an early foretaste of the military challenges ahead and a setback to morale. Deeply moved by the newspaper reports of the battle, the author Arthur Machen penned a short story called the 'The Bowmen'. As Machen later recalled, 'There were terrible things to be read on that hot Sunday morning between meat and mass. It was in *The Weekly Dispatch* that I saw the awful account of the retreat from Mons ... I seemed to see a furnace of torment and death and agony and terror seven times heated, and in the midst of the burning was the British Army.'[14] His story was printed in *The Evening News* on 29 September, and told of how, in the heat and desperation of battle, a soldier 'saw before him, beyond the trench, a long line of shapes, with a shining about them. They were like men who drew the bow, and with another shout their cloud of arrows flew singing and tingling through the air towards the German hosts.' St George had called up the spirits of the bowmen of Agincourt to aid them, and 'the singing arrows fled so swift and thick that they darkened the air; the heathen horde melted from before them'. Requests soon came in from several editors of parish magazines to reprint the story, and slowly but surely the account spread in print and by word of mouth; and as it did, it began to be taken as reality rather than fiction. It was in the following spring, with new versions of the bowmen appearing around St George's Day, that in Machen's words, 'the snowball of rumour that was then set rolling [and] has been rolling ever since' grew bigger and bigger, 'till it is now swollen to a monstrous size'.[15] The simple tale of the bowmen began to be embroidered and reformulated as reports accumulated of apparent first-hand sightings of angelic visions, knights in armour, and mysterious clouds at the retreat from Mons. The occultist and spiritualist communities obviously took a close interest, and reprinted every account they could gather of soldiers who had seen such visions. National and local newspapers joined the debate and the quest for verifiable testimonies. Pamphlet compilations of these accounts proliferated, most presenting the visions as undoubted proof of God's intervention.

The Reverend Forbes Phillips, Vicar of Gorleston, Norfolk, and his co-author complained in their book *War and the Weird* (1916), 'The Anglican Church has failed dismally to keep before people the teaching of the Church in regard to Angels and Angelic intervention in the affairs of men ... Soldiers tell their stories of angels and a few bishops cackle.'[16] But out in the parishes, it was Phillips's fellow Anglican clergymen who preached the message of a modern miracle and the divine preference it demonstrated for the British soldier. It is no surprise, of course, that the Reverend A. A. Boddy was evangelical in his promotion of the story. He published accounts in *Confidence* and reprinted them in a pamphlet *Real Angels of Mons*. On visiting the local regimental stores to hand out pocket Testaments and other religious literature, he was delighted that nearly every soldier also requested a copy of his pamphlet.[17] Sympathetic voices could also be heard among mainstream Anglican clergy. Preaching on the subject in September 1915, the Reverend John Hilton, of St Matthew's Church, Islington, London, told his flock that he had no doubt that God 'allowed some of those tired, weary, worn-out defenders of right, honour, purity and truth to see that there was a wall of protection between themselves and the Germans, and that that wall of protection was a body of His own ministers, whom we call angels'.[18]

But there were many sceptical voices too. How was it that all the accounts were of a second-hand nature? Letters from nurses and chaplains relating things soldiers had heard but not actually seen, army stories heard from a friend of a friend about strange appearances. What of the many soldiers who had not heard at all of any such apparitions? One private was reported as swearing that he had been fighting rearguard actions between 22 August and 6 September and had heard nothing from fellow soldiers about any supernatural visions, except on one occasion a sighting of the Devil that turned out to be an old blind cow.[19] Senior Anglicans were damning on the matter. The Dean of Durham, Herbert Hensley Henson, a liberal voice in the Anglican Church, was scathing about the 'eager haste' with which stories of the supernatural assistance given to British soldiers at Mons were circulated in the religious press. It was nothing more than 'grovelling superstition' and journalistic '*jeu d'esprit*'.[20] Berated for spreading superstition and worse, the spiritualist and occult periodical *Light* was actually one of the more perspicacious and cautious commentators on the Angels of Mons stories. It had quickly identified and notified its readers that Machen's piece was a work of fiction, and expressed astonishment that members of the public and clergymen were taking Machen's account as fact. In September 1915 it summed up developments: 'The subject is becoming a veritable Chameleon in its variations of hue and appearance, and the issue at times stands in danger of becoming confused.'[21] Helen Salter was in charge of the Society for Psychical Research's investigation into the Angels of Mons at the time, collating information, following up sighting reports, corresponding with interested parties. Her main conclusion from all this endeavour was concerned not so much with the evidence of supernatural intervention as the psychology of communication in wartime: 'The whole history of the case throws an interesting light on the value of human testimony and the growth of rumour.'[22]

While the battle *for* the Angels of Mons played out as part of the Anglican Church's struggle to respond to the spiritual and emotional demands of the war, the stories also had obvious political and military propaganda value. Although there is no evidence that the British War Propaganda Bureau, created in early autumn 1914, or the News Department of the Foreign Office, which was responsible for supplying news to the press, had any hand in creating the story, it has been suggested that the Propaganda Bureau may have involved itself in keeping the interest alive.[23] A satirical piece on the Mons accounts in the *Daily Herald*, in July 1915, observed, 'shells are useful enough in their way, but spectres are ten times more efficient—and cheaper. If there were any casualties in that ghostly company at Mons they cost the war Office nothing . . . the need of the moment is not a Ministry of Munitions, but a Ministry of Apparitions!'[24]

Visions of Mary

The pilgrimage trails to Marian shrines, such as at Lourdes in France or Marpingen in Germany, swelled with soldiers and their loved ones seeking succour and protection. The Bishop of Tarbes, who had spiritual jurisdiction over the famous Marian sanctuary of Lourdes, publicly called on the Virgin to aid France in its fight against the Germans. Apparitions of the Virgin Mary were periodically reported in times of exceptional communal stress and national crises over the centuries.[25] It is no surprise, then, that several new visitations by the Virgin were claimed during the period of the war. Numerous votive tablets in Italian shrines and churches depicted the Madonna and child appearing in a cloud over the battlefield, looking down upon and protecting Italian troops.[26] In April 1918, the *Irish Times* reported that several inhabitants in the village of Aughrim, Galway, had recently seen the apparition of the Virgin Mary in a nearby wood. Local legend had it that she had appeared before the bloody Battle of Aughrim in 1691, which marked the end of Jacobitism in Ireland. Her new appearance was thought to be a portent of great trouble ahead; whether for Ireland's independence or international peace was a matter of speculation.[27] It was around the time of the First World War that, in Italy, an illiterate peasant woman named Marietta D'Agostino, of Orta Nova, began to receive visitations from the Madonna, which bestowed upon her unusual powers of divination and healing. In February 1916 *La Stampa* reported that there was considerable excitement in the region of Puglia after an octogenarian peasant woman claimed tò have been visited by the Virgin in a dream. The Virgin had instructed her to go to the commune of Melendugno and dig at a certain spot. There she would find some blocks of stone, then some human bones, and finally, underneath, a chapel bearing the painted image of the Madonna of Peace. The war would then cease immediately. People in the area picked up their spades and an impromptu popular excavation took place to reveal the miracle.[28]

In Germany the 'Seer of Schippach', Barbara Weigand, who had for several decades attracted a devoted following for her professed visionary communications with Christ, the Virgin, and various saints, received a boost thanks to the war. By 1915 her followers had raised 500,000 marks to establish a pilgrimage site near Aschaffenburg, Bavaria, where she received her divine visitations. In one such communication she said the Virgin told her, 'German and Austrian soldiers will triumph!...Germany and Austria owe their victories hitherto only to those men that led you to My Son.' As she began to relay increasingly political prophetic messages about the war from her divine visitors, the ecclesiastical and secular authorities in the area sought to dampen her influence and prevent the founding of the pilgrimage grotto.[29]

There were also claims of Marian visitations on the battlefield. As the German Army pressed towards Paris in early September 1914, General Joffre made a decisive decision to counter-attack with British support. The Germans were pushed back, giving France a much-needed boost to military and public morale. The Feast of the Nativity of the Virgin had been on 8 September, and in churches and homes across the country prayers were said in her name for France's deliverance from the enemy. Claims quickly emerged that the unexpected success had been down to the divine intervention of the Virgin Mary, and so the literal 'miracle of the Marne' was born to complement the metaphorical military miracle. But, as with the Angels of Mons, the purported first-hand sightings of a Marian vision on the battlefield were few and problematic. The most detailed account was only printed in a French Catholic newspaper in January 1917, and concerned a letter apparently sent to the Carmelite monastery of Pontoise in January 1915, relating how nuns had heard of the miracle from the lips of a dying German priest who had been wounded and taken prisoner at the battle. He apparently said that he had been ordered to secrecy about the matter by the German military authorities, but his religious conscience won out: 'we saw the Virgin Mary, dressed all in white, with a blue waistband, leaning her head toward Paris. She turned her back to us, and with her right hand seemed to push us away...I saw her myself and a good number of my companions also.'[30]

But unlike the saga of the Angels of Mons, there was no clamour for or obsession with finding incontrovertible evidence for the Marne vision. The miraculous was engrained in Catholic religion at a theological and popular level. In sermons, diocesan newsletters, and Catholic periodicals it was held up as confirmation of the power of collective national worship.[31] Still, the clergy carefully tailored the religious message to ensure it did not undermine French military authority and prowess in the public mind. In 1917 the Catholic theologian Théodore Delmont published a series of morale-boosting war sermons and thought pieces, entitled *For the Crusade of the Twentieth Century*, in which he argued that the 'miracle of the Marne' was a 'relative' rather than absolute miracle. 'The visible protection of God and the Virgin Mary' did not alone save France at the battle, he observed, but rather facilitated the heroism and valour of the army. The Abbé Coubé followed a similar patriotic line of argument in his *Missel du miracle de la Marne* (1916). It was a victory inspired by the guiding tenet 'help yourself, and Heaven will help you'. The Virgin had intervened because God had been impressed by the bravery of the *poilus*.[32]

The Russian army also had its defining, soul-warming Marian vision early on in the war. In October 1914 newspapers reported that a Russian general fighting in East Prussia had written a letter describing how in the region of Suwalki, now in north-eastern Poland, one of his captains had seen a miraculous vision one night as his troops were bivouacked. A sentry rushed in to the camp and called the captain:

> The latter went with the soldier to the outskirts of the camp and witnessed an amazing apparition in the sky. It was that of the Virgin Mary with the infant Christ on one hand, the other hand pointing to the west. Our soldiers knelt on the ground and gazed fervently at the vision. After a time the apparition faded and in its place came a great image of the Cross shining against the dark night sky.

The next day the Russian army were victorious at the Battle of Augustov.[33] The scene was immortalized in a popular print published in hundreds of thousands of copies, entitled 'The Appearance of the Holy Mother from the Heavens to the Russian Troops before Battle, an Omen of Victory'. Other popular Russian prints, with titles such as 'I Shall Manifest Myself to Him', depicted Christ or the Virgin appearing on the battlefield to heal the wounded or comfort the dead. A further sky vision of the Virgin and child was apparently reported by Russian and Austrian troops above the fortress of Przemyśl, southern Poland, during the Russian siege in March 1915.[34]

The wave of battlefield Marian apparitions occurred during the early part of the war, and they were clearly a patriotic religious expression of confidence in the righteousness and hoped-for swift conclusion to the conflict. As the war ground on, heavenly signs and visions tailed off in the combat zone, and so it is no surprise that the most influential wartime Marian apparition of the period occurred far from the battle-fronts. It was in May 1917, in the small Portuguese village of Fátima, that a 10-year-old shepherdess named Lúcia dos Santos claimed to have been visited by the Virgin Mary. Portugal's involvement in the First World War receives little attention, but in March 1916 Germany declared war on the country and it reciprocated. Germany was a threat to its African colonies, while its U-boat blockade impacted severely on Portugal's crucial trade with Britain. By the time of Lúcia's apparent encounter, the first Portuguese troops had arrived at the French battle-front, but more significantly, the country was beginning to starve and bread riots had broken out. So it is not surprising that the Fátima apparitions spoke to the pressing national social and political concerns about the raging global war.[35]

The first apparition appeared to Lúcia and a couple of her friends on 13 May as they played where their sheep were grazing. Suddenly there were flashes of lightning and a ball of white light appeared above a small holm oak tree. In the centre of the ball stood 'a lady all of white, more brilliant than the sun'. After she told Lúcia not to be afraid, a brief conversation ensued in which the Virgin told her to come to the same spot for six months in succession on the thirteenth day. Lúcia then asked whether certain people she knew would go to heaven. Before she floated away into the sky and disappeared, Mary's last words were, 'Pray the Rosary every day, to obtain peace for the world, and the end of the war.' When Lúcia came home and told of her miraculous encounter, she was chastised by her mother for telling lies, and the local priest told her that the vision was the work of the Devil. Lúcia still did as the apparition had told her, and at her visitation on 13 July Mary reiterated that she desired Lúcia 'to continue to say five decades of the Rosary every day in honour of Our Lady of the Rosary to obtain peace for the world and the end of the war. For she alone will be able to help.'

Word spread quickly, excitement bubbled, and soon the Fátima visitation was a matter of national news, and religious and political debate.

Within a couple of months the holm oak had become a site of pilgrimage. A wooden threshold was constructed over it from which were suspended crosses and lanterns. Flowers and donations were left at a newly created shrine. Unlike at Lourdes, there was no blessed spring or well near the holm oak from which pilgrims could draw water to drink or apply to their bodies for cure of sickness and sin. Instead people took earth from the spot, with which they made infusions to heal the sick. People came to beseech Mary to save their loved ones fighting at the front, and when peace was finally declared, many saw it as confirmation of her prophetic and providential intervention to end the war.[36]

The White Comrade

'It had been said, again and again, that through that horror there walked a man in white—the men called him the White Comrade, but they knew who He was—tending the wounded.' So stated the Reverend C. E. Doudney, Vicar of St Luke's, Bath, to his congregation in July 1915. Doudney had recently returned home injured from chaplain duties on the Western Front. He accepted that some understandably thought the visions the result of the fevered minds of the wounded and sick. But looking across the battlefield with 'spiritual eyes', he was in no doubt at all that the White Comrade moved among the injured and dying giving physical and moral succour.[37]

Doudney's sermon suggests that accounts of the White Comrade were numerous, but I can find no references in the press to such sightings in the previous year or early part of 1915. As David Clarke has shown, the origin of the White Comrade legend derives largely from a short story by the Reverend W. H. Leathem entitled 'In the Trenches', which was published and widely reprinted in March 1915.[38] In the story a soldier named George Casey relates to the author that 'after many a hot engagement a man in white had been seen bending over the wounded. Snipers sniped at him. Shells fell around him. Nothing had power to touch him. He was either heroic beyond all heroes, or he was something greater still. This mysterious one, whom the French called the Comrade in White, seemed to be everywhere at once.' As the spiritualist paper *Light* observed in June, 'it is being quoted in some quarters as a piece of reality'.[39] It was given further public authenticity that month by the press coverage of a sermon delivered at Broughton Church, Manchester, by the Congregational pastor Robert F. Horton. He claimed to have received letters from the front describing various providential incidents, such as a captain who gave his men the order to pray as an airship passed over, and survived unscathed as the bombs fell harmlessly into the sea. Horton went on to state that he had come across a soldier who had heard accounts 'again and again' of men seeing the White Comrade. The soldier had put it down to 'hysterical excitement' at first, until finding himself in no man's land during one battle when he was approached by a white-robed figure who gave him joy and comfort.[40]

Once again fiction became fact, spreading from the home front to the battlefields, and returning in hearsay accounts from soldiers who said they knew of others who had seen the Comrade in White. In February and March 1916 Australian newspapers unwittingly printed Leathem's story of George Casey verbatim, stating that the account had been given in a letter from a Private Lindsay Rich, who was fighting in Flanders, to his local pastor in Wagga Wagga. The Australian *Shepparton News* headed the story with 'Strange Stories from the Trenches: Is it Nerves?' On reading the account, one man wrote to his local newspaper in June, saying that he had heard about the White Comrade from his cousin in England, who was helping at an invalid hospital in Cheltenham. She reported having heard 'accounts of the white comrade and his care of the helpless men on the battlefield given by many of those who have helped'.[41]

'In the Trenches' was republished in October 1915 in a collection by Leathem entitled *The Comrade in White*. He prefaced the slim volume by describing his writings as 'a reflex of the great religious stirring of the nation'.[42] He wrote subsequently that he did not realize that anyone would take the story to be a real case of supernatural intervention, though he did not doubt that such could occur. For Leathem, George Casey's story was 'of no evidential value whatsoever', but he thought it should be read as a 'spiritual truth' aimed at giving comfort to the families of soldiers.[43] Still, an international outbreak of artistic responses spread the legend further. In his collection of poems, Robert Haven Schauffler wrote in the foreword that he was inspired by Leatham's story, which he believed was 'written on the western front'.[44] His poem describes the battlefield encounter:

> Then, in the bursting shells' dim light,
> I saw he was clad in white.
> For a moment I thought I saw the smock
> Of some shepherd in search of his flock.

68

Alert were the enemy, too,
And their bullets flew
Straight at a mark no bullet could fail;
For the seeker was tall and his robe was bright;
But he did not flee nor quail.[45]

The most influential artistic expression was a painting called the 'White Comrade' by George Hillyard Swinstead. It depicted a luminous Christ in white appearing before a medical officer supporting a wounded soldier. It attracted considerable national press when it went on show at a 'War Exhibition' at Prince's Skating Club, London, in the summer of 1915.[46] A full-page copy, accompanied by a poem, was printed in the *Illustrated London News* that autumn, and photographs of it were reproduced in the regional press. Swinstead's oil paint version was on display in a Plymouth gallery early in 1916, with the *Western Morning News* describing how 'the two men typical of British heroes, although realistically treated, harmonize completely with the apparition presented with remarkable delicacy'.[47] By this time, colour prints were available for a shilling, photogravures for a few shillings, and facsimile oil paintings on canvas for 15 shillings. These copies were hugely popular and adorned many of the numerous public war shrines that sprang up from 1916 onwards, such as in Windsor parish church and the altar shrine at Oakham parish church. The one in Windsor consisted of the picture with the names of local men serving listed on either side, and a prayer desk at its foot.[48]

In November 1917, a letter from the widow of Colonel Cochran, formerly of the Hampshire Regiment, was printed in a local newspaper to relate news she had received from a chaplain at the front. A transport soldier had got entangled in some barbed wire during a gas attack. Knowing he was likely to be killed, he prayed to God, and suddenly a light shone close to him and in the centre of the light he saw Jesus. All fear drained from him, he was miraculously freed from the wire, and able to make his way back. He told the chaplain, 'You may think, sir, I imagined it, but as truly as I stand here I saw Him last night, and I don't think I shall ever feel fear again.'[49] As an article in an American Lutheran periodical explained in 1918, 'No one can explain this vision of the "Great White Comrade," but no one needs to explain it. Whether it is a real vision or a picture of the religious imagination makes no difference whatever; it is real; the Comrade is a real being.' As the author explained, the immaculate 'White Christ' of the Gospels had 'become in soldier language, "The Comrade in White"', ministering comfort to loved ones on the battlefield.[50] By this time 'The White Comrade' had been appropriated into official church language and iconography across the English-speaking combatant countries.

There were other white comrades roaming abroad than Christ. In October 1914 the Russian army fighting at Ivangorod were apparently given hope and valour from seeing an apparition of the great general Michael Skobeleff (1843–82). Skobeleff had risen to national fame for his role in the Russo-Turkish War of 1877. He made himself deliberately recognizable on the battlefield by wearing a white coat and riding a white horse. Legend had it that bullets could pass right through him, and after his death tradition had it that he would appear at critical moments when the Tsar's army was in battle. In the summer of 1915 a further sighting was recorded by Russian sentinels at Petrograd. An Irish journalist reporting on the story wrote that it was not 'surprising that the Russian soldiers have seen Skobeleff's ghost. They would be very strange soldiers if they did not see something in these desperate nerve-tearing, brain-racking struggles which they have endured so courage-ously.'[51] In January 1916 Sardar Narain Singh, of the 14th Sikhs, while recovering from six bullet wounds he received at Gallipoli, related how at the moment the bugle sounded to charge, he and his fellow soldiers saw a vision of the great warrior guru Govind Singh over the battlefield. He was also riding a white steed, and had a resplendent white egret on his turban. Singh said he could not express in words the courageous spirit this inspired in them. As men fell dead around them, they could think only of their devotion to the guru as they charged forward.[52]

Haunted Landscapes, Haunted People

Whether one believes in ghosts or not, it is an easy assumption that apparent sightings of ghosts must have been common on the First World War battlefields considering the sheer number of traumatic deaths and the intensity of individual and collective emotions. There is certainly a long tradition of the appearance of ghostly armies memor-ializing great battles, from the fields of Marathon in ancient Greece to the English Civil War of the seventeenth century and then to the theatres of conflict of the American Civil War. The aforementioned sightings of

Michael Skobeleff and Govind Singh are expressions of an old patriotic legend of being led into battle by the ghost of a great general. During the Balkan War of 1912, Serbian troops welcomed the news that the ghost of the medieval folk hero Marko Kralyevich had led troops into battle against the Turks, for example.[53] Elsewhere across the globe, particularly in Asia, terrible recent conflicts have generated accounts of tormented wailing spirits plaguing today's general population. But behind these general examples of mass military hauntings lie different types of legend and folk narrative relevant to different periods and cultures. The European seventeenth- and eighteenth-century examples of battlefield armies are usually described as sky battles, re-enactments fought out as portentous political visions far above the ground. Reports emerged again of such sky battles at Waterloo. The American Civil War haunted battlefields, populated by visions of soldiers going through the motions of war on the ground, are very much a modern creation driven by the growth of battlefield tourism. Meanwhile, the twentieth-century war hauntings involving massed anguished spirits tend to focus on the consequences of civilian massacres rather than the death of ranks of battlefield soldiers.[54]

So what sort of ghostly expressions of conflict might have been expected during and after the First World War? A convalescent Canadian lieutenant remarked that it was quite a common occurrence for soldiers to see the ghosts of their dead comrades in the war zone.[55] But apart from the various apparitions of historic armies conjured up during the Angels of Mons debate, we find very few contemporary references to ghostly armies of the recent dead being seen across the First World War battlefields either in the sky or on the ground. There are also few reports of battlefield hauntings in subsequent decades either. The First World War clearly generated personal hauntings rather than legendary phantom spectacles. The Canadian's own experience concerned talking to and feeling the icy cold touch of a private who had been killed three days before. He did not realize he was talking to a ghost until a comrade reminded him of the private's death. 'It takes away all fear of death, for I know that Private Rex lives, though dead.'[56]

But what did people mean by a 'ghost' at the time? It is a question that was rarely asked. In popular belief a ghost was the soul of the dead that had either never left the realm of the living, such as the sad, tormented spirits of suicides, or had returned to it. Some ghosts were purposeless, merely replaying over and over again the last moments before death, or some repetitive action that defined their lives. Others returned from heaven on missions to right injustices they suffered while living, such as identifying murderers, while others came back to warn of imminent danger or to frighten sinners. Once they had succeeded, they returned no more. Some ghosts haunted people and some haunted places. Towards the end of the war there were reports of mysterious lights flashing along the Cornish coastline. They were thought by some to be the ghosts of those drowned in enemy action, who were taking revenge by luring German boats and submarines onto the rocks.[57] But, as we shall see, the rise of spiritualism generated a new language about the spirits of the dead and their relationship to the living. Psychical researchers also redefined ghosts and hauntings in new ways. For some, they were real in the sense that the visions were telepathic hallucinations, 'a painted shadow, without life or meaning or purpose—the baseless fabric of a dream'.[58] So, all this considered, when a soldier or sailor said he encountered a ghost, we cannot always be sure what he meant by it.

Several of the haunting narratives from the trenches, and they are not legion, conformed to traditional purposeful ghosts. One type was the harbinger of imminent death, when a deceased family member returned fleetingly as if to say, 'We will be reunited shortly.' In 1915 it was reported that during the Battle of Mons two soldiers kept seeing the ghost of an old woman in a bonnet and bright blue skirt which interfered with their line of fire. At first they thought she was a Belgian farmer's wife, but such was the hail of bullets flying between the trenches they soon realized she was no living being. A sergeant overheard them talking about the ghostly vision and said, 'It's my old mother, who died twelve years ago, in her 82nd year. I believe she's come for me.' As he finished speaking a shell burst overhead and he was blown to pieces before them. One of the surviving soldiers said, 'we lay wounded there for some hours, but the old woman did not appear again'.[59] Then there were the ghostly family members who intervened to guide their loved ones away from certain death. An Australian private who found himself stranded between British and German lines wrote home about the experience. He threw himself on the ground to collect his thoughts and plan what to do next. As night descended, he attempted to head for the British position but met a bad welcome:

I jumped the barbed wire entanglement, when the officer in charge lifted his revolver and fired at me ten yards away and never touched me. Now, mother darling, comes the part you will find most difficult to believe. As I rose from the ground I saw as plainly as possible the form of my poor dead dad in front of me, and all that fearful fifty yards until I reached the trench he seemed to guide me. I have not a vivid imagination, and have never been given to a belief in the supernatural, but my own officer could not say I had a trace of fear on me when I returned ... I think it was the Almighty's way of guiding me to safety.[60]

In his memoir of the war, *And We Go On*, later reworked and retitled *Ghosts Have Warm Hands*, the Canadian front-line soldier Will Bird tells of a similar profound experience, which inspired the book's title. While deep in sleep under a groundsheet, he saw his brother Steve, who had been reported missing, probably killed, and felt his warm hand placed over his mouth. The apparition of his brother led him down the trench, through some ruins, before turning a corner and disappearing. When Bird woke up, he was in a different location from where he fell asleep, and several friends were looking on with astonishment. They led him back to the spot where he had originally fallen asleep. It had received a direct hit and the body parts of his sleeping companions lay scattered around.[61]

Some 'ghost' sightings in the trenches, and most of the visions reported on the home fronts by loved ones of those fighting abroad or at sea, were not ghosts as popularly understood. In November 1916, for example, the *Daily Express* carried a piece described as 'A real ghost story of the war', which was reprinted elsewhere as 'The Trench Ghost'. It concerned a regimental company in the trenches of Flanders and their former colonel. He had lost his arm fighting with them, and on recovering and being fitted with an artificial limb, he was appointed to lead a regiment destined for the Dardanelles. Shortly after arriving at Lemnos, he caught dysentery and had to be taken back to Britain, where he died. At the exact moment of his death, soldiers from his old company saw a fleeting apparition of him, his cap a little on one side as he always wore it, and with both arms intact.[62] In folklore terms this was a wraith or fetch, an apparition of someone fatally ill or in mortal danger that appeared as an omen to loved ones or to people with whom they were very close. The pre-war folklore archives are full of examples. In psychical research terminology the same phenomenon was called a 'crisis apparition', in other words a telepathic vision at the moment of death or profound emotional predicament. Whatever the definition, the percipient did not usually consider the apparition to be the soul or spirit of the dead.

As well as the conflation of terms and concepts, another reason why it is assumed that ghost sightings were a common feature of battlefield life is because of the First World War literary references to haunted soldiers. Ghosts were in vogue as literary figures, metaphors, and devices in the years leading up to 1914, and some of the poets and novelists associated with the war had already grappled with expressing death and the afterlife in their work.[63] While recuperating away from the front, the poet Siegfried Sassoon wrote in his diary for June 1916, 'If there really are such things as ghosts, and I'm not prepared to gainsay the fact—or illusion—if there are ghosts, then they will be all over this battle-front forever. I think the ghosts at Troy are all too tired to show themselves—they are too literary.'[64] Sassoon's good friend and fellow battalion officer Robert Graves wrote in *Goodbye to All That* of seeing the ghost of an acquaintance named Private Challoner while at Béthune. Graves was having a celebratory slap-up dinner when he saw Challoner look in through the window, salute, and pass on. It was unmistakably him, but he had been killed at Festubert the previous month.[65] *And We Go On*, which is considered by some a minor literary classic as well as a war memoir, has been described as 'a war story fused with a ghost story' as Steve accompanies and aids Bird, saving his life on numerous occasions.[66] In terms of fiction, the likes of Rudyard Kipling pursued ghostly themes in several war-related short stories, and J. M. Barrie's play *A Well-Remembered Voice* (1918) centres on a conversation between a grieving father and the spirit apparition of his son, leaving it open as to whether it is a figment of his melancholy imagination. Several French stories were also published at the time that involved armies of the dead rising from the battlefields, while the themes of real and psychological haunting have also been taken up and developed in the more recent fictional literature about the war, most notably Pat Barker's *Regeneration* trilogy (1991–5).[67]

There was and is a general feeling or assumption, then, that the battlefields *ought* to have been full of ghosts because the militarized landscapes were metaphorically haunted by the very real sight, sound, and smell of death and the dead. The living lived intimately with rotting corpses, and the trenches were full of macabre friendships with decaying bodies and body parts. French officer René Nicolas described the 'droll' stances of the three corpses with whom he shared his trench. One looked as though he was in the middle of a back somersault. His men hung their canteens over a foot that poked through the trench wall. 'They not only cease to make us uncomfortable,' he wrote, 'but they even make us laugh.'[68] But for the religiously minded, the apocalyptic environment conjured up biblical imagery of the end times and the final resurrection of the dead. So, as the Anglo-American soldier Coningsby Dawson, who fought on the Western Front with the Canadian Field Artillery, thought, 'surely the places in which I have been should be ghost-haunted'.[69] But maybe the very intimacy with the physical remains of the dead, and the daily experience of incoherent mass death, actually inhibited the creation of ghosts in a cultural and psychological way. The ghosts of the First World War haunted people, not places. They were not required to make concrete the lasting propinquity between life and death in the physical environment of everyday life. Spiritualism, as a faith, did, however, provide a very clear road map for such an ongoing relationship, one that challenged the popular and orthodox religious views of the afterlife. When the Canadian soldier mentioned earlier said, 'I know that Private Rex lives, though dead,' he was speaking the language of spiritualism, and so we now need to assess its influence on all fronts.

Spiritualism and the War

Spiritualists did not accept death as understood by the vast majority of people. In a sense, spiritualism precluded the creation of ghosts. While ghosts in popular culture were the spirits or souls of the dead, spiritualists rejected the traditional concept of mortality entirely. Physical and spiritual life was a continuum involving a transmission of the soul from the earthbound realm to the spirit realm. Mediums acted as a telegraph that enabled a regular two-way conversation. If the spirits appeared, it was usually in the seance room as part of what was effectively a religious ceremony with the medium as minister. The profundity and distinctiveness of the spiritualist conception of life is well illustrated by a very mundane grumble. In late 1917 a Surrey spiritualist complained to the movement's press that he was fed up with fellow spiritualist speakers crying off meetings because of concerns over imminent air raids: 'Surely we who preach that there is no death should not fear death! We who believe in spirit guardianship, should show more courage than the average man in the street.[70]

In his history of spiritualism published in 1920, Joseph McCabe, a former Catholic priest turned campaigner for rationalism, concluded that the impact of the war on American and British interest in spiritualism could not be 'overestimated in its general influence, but the careful student will realise that it must be studied carefully'.[71] This caution derived from McCabe's analysis of American national census data to dispute the inflated membership figures provided by some spiritualist organizations during and after the war. The statistics suggest that while membership of spiritualist churches certainly grew in America, there was hardly a huge jump during the duration of the war. This is also reflected in Britain, where there were 145 groups affiliated to the Spiritualists' National Union in 1914, rising modestly to 158 in 1916. Dig further down amongst the membership records of individual spiritualist churches and we are likely to find some mixed patterns. The York Spiritualist Society records show, for example, that between 1899 and 1909 there was a total of 357 full and associate members, but only 137 during the war years.[72]

Just as advocates of spiritualism sometimes made exaggerated claims about the growth of the movement, so its many critics had vested interests in overinflating its spread and influence as a call to action for their own causes. The Catholic Church denounced spiritualism as superstition and even diabolic in inspiration. It was blasphemous for Catholics to attempt to contact the spirit world. The dead had received the sacrament of the last rites and rested in peace. Intercession with the dead was a matter of prayer and priestly service. In 1898 the Holy Office forbade 'spiritistic practices, even though intercourse with the demon be excluded and communication sought with good spirits only'. In 1917 it was presented with the following question, which was no doubt inspired by wartime concerns:

Whether it is allowed either through a so-called medium or without one, and with or without hypnotism, to assist in any spiritualistic communications or manifestations, even such as appear to be blameless or pious, either asking questions of the souls or spirits, or listening to their answers, or merely looking.

The Vatican's response was a firm negative.[73] Deemed incompatible with the Catholic faith, spiritualism as a religion did not gain the same foothold in Catholic Europe as it did in Protestant Britain and America, and there were some Catholic clerics who were tireless in their wartime attacks on spiritualism. In France we find Father Stéphen Coubé, who in early 1917 organized a series of anti-*Spiritisme* conferences in the Church of the Madeleine, Paris.[74] The former Anglican priest and convert John Godfrey Raupert made a career out of attacking spiritualism in Britain. His book *Dangers of Spiritualism* (1901) went through a third edition shortly after the outbreak of the war, and in 1918 he was commissioned by the Vatican to conduct an anti-spiritualist tour in America.[75] Another vocal public critic was the Jesuit priest Bernard Vaughan, who warned of spiritualism that people should 'shun it as they would cocaine. In neither drug is to be discovered the will of God.'[76] The likes of Coubé and Raupert did not doubt that mediums were in contact with the spirit world; the grave problem was that they were channelling demons and not the dead. Spiritualists were opening the gates of hell, and seances were enabling the Devil's desires to undermine true Christianity at a time when talk of the biblical Apocalypse was widespread.

Some clergy from the Nonconformist and evangelical wing of Protestantism shared the Catholic concerns. In a febrile atmosphere with apocalyptic claims that the war was a sign of the imminence of Armageddon, the Kaiser playing the role of the Antichrist, talk of the Devil and demons was common. The London Baptist minister Frederick Brotherton Meyer denounced spiritualism as 'an outbreak of Demonism'. The Pentecostal Anglican the Reverend A. A. Boddy thought spiritualism a 'terrible thing', and claimed in 1916 that mediums were 'yielding to the power of demons who personate departed ones'. Those present at seances might have been awestruck and convinced by the apparent intimate knowledge that the so-called spirits of the dead divulged to their living loved ones, but, according to Boddy, it was all demonic deception. Demons were consummate eavesdroppers: 'they can hear and they can remember. They can tell one another any things, and they can be present in the secret places, and so they can reveal things that happened in the past life, and speak of things which seem to be from those who have departed. But they are really only impersonating them.'[77]

The attacks on spiritualism during the war also came from a secular, rationalist perspective. In 1917 the eminent folklorist and evolutionary theorist Edward Clodd published a scathing critique in his *Brief History and Examination of Modern Spiritualism*.[78] For Clodd, the premise and practice of spiritualism were founded on nothing more than fraud, ignorance, and irrationality. When the novelist Thomas Hardy read the book, he wrote to his friend Clodd, 'What a set-back this revival of superstition is! It makes one despair of the human mind. Where's Willy Shakespeare's "So noble in reason" now!'[79] The ghost hunter Elliot O'Donnell pressed home how spiritualism engendered physical and mental ill health. Yet far worse in his mind was that spiritualism, through its predominantly female mediums, was promoting the cause of 'free love without men'; if this remained unchecked, it would 'prove to be the biggest calamity that has ever befallen the world—far bigger, even, than the late Great War'.[80] The stage conjurer and mentalist Stuart Cumberland wondered whether there was a more sinister explanation behind what he saw as the irrational flourishing of spiritualism, 'beyond that provided by the emotional longings arising out of the Great War and mediumistic desire to make money out of the craze'.[81] Was an Unseen Hand fostering British thraldom to the Unseen World? Cumberland thought so. He explained how Germany used Rasputin's mystical reputation to undermine the Russians, and implied that they had also employed an unwitting Madame de Thèbes to their own propagandist ends. The world was 'literally a-crawl' with Central European spies, according to Cumberland, and they had ample opportunity to manipulate the foolish masses and exploit what he dismissed as 'weak-kneed isms' such as conchyism, pacifism, and spiritualism.[82] These were nothing but dark, paranoid mutterings. Cumberland produced no evidence. He was a vocal anti-spiritualist who considered all mediums frauds, and like other British critics turned a blind eye to the espousal of providentialism by the clergy of the mainstream churches. The notion of an Unseen or Hidden Hand organization of German sympathizers on the home front trying to undermine the British war effort through assassination and, more insidiously, eroding morale became a popular theme for jingoists like Horatio Bottomley.[83]

By the time of the First World War, mainstream Anglicanism had long expunged the providential and the miraculous from its teachings, and demoted the afterlife in its tenets, services, and public engagement. It is no surprise, then, that, come the war, senior Anglican clergymen denounced spiritualism in print and from the pulpit in familiar ways.

The bishop of Oxford opined that spiritualists were probably 'the victims of clever demons'.[84] But the sheer scale of mass death amongst their parishioners challenged the rank and file of curates and vicars, who found that they were increasingly required to act as comforters and consolers of the dead as well as the bereaved. There was a desire and need to focus on the afterlife and reflect on the spiritual state of the dead.[85] The imagery of and inspiration drawn from the Comrade in White was one such expression of this modest flourishing of a more spiritual Anglicanism on the ground.

We have already seen how some Anglican clergy endorsed and even appropriated the Angels of Mons. So some Anglican clergy, such as Charles Tweedale, Vicar of Weston, North Yorkshire, took a step further and fully embraced spiritualism, arguing that the Church had to restore the 'ancient gifts' of spiritual connection, and that it should emphasize the communion with the dead. He stated, furthermore, that psychic and spiritualist means were the only effective ways of communication with the afterlife.[86] The Reverend F. Fielding-Ould, Vicar of Christ Church, Regent's Park, London, was another enthusiastic supporter. In March 1917 he gave an address to the London Spiritualist Alliance on the topic 'Is Spiritualism of the Devil?' 'The war has brought things to a head,' he said. There was widespread dissatisfaction with the procedure and method of the Church. 'People are educated in these days and can think for themselves; they will not be soothed or put aside with the old forms of speech and pious opinion—besides, as never before they are earnest: their husbands and sons are being killed every day, and they demand some instruction and teaching which is alive and reasonable.'[87]

There was a strong vein of pacifism in the spiritualist faith. In 1915 a Dutch adherent called for the movement to unite and protest, albeit from the distance of national neutrality: 'War against the War! Down with your weapons!,' he cried.[88] Two years later, the motion 'All War is Murder' was passed at the British Spiritualists' National Union (SNU) conference. When conscription was introduced in 1916, we find members of fighting age being brought before military tribunals for conscientious objection, though certainly not in significant numbers compared to denominations such as the Quakers and Christadelphians.[89] One such appeal was heard by the Warwick County Tribunal for Birmingham and district in April 1916. Alderman Pritchett gave it as his opinion to the tribunal that spiritualism was not a religion, to which the applicant countered that it was, indeed, a religion and a science. Speaking with great emotion, the spiritualist addressed the panel: 'How can you do it, brother? We are all brothers. How can you force me into it?' He had already declined to enlist in the army medical corps, and when asked why he refused to care for the wounded, he replied, 'I have to look at the other side as well. The Germans and the Austrians are also our brothers.'[90] As this exchange suggests, this particular spiritualist's pacifism derived from his adherence to international socialism, which had significant reach in the spiritualist movement. At a tribunal in Preston the same month, another spiritualist appellant, who had two brothers fighting in France, said he refused to fight because he ascribed to the international socialist view that the war was only a means of bolstering capitalist commercialism and private ownership. He then referred to passages in the Bible and what the *Lyceum Manual*, the guide and reference book for the spiritualist faith, had to say on the matter. While he was prepared to sacrifice himself, he would not do so in any act of force or even self-defence. His appeal was unsurprisingly also refused.[91]

The 1917 SNU conference may have passed a motion denouncing war, but another motion supporting conscientious objectors was voted down. It is clear that the majority of spiritualists supported the war effort to varying degrees. The roll of honour of the Sowerby Bridge Spiritualist Society shows that thirty-one members enlisted, and six of them were killed in combat. A hundred 'Lyceum lads' joined the army from the Burnley district—'not for love of fighting' but out of a 'sense of striving to do their duty'.[92] In February 1917 John G. Wood, press correspondent for the Midland District Union of Spiritualists, wrote to a local newspaper to stress that few spiritualists were to be found in the ranks of the conscientious objectors, and that while all spiritualists abhorred bloodshed, some of his personal friends who had been brought up in the spiritualist faith had already given their lives, and one of his sons currently had trench fever. 'Wild beasts must be treated as wild beasts,' he concluded, 'and the German brutes must be taught a much-needed lesson ere the angel carol of "Peace on earth goodwill to men" will be heard again.'[93] Spiritualist organizations also raised money for food parcels, medicines, and cigarettes. The leading spiritualist journal *Two Worlds* sponsored a Spiritualist Motor Ambulance Fund, which was also supported by *Light* and *The International Psychic Gazette*. The sum of £931 was raised and six ambulances were purchased from the Ford Company and presented to the War Office. They bore the words 'Jointly subscribed for by the Spiritualists of the Dominion of New Zealand and Great Britain'.[94] These expressions of support for the war effort did not pass without criticism from the radical sections of the faith. One correspondent accused the editor of *Two Worlds* of being 'a bloodthirsty Spiritualist who believes in and condones murder'.[95] One suspects that he would not have been happy with Arthur Conan Doyle's short note 'The Military Value of Spiritualism', in which he argued that spiritualists were ideally equipped for the battlefield. By way of illustration, he cited a letter sent to him by a soldier with whom he had previously discussed the faith: 'It takes all the horror away from being killed,' wrote the soldier. 'I feel now that I can go into the line and stick it ever so much better than I could before.'[96]

We know there were hundreds of spiritualists on the battlefields either as soldiers or in non-combatant roles. One well-known figure in the movement, Ernest Vickers, President of the British Spiritualist Lyceum, was killed in Flanders in July 1917 during service in the Durham Light Infantry.[97] But, as was explained in *Two Worlds* when it printed its spiritualist roll of honour, those listed did not represent all who fought because army officials did not accept spiritualism as a religion and therefore did not register the faith in official documentation. Some spiritualists were reluctant, furthermore, to state their real religious affiliation for fear of ostracism, particularly in light of the public perception that they were lukewarm on the war.[98] The censor was also at work, of course. One Private A. Bamford, a spiritualist in the 19th Rifle Brigade, wrote to *Two Worlds* in the summer of 1916 to express his delight at seeing one of the spiritualist ambulances while he was resting in Egypt: 'I have been out here some time. Coming in touch with all classes and creeds, I have seen some very strange sights. But you know there is the Censor. I wish you and all friends at home good luck.'[99]

There is little evidence to suggest, though, that spiritualism expanded amongst the armed services.[100] The Spiritualists' National Union was not averse to spreading its message, but it was far from using the war as an evangelical mission in comparison to other churches and denominations. It was not interested in sending its members to preach the faith at the front, though in early 1915 it organized the sending of what it called seven thousand 'propaganda' pamphlets to the French war zone, and

> so supply comforts for the mind as others have for the body. The consignment has been sent through the War Office arrangements to the Military Base at Boulogne, where a somewhat over-zealous officer has taken upon himself to become mildly obstructive because of the character of the literature! However, it is quite expected that by the time these lines are read all difficulties will have been overcome, and the pamphlets will be doing their good work.[101]

Seven thousand pamphlets were a drop in the ocean compared to the millions of other religious publications that mainstream Christian organizations sent to the war zones.

Spirits on the Battlefield

Despite concerns expressed by a few chaplains and officers at the time, there is hardly any evidence of seances or informal spiritualistic services being conducted at the front.[102] The practice of faith was personal and private. Those serving in the army and navy might attend spiritualist services when back home on rare and fleeting periods of leave, but in the meantime they relied on family and friends to communicate with the spirit world on their behalf. Throughout 1917 a spiritualist and sapper with a Distinguished Service Order was a periodic correspondent to *Light*, writing from the trenches about his faith. He had been on the front line in Flanders and France. He was not psychic himself, but from the seances he attended back home he knew that 'While serving my country on and about the front-line trenches I have been happy in the knowledge that my spirit friends have always been near me to guard and protect me. When days and nights are wet and gloomy they cheer me up; they have brought me unscathed through storms of shell and shrapnel.' He explained in one letter that he did not actually see his spirit friends, but he knew they were looking over him, 'either by strong impression or a direct message given to a "sensitive" friend of mine and sent to me in writing'.[103]

Even if spiritualists were not actively engaging with spirits at the front, back home some followers were convinced that the spirit world was just getting on with it anyway and constantly intervening in the conflict in myriad beneficial ways. In July 1914 the *Revue Spirite* published a supposed mediumistic communication from the spirit of Joan of Arc in which she confirmed that she and other spirits would be invisibly leading the French military strategy against the Germans, working through the generals.[104] Leading French spiritualist Léon Denis suggested that France might have succumbed to the Germans early on if it had not been for the support of the innumerable legions of spirits who increased the energy and stimulated the courage of the *poilus*. Even the best strategies of General Joffre were probably inspired from the other world.[105] In England, a spiritualist from Hull wrote a rather bumbling letter to the *Leeds Mercury* in October 1915 explaining how the spirits organized themselves:

> Sir.—All who die in the performance of any duty go to Valhalla—one of the heavens—the third, I believe, though I am not quite sure. Of one thing I know they are supremely happy. Their sphere of action is glorified and enlarged, and as spirit forces they are engaged in service in different parts of the universe. As a psychic I distinctly affirm that councils of the spirits are often held to see what can be done in the war.[106]

In November 1914 the veteran medium and author Mrs M. H. Wallis gave a talk to the London Spiritualist Alliance on the practical work of the spirits on the battlefield. She explained that those spirit friends who ministered were enabled to do so by their purity of heart and singleness of purpose. While some spirits favoured the soldiers of their own former country, admitted Wallis, others assisted the dying and the suffering irrespective of which side of the war they were on. Through mesmeric means the spirit doctors were thought able to give comfort to those soldiers suffering agonizing pain by inducing a state of torpor. In this line of work, doctors and nurses who had passed over to the spirit side of life were particularly well equipped, as they could identify both the external and internal conditions of the injured. One such American spirit doctor, communicating through a medium in 1916, explained a bit about his work, though he said, 'It's hard to talk about it; we are too near its carnage.' When asked if he was working on the battlefields of France, he replied, 'Mostly, but not entirely. I have offered my services as a physician should, where they are most needed. Last month I was in

Serbia.'[107] The bulk of the spirits' work, though, was in assisting the battlefield dead in their transition to their new life.[108]

Away from the battlefields, the spirits intervened in other unexpected ways. In June 1915 a Hull manufacturer named Alfred Donnison was escorted to a police station by soldiers after a woman reported that he had been talking German loudly in Chariot Street, and had said 'God bless the Kaiser.' Donnison denied he knew German or had German sympathies. He fell ill at the police station and died shortly after. On reading about the incident in the newspapers, the psychic investigator Reginald B. Span suggested that Donnison's organs of speech had been temporarily possessed by the spirit of a dead German. 'I think my explanation should be sufficient to clear his character,' he concluded—'at any rate in the eyes of Spiritualists'.[109] While, from scruples and concern over prosecution, mediums did not generally seek to find out military secrets from the other world, claims were occasionally made that spirits had made unbidden confidences. In late November 1918 a correspondent to the *Dundee Advertiser* stated that on 29 October he and five others were engaged in psychical research with a medium when a communication came through from the other side warning that the German High Command was planning an all-out U-boat attack against British and Allied navies. The spirit also described the German peace talks as a trick.[110] A few days later the Kiel mutiny broke out after the German navy planned one last great battle.

Spiritualists felt they also made a valuable contribution to the war effort by supporting the spirit world in their endless battlefield ministrations, easing the transition of spirits from the bloody, muddy trenches to their new life. Mrs Wallis believed that groups of 'strongly-convinced' spiritualists acted as psychic batteries from which the spirits drew the power required to conduct such earthly work. H. Pemberton, of Dublin, explained how his wife, an automatic-writing medium, and her spirit guide were also doing their bit for the war effort. Since the beginning of the war their spirit guide had been engaged in helping Allied soldiers whose spirits were 'passing over' from the front. Pemberton suggested to the spirit guide that he encourage some of those he was supporting to join the Pembertons' Sunday evening seance conversations. This proved a smashing success, with some two to three hundred Allied soldiers of all nationalities being comforted as they passed over. 'We have had a few lines written by a French officer', wrote Pemberton, 'and a most grateful, touching and dignified message from an Indian.'[111]

Being blown to bits on the battlefield amidst mass slaughter was not conducive to a calm transition from one life to the next. Seance communications suggested that anxieties and trauma were evident amongst those released from their earthly bodies. In a talk entitled 'Occult Aspects of the Battlefield', given to the International Club for Psychical Research, London, in 1915, the theosophist Robert King described 'swirling groups of combatants who had left the body, locked together in an intense emotional stress, fancying they were still engaged in slaughter'.[112] During a seance held by the medium Violet Burton, a spirit called Father John, who said he had been a contemporary and disciple of St Francis of Assisi, explained how he had given succour to an officer who had been blown up by a bomb during his confession with a priest. The shock to the officer's whole being was so overwhelming 'as to cast him into unconsciousness on both planes...It was impossible to break the shock of dissolution to the spirit, which also became unconscious.' As a physician of the soul, Father John regained the consciousness of the spirit by laying hands on the officer's spirit body and filling his lungs with 'prayer ether'.[113] Still, not all spiritualists were happy with such missions. A Dutch spiritualist magazine included a piece suggesting that the angels and spirits were so busy ministering to and escorting soldiers and sailors to the other world that they were proving frustratingly less contactable in the seance room.[114]

Despite the attacks on spiritualism, mediums clearly played a recognizable role in comforting the bereaved in this world. The seance acted as a blend of theatre, religious service, and therapy. The high-profile experiences published by Arthur Conan Doyle and the eminent physicist Sir Oliver Lodge (1851–1940) were powerful and engaging expressions of the comfort brought by the conviction that there was no such state as death.[115] Conan Doyle's scepticism of seance phenomena and the possibility of communication with the dead was completely eroded following repeated family bereavements due to the war. First his brother-in-law was killed at Mons, and then in 1918 his brother was killed in action. What affected him most was the death of his precious son Kingsley, who succumbed to pneumonia in 1918, in part due to his weak health after being wounded at the Somme. In March 1916 Doyle wrote to the occult newspaper *Light* on the issue of the location of the soul during unconsciousness, and expressed his hardening spiritualist convictions. 'Personally I know of no single argument which is not in favour of the extinction of our individuality at death, save only the facts of psychic research. But these are so strong that they must outweigh all others.'[116] Four years later, following a series of seance communications with Kingsley, he wrote of 'the relief afforded by posthumous messages', and how great a solace could be brought to a 'tortured world' if it accepted that the spirit realm of loved ones was only a medium away.[117]

Lodge's long-standing interest in spiritualist phenomena became deeply personal when his son Raymond was killed in Flanders in September 1915. He and his wife participated in a series of seances in which they communicated with him, and their conversations inspired a book in 1916 named after their son. Although hardly cheap, *Raymond* sold very well, and found its way to some soldiers in the war zone.[118] It also had an eager international audience. It went through at least ten editions during the war, and a survey of public lending libraries across the United States in 1920 revealed that *Raymond* was the fifth most borrowed book under the 'General' category, with James Maynard Keynes's *The Economic Consequences of the Peace* at number one.[119] Still, Lodge complained in 1918 that he had been unable to get it published in France, because, he suggested, there was less interest there in survival after death as a psychical matter.[120] The book inspired a new genre of British and American wartime spirit memoirs. After reading it several times for solace, the mother of the soldier Rolf Little, who died in the Chelsea barracks in 1915, decided, 'Well! If Sir Oliver Lodge can speak to *his* boy *I* can speak to *mine*.'[121] She got in touch with Lodge, who helped her arrange an appointment with a trusted medium named Gladys Leonard. She was the spiritualist who had channelled the conversations with Raymond. Some of the resulting communications, and Mrs Little's own spiritual journey, were published in her book *Grenadier Rolf: By His Mother*. Leonard's mediumship also enabled another such publication, *Claude's Book* (1918), which apparently contained the 'new life' thoughts of a member of the Royal Flying Corps who died in a dogfight with two German planes over Flanders in November 1915. As was explained in the preface to a subsequent volume, *Claude's Second Book* (1919), 'Judging from the very large number of letters I received on its publication, it is obvious *Claude's Book* proved a comfort to many by helping them to realise that a further, fuller life follows on from this one.'[122]

It is difficult to assess how many people attended spiritualist seances during the war, but talk of hundreds of thousands or even tens of thousands turning to mediums for spirit communication is just not feasible. The British spiritualist John Arthur Hill observed in 1918 that trusted mediums, like Leonard, who professed to communicate with the war dead were only available to the public in London, and even then 'were rare and uncertain'. The few good mediums elsewhere in the country 'confine themselves to religious and semi-religious work in their own sect'. And, as we have seen, there was no huge upswing in spiritualist membership during the war.[123] Furthermore, many of those who were consulted as mediums by the paying public were actually being asked to divine the fate of the living on the battlefields rather than to communicate with those killed. The term 'medium' and 'seance' were used in a very broad sense by the police, journalists, and commentators. The report of the trial of a fitter from Hull named George Albert Rivers is a good example. The article was headed 'A Fitter's Spiritualistic Séances', and Rivers was described as 'conducting meetings of a spiritualistic character' and acting as a 'spiritualistic medium'. While he professed to be in contact with the spirits, he was basically telling fortunes. One client gave him a photo of her soldier brother, and Rivers told her 'I am afraid it is very bad news. I get him killed [sic]. I will lay a thousand to one on it.' He told another lady who was expecting a letter from Italy, 'I can see Italy written over your head.'[124] This was the sort of seance going on up and down the country and amongst all classes.

There is also little evidence that considerable numbers of people were casually dabbling with table-rapping seances in their own homes. Mediumship was generally considered to be a rare gift rather than a practice that could be learned from books. While a mass-produced Ouija board game was being widely marketed by an American toy maker in the war years and before—'its mysterious moves, directed by what forces no man knows, never fail to captivate and enthral the most sceptical'—they were very rare items in homes, and they only became more widely known to the public outside America from the 1920s.[125] Behind some of the overinflated concerns about the popularity of the Ouija board for spirit communication at the time, we find the Catholic propagandist Godfrey Raupert. While on tour in America in 1918, Raupert wrote about the growing pernicious influence of Ouija there, stating 'so rapidly has this practice spread in this country that there are few families to-day who have not come in touch with these experiments in one way or another'. His article was reproduced again the following year in his anti-spiritualist book *The New Black Magic and the Truth about the Ouija-Board*.[126]

Psychical Warfare

The Anglo-American psychical investigator Hereward Carrington (1880–1958) dedicated his book *Psychical Phenomena and the War* (1918) 'to those brave souls who have, while fighting for their country, solved the problems with which this book deals'. Just as the war was taken as a unique experimental opportunity by continental folklorists, so psychical researchers saw the potential for unlocking the secrets of the mind and spirit. As Carrington put it, 'The importance of psychical investigation has never been so forcefully demonstrated to us as by the present great World War. Is man essentially body or spirit? ... Every month that passes, thousands of souls are being shot into the spiritual world—*or* obliterated altogether.'[127] Some psychical researchers were spiritualists, some, particularly Catholic researchers, were ardent critics of spiritualism. The well-known ghost hunter Elliot O'Donnell felt it necessary to preface his book *The Menace of Spiritualism* (1920) by stating that he wanted to make it absolutely clear that his criticism did not extend to psychical research and the investigation of haunted houses, and did not detract from the supportive opinions he had exhibited in his writings on spontaneous ghostly phenomena.[128] Of those psychical researchers who did engage in experimenting with spirit mediumship, moreover, one has to make a distinction between those who were interested in the phenomena alone as possible examples of untapped natural psychic powers and those who sought confirmation of life after death as a religious enquiry. But strip spiritualism out of the psychical equation, and there were other phenomena that the war provided unprecedented conditions for testing and observing, such as telepathy, clairvoyance, and psychical healing.

In several respects, though, the Society for Psychical Research had a frustrating war. There was no boost to its membership due to public interest in the occult or spirit matters. It had 1,212 members at the beginning of 1915, but its council noted the creeping influence of the conflict. There had been a net decrease of thirty-one members, with the society reckoning that the war accounted for half the number of resignations out of those who mentioned any reason for their resignation. By March 1917 membership had dropped further to 1,085, though numbers slowly began to pick up again thereafter.[129] The society's council remarked in March 1915 that the war was also sapping its members' time and energies to conduct psychical research. Most of its medical members were preoccupied working in war hospitals. Council member Mr Feilding accepted an appointment to the Naval Press Bureau, Dr M'Dougall went to the front in charge of a motor-ambulance, and Mr E. N. Bennett took command of a Red Cross contingent that was sent to Serbia. Later that year it commented that, 'owing to the fact that public interest is now so largely centred upon the war', it had proved unusually difficult to obtain relevant material for the journal, resulting in its delayed publication.[130] Furthermore, the anticipated windfall of research material as a consequence of the war never materialized. The council minutes for March 1916 observed, 'One might perhaps have expected that the war, with its large tale of casualties and with the increased emotional tension accompanying it, would have produced a number of interesting experiences.' But the low number and quality of reports it was receiving was very disappointing. 'On the whole, evidence of apparitions at the time of death or wounding has been conspicuous by its absence. Such cases have doubtless occurred, but practically none of those which have reached us have come up on investigation to the standard of evidence required.' The following year the council heard once again that the number of publishable cases concerning the war was small, a mere handful.[131]

The Society for Psychical Research generally represented the sober, scientific face of psychical research. Its business was primarily testing the evidence for such phenomena, not promoting or exploiting its potential. But there were those on the fringes who wondered whether psychic powers could be used to aid the war effort or influence its course. The theosophist and occultist A. P. Sinnett thought the war was an earthly expression of a fundamental cosmic battle between the powers of good and evil, and that the German nation had summoned up elemental organisms from the lower astral plains to spread disease among the allied troops. What to do? Writing in *The Occult Review* in December 1914, Sinnett suggested that if the people of London devoted ten minutes a day to concentrating on driving the elemental organisms back, then the aggregate value of such thought power 'would be worth many army corps in the field'.[132] Others proposed more direct militaristic interventions. In the second month of the war a woman signing herself 'Soldier's Daughter' wrote to the English press urging all non-combatants to aid psychically the armed forces by intensely 'willing a victory'. In 1916 an Italian architect named Vittorio Galli published a pamphlet entitled *Guerra telepatica*, in which he, likewise, called for a psychic union to collectively will the defeat of the Germanic enemy. Such psychic interventions were generally not very well received in the psychical community, though. It was pointed out that both sides could play that game, resulting in a titanic 'struggle between contending wills' that would not be conclusive, and might ultimately be detrimental to the military effort. Besides, from a spiritualist perspective, willing the death of others was immoral. Arthur Lovell, the founder of the London Society for the Prevention of Premature Burial, responded by advising that 'willing hard' was not to be indulged in, full stop: 'it exhausts nervous energy, heats the cerebellum, and generally ends in a complete breakdown of mind and body'. Better, he said, to assist the war effort by nursing, praying, paying, and the like: 'you can then rest content that you are "willing" success to your country in the right way'.[133]

Despite such advice, in May 1916 a new campaign group was afoot with the impressive title of the Householders' War League of Thought, which aimed to tap the 'mighty energies of organised collective thought' to bring about peace through overwhelming victory. The occult principles behind the campaign were explained in an essay written by a student of occultism entitled 'Can We End the War by Thought?', which was published in the *Herald of the Star*, the periodical of the theosophical Order of the Star in the East. It appealed to ministers and priests of every creed to encourage their flocks to join in this world-changing endeavour to end the war quickly and so retain sufficient collective energy to support the power of good in the anticipation of the new era to come.[134] The article was quickly reprinted as a pamphlet to accompany the following advertisement that appeared in the local press in England and Australia in May 1916:

Every householder in the Empire is invited to gather the inmates of his house together for a few minutes daily, for silent concentrated Thought directed to the helping of the Powers of Good, each one throwing all his thought and energy on the side of Right, so as to bring this war to a successful close as soon as possible. Where desired, the few silent minutes could open with these words:

> We ask that the Divine Will shall find in us clean and deep channels through which It may deign to flow.

If hundreds of thousands, either as householders, or singly, who are unable to be at the Front, would help in this practical way, we should create an effective force, a thought regiment to reinforce those who are struggling on land, sea and air for the triumph of Right and the upward progress of humanity.

Those interested are invited to communicate with the Householders' War League of Thought 314, Regent Street, W. (near Queen's Hall).[135]

When the advertisement appeared in a New South Wales paper, it was accompanied by a letter from a man in Lismore, in the north-east of the state, who offered to collate positive responses and pass them on. He hoped the exercise would empower the soldiers to bring about a success-ful issue to the anticipated Allied offensive.[136] He was referring, of course, to the coming Battle of the Somme. Few newspapers printed the adver-tisement, however, and there was practically no press interest in the Householders' War League of Thought more generally. The Order of the Star in the East supported the campaign but it is not clear from the article whether it was the inspiration for it. But it is telling that during the war 314 Regent Street was, in fact, the address of the Star Shop, which sold the order's books along with a wider array of works on mysticism, Christianity, Buddhism, theosophy, and 'Higher Thought'.[137]

Instead of a psychic offensive, others argued that pursuing a psychic peace was a more productive and moral way to go. On 27 August 1914 some notable psychical researchers gathered at the Occult Club, Piccadilly Place, London to explore whether they should form a society to lay down rules as to using collective mental concentration to bring about peace through international friendship and understanding. This would involve agreeing to observe certain times for collective thought power.[138] Louise 'Lizzy' Lind-Af-Hageby (1878–1963), a pioneering feminist and co-founder of the Animal Defence and Anti-Vivisection Society, was a leading voice at the meeting, and she guided the discussion at a subsequent gathering of interested parties where it was proposed to set up an Occultists' Peace Union. The title was a cause of some disagreement amongst those attending. The engineer, prophet, and former Christian Scientist Frederick

L. Rawson, who we shall meet again in a later chapter, thought that the term 'occultist' was too closely associated with black magic in the popular mind and so would detract from the proposed union's aims. He had personally suffered from the term being directed at him, and so he suggested instead 'The Thinkers' Peace Union'. One of those present, Mrs Gaskell, agreed with Rawson about the problem of public misinterpretation, but proposed an alternative title, 'The Rose and the Lily Peace League', because its poetic appeal 'would stir the spiritual nature of the people'. There was not much support for this floral title amongst those present either. After further discussion, Rawson and others were won round, and all but one of those present agreed on the original proposition—Occultists' Peace Union. They would seek to educate and promote the term 'Occultist' as standing for all that was 'divinest and most spiritual', and a small committee was created to draw up the OPU's statutes.[139] Mrs Gaskell had predicted at the meeting that the war would be over within a month, but this applied more accurately to the future of the OPU, which seems to have fizzled out shortly after.

In an article entitled 'Psychic Help for Soldiers and Sailors', the occultist and ritual magician J. W. Brodie Innes put forward that the sick and hopeless on the battlefield could be comforted and supported through telepathic thought. One could also use the power of dreams to bring about such psychic succour. He had tried this himself, and was pleased to report that a convalescing young soldier he knew reported feeling much better after having seen a vision of Innes and a beautiful woman by his bedside.[140] Such dream healing was also promoted by some on the mystical fringes of Anglicanism. At a meeting of the international Club for Psychical Research in February 1915, Mrs Camus, wife of a London Anglican vicar, related how on the morning of 7 November she dreamed that she was at the front shortly after a battle had taken place. There were casualties strewn everywhere. She saw a female form walking among them tending to the wounded, and recognized her acquaintance, fellow Anglican worshipper Dorothy Kerin. Only two years earlier Kerin, then in her early twenties, had been the focus of press attention when it was claimed that she had been divinely cured of tuberculosis after seeing a vision of Jesus and two angels.[141] In Camus's dream, Camus walked over to Kerin and asked if she could help her. Kerin requested that she look over the bloody field and identify those men most in need, and that she would then go over and lay her hands on them to relieve their suffering. Camus duly obliged before waking up. The next day Kerin visited the vicarage and much to her surprise said that she had similarly dreamed of meeting her on the battlefield that morning. 'I do not think it was a dream,' said Kerin. 'I was helping the poor wounded men.' Later, in January, Kerin said she received a letter from a captain in which he asked, 'were you conscious that on the 8 January you came to me in spirit and laid hands on me to heal me when I was wounded with a shot?'[142]

Over in France, at a conference of the Sociétés Savantes in February 1916, psychical researcher M. L. Bardonnet gave a lecture in which he set out his plan to use clairvoyance to identify the location of German troops, batteries, and fortifications. The idea attracted a lot of interest, and it was agreed to set up a commission to investigate.[143] Later in the year he published an experiment with the clairvoyant Madame de V., during which she apparently visualized a possible military site. She talked of a large house and heavy iron objects that were not guns 'but something similar'. 'You don't see other things of war?,' he asked. She replied, 'There are some things a little in the air.' As the seance progressed, she saw five cannons, but most significantly the carcass of a Zeppelin.[144] This was one of the very few attempts to use clairvoyance for military purposes at the time, as there was considerable scepticism among psychical researchers as to its value. It was considered an imperfect and inconsistent psychic state that would not allow for sufficient accuracy to be able to identify exact locations. The psychical researcher and former Rector of the Academy of Dijon Émile Boirac concluded the following year that it was not worth 'risking an instrument of which we are not quite sure' for military advantage.[145]

Premonitions

The main field of psychical war research on both sides of the channel concerned the evidence for telepathic visions and clairvoyant premonitions of death and danger in the trenches or at sea. Other than spiritual mediumship, these had been the key areas for psychical researchers for a couple of decades. Across the channel, in 1917 the leading French psychical researcher Charles Richet gained agreement from the French government to place a plea in the army journal *Bulletin des Armées de la République* for testimonies asking, 'Do you have any premonitions?'

He received around a hundred letters, a few of which were printed in the *Annales des Sciences Psychiques*. Numerous examples culled from such sources were also gathered together in books published during or shortly after the war, such as Rosa Stuart's *Dreams and Visions of the War* (1917), and Carrington's *Psychical Phenomena and the War* (1918). In Britain, the local and national press also periodically printed stories of premonitions experienced by the mothers and other family members of military personnel.

Many of these accounts were presentiments, in other words intuitive, mostly foreboding feelings about the future. Out in the battlefields these were sometimes referred to as 'the call', a sense that one's death was imminent. Indeed, such presentiments were perhaps the most openly talked about psychic phenomena amongst soldiers themselves and in their letters home. In 1917 an American soldier, Daniel W. King, who fought through Verdun, said he could give the names of half a dozen men in his own company who had felt the call: 'I have never known it to fail. It always means death.' There was the account of two soldiers sheltering in a stable near the front. It was bitterly cold, and one suggested to the other that they huddle up to keep warm. The other said, 'No. I shall be killed to-night.' His companion scoffed, but the other moved to an upper part of the stable. That night, at midnight, a dud shell came through the roof and killed him.[146] When, in the summer of 1915, Private William Terry of the 3rd Coldstream Guards came home to Eridge, East Sussex on leave, he had a premonition that he would not return from the front the next time. He was killed in action on 11 August.[147] A correspondent to *The Scotsman* related how a sailor on the *Pathfinder* had told him that he had just sent off a parcel to his wife containing all his money and valuables. 'There is something coming to me,' he said quietly. Within thirty hours he was dead after a torpedo sank the *Pathfinder* on 5 September 1914.[148] In the summer of 1915 Private Tom Arnold, of Briton Ferry, west Wales, wrote to his parents from the trenches of Gallipoli, 'I have a strange presentiment that something is going to happen, and if I lose my life in to-morrow's battle I want you to banish all grief or sorrow for me.' He was found dead in a gully the next day.[149] An inquest on a drowned woman in Hackney, London, heard, in January 1918, that before she was found dead, she had had a premonition that her husband had been killed in action. Notification of his death was received two weeks later. The coroner observed that it was a curious premonition, but 'it had proved to be true'.[150] Such presentiments were not always ominous. It was reported that despite receiving a letter of condolence from the king, the mother of one Private Potter, in Dudley, had a presentiment he was still alive, and refused to give consent for a memorial service. A letter subsequently arrived from her son saying he was alive and well in a Turkish prisoner of war camp.[151]

A second category of wartime premonition, which was also represented in literary works of the time, concerns the aforementioned crisis apparitions or phantasms.[152] These were 'veridical' or 'truthful' hallucinations experienced while awake. Psychical researchers attempted to explore whether the mind of the person experiencing the crisis could unwittingly or willingly telepathically impress the vision of what they were experiencing or was about to befall them on the mind of a loved one. The day that Rifleman John Middlebrook was shot in the arm his mother reported to her family that during the night he had appeared to her in her bedroom, pointed to his shattered arm, and said 'Look, Mother.' Middlebrook, who was a theology student and future Baptist minister, believed that he had been able—thanks to the providence of God, 'to tell my mother myself—an answer to most urgent prayer'.[153] As we have already seen, crisis apparitions could also work the other way, with loved ones on the home front appearing on the battlefields. A soldier wrote to his mother, for instance, that while he was involved in the dangerous task of carrying bombs, he had to take cover. Some twenty yards off, he saw his mother 'as plain as life'. Leaving his bombs, he crawled close to the place where the apparition appeared, when a German shell dropped on them, 'and—well—I had to return for some more. But had it not been for you, I certainly would have been reported "missing."...You'll turn up again, next time a shell's coming?'[154]

Our third category concerns the interpretation of dreams and dream premonitions. A German soldier named Walter Lange wrote home in June 1915, 'I am always dreaming such strange things now.' In one of them he met an old friend. 'You were killed long ago!,' Walter exclaimed. To which his friend replied, 'Yes, of course I was, and so were you.' Walter wrote in his letter, 'What do you think of such a curious dream? Is it a premonition?' Indian cavalryman Mirza Ahmed Baig, who was stationed in France, wrote to a friend about a strange dream in August 1916, and requested 'a complete and precise interpretation'.[155] For others, some dream omens were all too clear. It was a widespread conviction amongst northern French soldiers, for instance, that to dream of a bus was a certain omen of death.[156] On the home front there were numerous accounts of mothers and wives dreaming of the imminent death of loved ones. On 11 October 1914, for example, the mother of Gunner Thomas F. Johnson, Stoke Grove, Guildford, said that she had dreamt 'that he had died from his wounds, and she saw him standing by her side, and heard him call her'. Her son died in a Rouen hospital three days later.[157] In October 1915, the mother of Private Frank Wright, West Riding Regiment, who lived in Hebden Bridge, had a vivid dream of her son 'lying dead in a trench, along with another soldier, and they had been dug out and returned'. Four days later she received the news he had been buried in a collapsed dugout.[158] There was also the British mother who dreamed one night of seeing her son wounded on the battlefield with his throat bound with lint. She walked up to him to find he had been shot in the head and throat. On awaking she feared her son was dead, and soon the news arrived that he had, indeed, been killed as she had seen.[159] The sinking of ships and the consequent loss of life also entered the dreams of some. The Society for Psychical Research thoroughly investigated one such premonition experienced by a Miss Ann Jones (pseudonym) on 6 August 1914. She was sitting in her room and felt a great depression overpower her. She fell into a kind of swoon for several hours during which she had an impression of a sinking ship. She wrote it down in her diary, and when friends arrived at nine in the evening, she also told them of her dream. The next day the newspapers reported the sinking of HMS *Amphion*, with over one hundred dead.[160]

Of the hundred premonition accounts Richet received he considered only thirty of them worth preserving, and only seven or eight as being of great interest.[161] The council of the SPR also expressed its disappointment with the quality of reports in March 1916:

> Such cases have doubtless occurred, but practically none of those which have reached us have come up on investigation to the standard of evidence required. There was, for instance, one where the parents of a soldier reported that they had dreamt of him, and his sister that she had seen a vision of him, on the night he was killed. But no first-hand evidence of their having mentioned their experiences before they knew of the death was forthcoming. Another case reporting that a vision of a son by his mother had occurred at the time of his death, turned out to have no foundation whatever.[162]

96

The following year, the council noted that between 1911 and 1915 it had reported only five cases for which the evidence was sufficiently strong to warrant publication. But it welcomed a recent modest increase in reports of veridical apparitions of the living, including that of an officer, shortly after he had been wounded at the front.[163] One of the handful of cases it considered worthy of printing concerned a newspaper report on 6 June 1916 that one Mrs Baxter, the sister of Seaman George Malpress, of Peterborough, serving on the Queen Mary, dreamed that her brother came to her bedside shortly before the ship was sunk by a German battlecruiser during the Battle of Jutland. The SPR investigated, interviewing Mrs Baxter, her mother, and her doctor, and meticulously checked the details and timings they gave with the known facts about the sinking. It transpired that Baxter was not asleep when she saw the vision of her brother but was ill at the time, suffering from erysipelas. The SPR normally excluded hallucinations reported by individuals suffering illnesses, but on this occasion, perhaps with a degree of desperation, it considered the Baxter case worthy of printing because it was the only such hallucination Baxter had experienced.[164]

There was a further fundamental problem with premonition research, in that only those instances that had apparently come true were recorded or researched. Many presentiments and dreams were not borne out, as several soldiers noted at the time. The Canadian infantryman Charles Savage observed that he 'had known quite a few who at various times had such presentiments and I also knew that they were as often wrong as right, but statistics are poor consolation when you feel that way'. The French soldier and academic Fernand Baldensperger similarly noted that '"false coincidences" might entitle a casual observer to dismiss entirely that sort of premonition'. He had, himself, been utterly convinced on several occasions that he was not going to return home, and had begun measures to deal with his affairs:[165]

As a social historian it is not my task to reason away the range of phenomena described and discussed in this chapter. Many others have attempted to do that at the time and since. In 1917 popular science journals reported, for instance, on an engineering explanation for the Przemyśl Marian visions of March 1915. It was suggested that Austrian scientists had projected the image onto low-lying clouds using a stereopticon (a magic lantern projection involving two slides to create a three-dimensional effect) carried by an aeroplane, using slides of a well-known holy painting in the monastery of Częstochowa. The intention was to bolster the faith of the besieged Austrian troops. It was also proposed that the apparitions seen by soldiers from the trenches were macabre will-o'-the-wisps, luminous gases produced by calcium and phosphorous emitting from the myriad decaying bodies on the battle-field.[166] Far more convincing are the psychological explanations for hallucinations and convictions of imminent death that were proposed at the time, and have been examined at length since. The fatigue, sensory deprivation, and sensory overstimulation engendered by trench warfare created distorted perceptions and mental aberrations, while stress and anxiety undoubtedly led to some of the uncanny experiences of those affected by fear and loss on the home fronts and battlefields.[167] One of the themes of this chapter has been to show, furthermore, how tradition, fiction, imagination, rumour, wishful thinking, poor memory, deception, and embroidery of the facts generated convictions and impressions of divine, spiritual, and supernatural influence.

Yet, whatever the spurious or mundane origins of wartime visions, spirits, and psychical experiences, they have important social and cultural significance in their own right. What may look like the bizarre or fantastical expressions of religious enthusiasm or psychological trauma, or the fervid imaginings of the occult fringe, actually often had deep roots in popular faith and tradition. There was no great retrogressive recrudescence of mystical tendencies in wartime societies, and neither was there a profound new public relationship with the spiritual side of life. The interest in spiritualism has been used to confirm the concept of a post-war societal cult of the dead regarding the war. But that was much more a result of ritualized Anglican and state-sponsored memorialization, which we are still asked to engage with today through politics, media pressure, and royal presence. But the war did generate new expressions regarding familiar supernatural notions, and spiritualism and psychical research provided a modern language for understanding apparitions and the afterlife.

4

TELLING FORTUNES, TELLING TALES

Troubled waters created by the war have favoured the operations of those who dangle the dazzling bait of "magic" before the less wary fish of the human shoal.

(*Justice of the Peace*, 20 January 1917)

The popularity of fortune tellers during the war was widely reported in the press of the combatant countries. The propaganda message was obvious from all sides. Clearly the enemy was weakening under pressure, riddled with doubts and losing its collective reasoning if its people were resorting en masse to fortune tellers for succour and comfort. In November 1914, a widely reprinted article by *The Times*'s correspondent in Lübeck reported how fortune tellers had been banned across Germany because of the reliance on them by womenfolk, who, he stated, had 'undergone an even greater strain than those of this country'. Only a month later it was further observed in the British newspapers that fortune tellers, hitherto not tolerated in 'moral Germany', were now booming in the country's savage wartime culture, with hundreds of German women turning to it as a living. According to the press, this was connived at by the police because the fortune tellers served up a patriotic story of Britain's eventual defeat.[1] From the other side, in 1917 the *Deutsches Volksblatt* took great pleasure in relating an article from the *Daily Mail* that reported how London was inundated with fortune tellers feeding off the gullibility of its superstitious citizens. As it looked increasingly likely that America would join the war, the Austrian *Illustriertes Oesterreichisches Journal* published an article entitled 'Superstition in America' in which it told its readers how American cities were a 'paradise' for *Wahrsager* or fortune tellers of every hue. Astrology books were very popular, it reported, because gullible Americans took it as a serious science.[2]

Putting the propaganda to one side, there is no doubt that many thousands of fortune tellers profitably plied their trade during the war. While the crowds of prophets, almanac compilers, and soothsayers pronounced on the fate of nations, the myriad high-street and back-street palmists, card readers, and clairvoyants serviced the popular desire for personal enlightenment as to the future, assuaging—and sometimes fuelling—private hopes, fears, and anxieties. The headache for the authorities was not knowing what wartime messages were being relayed by such operators in front rooms, parlours, and meeting halls. As we have seen, the astrologers and prophets uniformly toed a patriotic line in their predictions, but were the fortune tellers also on message? Or were they undermining public confidence in the war effort? What effect were they having on the morale of the soldiery? There is a real sense of frustration with a popular culture of divination that proved impossible to harness let alone suppress. The prosecution of fortune tellers also exposed some tendentious areas regarding the freedom of religious and scientific expression, and the porous boundary between occult *practices* and occult *purpose*. Applying hindsight, then, to the wartime history of foresight uncovers some intriguing insights into personal anxieties, the limits of state control, and the place of mediumship in popular culture.

The Business of Fortune Telling

The classified advertisements in the national and regional press are a good place to start getting a feel for the range of fortune tellers during the war, and also how they promoted themselves in an increasingly competitive market.[3] Let us have a peek, for example, at the *Sheffield Evening Telegraph* for 10 March 1915. There we find Professor Swallow, 'who predicted the German War. Hundreds grateful. Don't procrastinate.' Meanwhile, the astrologer, phrenologist, and palmist 'Zampier' claimed to be the 'People's Advisor'. Professor Hatfield, a phrenologist, informed that he gave 'consultations daily relative to character and mental capacity'. Madame Flora, clairvoyant, palmist, and crystal seer, advertised she was only in town for a few more weeks. A few months later Madame Martino, Madame Naomi, and Madame Doreen joined the Sheffield throng, advertising their palmistry and clairvoyant services.[4] Over in France, the following month we find a similar series of advertisements in the daily newspaper *Le Matin*, though the offer of magic and the use of the Tarot were more evident. There was Mme Sauton the celebrated cartomancer, and Madame Luchatel who used the Egyptian Tarot and had 'surprised the most sceptical'. Madame Cléopâtre, of Chalon-sur-Saône, described herself as the most celebrated medium in the world. M. Rhodes of rue Fidélité, Paris, offered to foretell the destiny of loved ones present, absent, and disappeared. The medium and clairvoyant Mme Henry described herself as the 'witch of Mont Ventoux' and boasted her predictions were always right, while a 'scientific' medium named Adi advertised her knowledge of magical secrets.[5]

As the advertisements suggest, quite a few professional fortune tellers were itinerant, moving from town to town, renting out premises, promoting their availability in the press or through notices, and then moving on, either to avoid the police or to try out new, more prosperous divinatory pastures. In 1915, for instance, palmist Gertrude Garrett decided to move on after stints in Yarmouth and other seaside resorts. She settled in Luton, rented out a consultation room a few houses down from her new abode, and placed the following notice inside the window: 'Madam Lee, a relative of the old established Gipsy Lee family, now nearly extinct, patronised by the leading aristocracy, nobility and gentry, and thousands of the appreciative public.' Trade was brisk, including amongst soldiers.[6] Other practitioners were long-established and well-known figures in their villages or neighbourhoods who were just as happy to visit their clients' homes as receive them at their own premises.[7] Well-established backstreet fortune tellers charged between six pence and a shilling for a consultation. While earnings obviously fluctuated from week to week, good money could be made, with some regularly receiving dozens of people a day. As a comparison, a captain in the British infantry earned a minimum 12s 6d a day, while wages in the Women's Land Army were between 14s and 20s a week.[8] London fortune tellers catering for the well-heeled could earn several pounds a day. When the American medium and fortune teller Almira Brockway was arrested in December 1916, her confiscated ledger revealed she had received £115 over thirty-four days.[9] For the numerous itinerant practitioners, earnings could be erratic as they tried to whip up a clientele from scratch through advertising. The confiscated notebook of Rupert Eric Costello de Montmorency, alias Rupert Ghansaka, an itinerant West African fortuneteller known as

'Professor Rajah', makes for interesting reading. Regarding the first half of 1916 he recorded:

Glasgow: Nothing doing, 12s in two weeks.
Cork: No good; 3s in four days.
Cardiff: Rotten; Welsh artful dodgers; no good.
Blackpool: No good.

Manchester proved profitable, though, and he made £8 15s in his second week there, and £9 6d in the third week. He had been prosecuted several times previously, and in June 1917 he was picked up again by the police in Birmingham under the Vagrancy Act, claiming to be a phrenologist.[10]

There were other means of obtaining divinatory knowledge than attending the consulting rooms of fortune tellers. While much of wartime astrology was concerned with the advent and course of the war, there was also a thriving trade in mail-order horoscopes for individuals. This business model was pioneered by Alan Leo (1860–1917). When he founded The Astrologer's Magazine in 1890, he offered new subscribers a free horoscope. This proved a popular offer but hugely time-consuming for Leo to produce, and he began to charge for his horoscopes according to the detail demanded by the customer. The key innovation, though, was the creation of a series of simple, formulaic horoscopes for the relevant sun sign or ruling planet that could be mimeographed in their thousands and sold for a shilling each. He hit upon this because of the number of requests he received from customers who did not know their time of birth, but nevertheless asked, 'Please try your best for me.'[11] During the First World War there were numerous unscrupulous operators adopting the same modus operandi without Leo's genuine commitment to astrological principles. In February 1916 one Professor Wharncliffe, who described himself as 'the famous English Astrologer', paid for an advertisement masquerading as a news item in which he stated how in 1913 he had foretold the coming of the war through the science of astrology, and that he now offered astrological readings if given name, address, and date of birth.[12] Wharncliffe was, in fact, neither a professor nor famous. He may not even have existed—as we might divine from the trial in Belfast of William J. Harrison in July 1917. Earlier that year advertisements appeared in a monthly magazine stating:

'Fate. Money returned if horoscope untrue.' For a one-shilling postal order and two pence in stamps, Newton Verity of Duke Street, London, offered to draw up a typed seven-page horoscope. But Newton Verity was not a real person but a trading name for a mail-order horoscope business set up a few years earlier by a man in Cornwall called Hepps. Harrison bought the business from him for £500 in 1911, and it had proven very lucrative, with a global customer base. One of those who sent off his money was a wounded soldier from Northern Ireland named Leslie Adamson. So did a vigilant detective police officer in Portadown, who saw the magazine advertisement and thought it needed investigating. It transpired that the horoscopes both men received were identical. They were from a generic job lot of horoscopes, some twenty to thirty thousand, that Harrison had bought from Hepps.[13]

Automated fortune tellers had also become popular enough in Britain by the 1890s that a newspaper bemoaned, 'are not these fortune-telling automatic machines now in the railway stations a significant proof of the silliness of the age'.[14] During the early twentieth century sophisti-cated electric versions were developed, with names such as the Hindoo Fortune Telling Machine and the Wizard Fortune Teller, which usually dispensed a card or piece of paper bearing stock predictions rather like Chinese fortune cookies. They became a staple of American and British working-class seaside arcades, and exercised their charm amongst sol-diers on leave during the war. An American correspondent in Paris described the pleasures available to soldiers sauntering around Paris's annual Foire aux Pains d'Épices (Gingerbread Fair) in the Place de la Nation: 'innumerable roulette wheels, shooting galleries with scores of Kaisers as targets, and fortune telling machines are ready to lure Mister Doughboy'.[15] In June 1915 a Viennese newspaper grumbled at the popu-larity of a German machine called the 'Chyromant-Automaton'. 'You see, the soothsayers are progressive, they use the new inventions of technol-ogy,' it observed, reporting that day after day crowds of peasant recruits and convalescent and injured soldiers could be found crowding around it in the *Prater-Ausstellungsstraße*. For 20 *Heller* (a small coin) it produced a piece of paper containing 'the study of the lines of your palm' and a prediction of the future.[16]

Such machines were twentieth-century novelties, a bit of fun, but in all the combatant countries there was a long tradition of popular printed guides to the future that continued into the war years and beyond. We have already encountered almanacs and prophecy literature that foretold general events, but there was a thriving market for dream interpreters and manuals on chiromancy and cartomancy. In Russia, before books of divination were banned following the 1917 revolution, some of the best-known cheap books on dream interpretation, divination, and spells were attributed to James Bruce, the son of a Scottish nobleman who rose through the ranks to become a general under Peter the Great, who reigned from 1682 to 1725. Bruce also acted as Peter's royal astronomer, and when he was put in charge of printing, he produced the first Russian almanac. His life and his almanac were the basis of numerous legends and divinatory manuals over the next two centuries, such as *Bruce's Pocket Oracle*. Between 1916 and 1917 three editions appeared of a publication entitled *A New Book. Household Remedies. The Bruce Calendar for 200 Years. A Course in Folk Healing, Magic, Sorcery, and A Complete Collection of Russian Folk Spells*.[17] The popularity of Madame de Thèbes's works on chiromancy in France has already been noted, and there were numerous other guides available during the war. In 1916 there appeared *La Cartomancie; ou, L'avenir dévoilé par les cartes*, for example, and the following year *Cosmogonie humaine*, which contained a key to chiromancy, physiognomy, graphology, and phrenology.[18] In Germany, Gustav Wilhelm Gessmann's *Catechism of Chiromancy*, first published in the 1890s, was republished in 1915, while the anti-Semitic esotericist Willy Vierath wrote *Die Handlesekunst und das Wahrsagen aus der Hand* ('Palmistry and Divination from the Hand') three years later. Dream divination manuals were popular in Britain. In late 1914 Scottish newspapers carried the following advertisement: 'Do you believe in the interpretation of dreams? If so, you will find "The penny Dream Book" a source of never-ending pleasure and interest.' It was available from newsagents and post free for two pence.[19] Numerous palmistry manuals were available, including the *Catechism of Palmistry* by the well-known Blackpool fortune teller Ida Ellis.[20] Those wishing to learn tasseomancy (reading tea leaves) could purchase *The Art of Fortune-Telling by Tea-Leaves. By a Highland Seer* (1917), or purchase the *Weekly Companion*'s giveaway guide in August 1915. 'You will learn the whole art of reading fortunes in the teacup in a few minutes,' it promised. 'You will be able to reveal the future to your friends.'[21] The secrets of cartomancy were explained in numerous publications, such as *Indian Card Reading: The Art of Fortune Telling by Means of Ordinary Playing Cards Explained in Six Lessons* (1916), and *Old Moore's Fortune Telling by Cards:*

An Easy Guide (1918). Finally, for those wishing to experiment with a crystal ball, an English publisher reprinted a guide by the American mystical spiritualist Jesse Charles Fremont Grumbine, *The System of Philosophy Concerning the Divinity of Clairvoyance; Also a Treatise on Divination and Crystal Reading* (1915).

The extent to which, during the war, people sat in their homes with such manuals, earnestly examining their palms or laying the cards to see what would befall them or their loved ones, is unknowable. But the long history of popular divination suggests that if people seriously wanted to divine the future, they consulted the professionals rather than set about learning a divinatory art. Telling fortunes could also be practised as a mere amusement, of course, and tasseomancy was popular in this respect. As the *Weekly Companion* advertised in 1915, 'at parties at home—in fact, at any place where you take tea—you will be the centre of attraction if you can read the teacups'.[22] By the war it had been demystified and commercialized. Specially designed china fortune teacups were in vogue, which bore illustrations of cards or astrological signs on the inside, and came with instruction booklets with their own original interpretive systems. With tasseomancy mass-marketed in this way, it is telling that very few professional fortune tellers advertised or practised it for payment.

Magical Services

Some fortune tellers also offered services that were in the realm of popular magic. This might simply concern giving advice on how to conduct protective rituals. Mary Anne Lowther told a client that her soldier husband would return if she placed her left garter under her pillow at night and said her prayers.[23] In July 1915 a German woman named Minna Falkenhain wrote to her husband serving on the Russian front to inform him that a wise old woman had advised that he would be protected if he sent her some of his hair. Not any old hairs, though: they 'must be from below your stomach: you know, of course, from your genitals', she explained. Furthermore, they had to be 'approximately half a measure long'. 'If I had already known that when you were here, it would have been better,' she explained, before concluding, 'Please be so good and cut some from you and send them to me in a letter.'[24] The venerable trade of those magical practitioners known as cunning folk, or wise men and wise women, was perfectly adaptable to wartime needs. Such people claimed to be able to solve a wide range of problems through their magical powers, which they professed to have either inherited, learned from books of magic, or gained from supernatural beings such as fairies and angels. In November 1917, for instance, Mary Lilian Trenery, a cunning woman of Penzance, Cornwall, was prosecuted for extorting £14 15s from Mary Jane Pascoe for services that included taking off an evil spell from her cattle, procuring good fortune, and, for £1 each, promising to protect her three boys who were in the army and one in the navy, and ensure they came home. Trenery even had the nerve to ask Pascoe for a five-shilling 'war bonus' for her work, which was duly paid. She also took money from Lilie Bourgoyne, of Camborne, to quieten her troublesome husband. For 30 shillings she said she could resolve her problems by magically ensuring that he was conscripted into the army. Trenery had even greater war ambitions, though, as the magistrates' court heard how she had claimed that if she could go to see the Kaiser, she could influence him to stop the war.[25]

Quite a few diviners did a sideline in protective charms and amulets. The Rotherham fortune teller Sarah Ann Flint sold little sachet charms for 3 shillings to local female munitions workers, telling them that they would bring good luck if worn next to the heart. She said they contained quicksilver and a special cream. When one of them was opened, however, it was found to contain only table salt.[26] As was noted earlier, French fortune tellers and occultists were more open in their advertisements about the magical aspects of their services. One practitioner condemned by the Paris authorities was found to have made hundreds of thousands of francs selling talismans to soldiers for protection against bullets and shells. In the summer of 1915 a cartomancer named Camille Mercier, who lived near Lyons and claimed to be the daughter of Madame de Thèbes, was arrested for charging 20 francs from women for sachets that would protect their soldier husbands and boyfriends from bullets and artillery shells. Higher up the scale, an expatriate Argentine astrologer named Jean Berecochea was prosecuted in part for offering white metal medallions for sale which he said had magnetic powers and would protect those who wore them from all harm. One of his happy clients testified that it was thanks to these talismans that, in October 1914, her son had survived the Battle of Yser unscathed while his battalion was decimated.[27] The Parisian magician Jean Talazac, also known as the 'Red Sorcerer' or 'Occultus', became something of a media celebrity when he was prosecuted in 1916. His shop and brochures advertised a range of talismans and magical ingredients, including moles' feet at 10 francs each, wolves' teeth for just under 5 francs, snake skins, vultures' lungs, and hangman's rope.[28]

The Campaign against Fortune Tellers

The practice of fortune-telling for profit was a criminal offence across the European combatant countries. It was sometimes classed gener-ally as a fraud, but in some states there were long-standing laws specific to such occult 'pretences'. Article 54 of the Bavarian criminal code, for instance, included a paragraph against *Gaukelei* or charla-tanry or trickery:

> Whosoever for payment or for the attainment of some other advantage concerns themselves with so-called magic or spirit conjuring, with prophecy, card reading, divination, sign and dream interpretation or other charlatanry of the same kind, will be punished with a fine of up to 150 marks or with imprisonment.

By the end of the conflict the Bavarian wartime legal code was further extended to forbidding unauthorized lectures and demonstrations of the occult sciences.[29] Similar statutes also operated in the German states of Baden and Hesse. In France, Article 479:7 of the Napoleonic penal code punished those who made 'a profession of divination and predic-tion, or of the explanation of dreams'. By the time of the First World War further articles added to the code required the confiscation of 'all instruments, tools, and costumes serving or intended for the practice of the profession of fortune-teller or interpreter of dreams'. Punishment under the Article usually consisted of no more than minor fines, with prison sentences only applicable in circumstances such as recidivism. But in January 1915 the Paris prefect of police Émile Marie Laurent wrote to the Minister of the Interior noting the failings of Article 479:7 for dealing with the 'great number' of soldiers' wives and unemployed workers who were using their state relief payments for visits to fortune tellers. A few months later Henri Guernul, the general secretary of the

Ligue Française pour la Défense des Droits de l'Homme et du Citoyen, or Human Rights League of France, born in 1898 out of the Dreyfus scandal, wrote to the Ministry of Justice reporting that numerous of its members were also concerned about the insufficiency of the law to deal with the swarms of fortune tellers trading on the fate of missing soldiers. He highlighted with frustration that the judiciary rarely applied the Napoleonic Article 405 against fraud and false undertakings, which allowed much heavier penalties. His members thought that this law would prove a stronger deterrent. 'This exploitation of the anguish of families is at this hour particularly condemnable,' Guernul concluded, 'and its repression must be ordered.'[30]

British fortune tellers were liable to prosecution under section 4 of the Vagrancy Act of 1824, which punished 'persons pretending or professing to tell fortunes, or using any subtle craft, means, or device, by palmistry or otherwise, to deceive and impose'. Those convicted could be sentenced to three months' hard labour and receive a substantial fine of up to £25. By the time of the war, the guiding principle as to whether to prosecute fortune tellers under the Act had been set out in a letter from the Home Office to the Commissioner of Police in 1892. The Secretary of State, Herbert Asquith, advised that the police were only to pursue fortune tellers if the 'young and ignorant' were in danger of being defrauded. This was reiterated by Charles Masterman, the future head of the British War Propaganda Bureau, in the House of Commons in May 1911, with Asquith now prime minister:

> the mere practice of palmistry is not, so, far as I am aware, illegal; the essence of the offence created by the Statute is the intention to impose, and the object is to protect the young and the ignorant. The police have instructions to watch cases of suspicion, and whenever there is good ground for believing that fraud or imposition is being practised they will be directed to prosecute.

As was abundantly clear from Metropolitan Police prosecutions in 1912, though, many of the clients of fashionable West End fortune tellers were neither young nor ignorant.[31] The war then shifted the parameters and concerns.

On both sides of the conflict there was considerable anxiety amongst the authorities and the press about the pernicious influence of fortune tellers on public morale. Concerted efforts were made to suppress their trade and to warn people of the dangers of resorting to them. One widely reported case in Germany concerned a Munich practitioner who was sentenced to jail for six weeks in February 1915 for telling numerous clients that their husbands would be killed or return crippled.[32] Later that year a number of German newspapers reprinted an article by the criminologist and campaigner against occultists and 'superstition' Albert Hellwig (1880–1950). He commended the authorities for their concerted attempts to suppress fortune tellers. Military commanders had ordered the arrest of some and had forbidden them from advertising in newspapers. In the article, and a subsequent book published in 1916 entitled *Weltkrieg und Aberglaube* ('World War and Superstition'), Hellwig not only complained of the diviners who perniciously forecast the deaths of soldiers at the front, but equally condemned those who predicted positive futures for soldiers and their loved ones. Hellwig urged that if more funds were made available, then further penal measures should be taken to end the divination trade for the sake of the war effort. Cases like the suicide of 21-year-old Lucie Oldenburg, of Berlin, after consulting a fortune teller about her fears regarding a loved one in the war served to confirm the concerns.[33] But the nature of different local and regional ordinances and laws in Germany meant it was not so easy to enforce a blanket ban across the country. Indeed, in March 1916 a fortune teller in Neuss, North Rhine-Westphalia, even lodged a formal complaint against the police for threatening to fine her 150 marks for each infringement. She claimed she had paid a tax that allowed her to operate legitimately. While she was technically correct, in the circumstances it was not a good move on her behalf. She was denounced in court and in the press for profiting from the many 'mischiefs' she had made against the relatives of those at war, and she stood accused of violating moral sentiments. The police's warnings were upheld.[34] But despite the most proactive anti-divination campaign of all the main combatant countries, the prosecution in September 1918 of the popular Leipzig cartomancer Agnes Kropaczewski is indicative of the resilience of the German fortune-telling trade throughout the war and beyond.[35]

The British authorities had their own problems applying the Vagrancy Act as a weapon against fortune-telling. It became quite a common practice for fortune tellers to charge for other innocuous activities, such as a lecture or religious service, with clients paying at the door and then being invited to have a 'free' consultation. The Luton fortune teller Gertrude Garrett tried to get around the same problem by charging 1 shilling for a copy of a book she gave each customer entitled *An Epitome of Palmistry*.[36] Some simply made no formal charge but expressed their gratitude for any donations clients wished to make. There was also an issue of double standards in the application of the law. Fortune tellers were frequently employed as an entertainment at charity bazaars and fundraisers for the war effort. In July 1918, for instance, the *Dundee Evening Telegraph* reported that one Mrs Stark of Cupar had held a tea and fortune-telling entertainment for the Red Cross.[37] Well-heeled society women sometimes dressed up and 'played' the fortune teller at such fundraisers, but the professionals were also called in. The former soldier and First World War correspondent Charles à Court Repington recorded in his diary for August 1917 a visit to Alloa House, Scotland, the residence of Lady Mar, when a number of other military personnel were present. The day before, there had been a bazaar in the grounds and a fortune teller named Madame Dubois had been in action: 'All the Admirals in turn went to see the fortune-teller ... all came out from their consultation with the lady, looking flushed and pleased, and with a glint in their eyes, showing that the lady had prophesied great careers for them all.'[38]

This vogue for charity fortune tellers, which had begun in the previous couple of decades, muddied the boundary between fortune-telling as a pernicious prosecutable crime and as a charming, frivolous entertainment.[39] In legal terms the distinction resided in whether the fortune tellers set out 'to deceive and impose'. But was it still an imposition if the money that changed hands was for charity rather than personal profit? Some charitable events evidently avoided the matter by laying on fortune tellers as free entertainments. The whole issue smacked of blatant hypocrisy to some wartime fortune tellers, though, who found themselves in court tacitly or explicitly accused of undermining the war effort. The defence lawyer for the Clapham fortune teller Elizabeth Sixsmith, alias Madame Betty, argued that she had given much of her time to charity bazaars without payment.[40] At one of his various trials, Rupert de Montmorency, 'the Rajah', similarly complained that he had performed at charity bazaars to raise money for wounded soldiers, so why should he not do so to gain, as he put it, 'a little bit on his own'?[41]

In early 1915 the activities of a London fortune teller and astrologer named Zazra caused legal consternation and a flurry of communications between the Consul General in Barcelona, the Home Office, Foreign Office, and the Metropolitan Police. It began when a poor boy of Granollers, near Barcelona, received an advertisement in Spanish setting out Zazra's mail-order astrological services and a cut-out coupon to be sent to his home at 91 Maida Vale, along with the relevant sum of money in pesetas or dollars. It was headed with a picture of Zazra in a turban and Indian dress. We know from other sources that he described himself as the Chief Mystic of the Hindoo School of Protection. A resident of Granollers sent the flyer to the Consul General requesting that action be taken against Zazra. The Home Office and Foreign Office took the matter seriously and asked the Metropolitan Police to provide a report on Zazra, which they duly received. It transpired that Zazra was an Englishman named Arthur Drew Clifton who had for many years operated as a palmist, astrologer, and clairvoyant at 90 New Bond Street. He ceased operating from there in September 1912 after receiving a warning from the police that if he continued to advertise his services, he would be prosecuted under the Vagrancy Act. Clifton duly complied, saying he and his wife could live comfortably without having to maintain his business. He had, indeed, done well, with a large house, cars, and horses. The police described Clifton as 'a very shrewd man, and one not easily scared'. This would appear to be the case, because after removing himself from the high street and the British newspaper advertisement pages, he turned to offering his services to overseas clients, operating from his private residence. The Home Office looked into the possibility of prosecuting Zazra but ultimately advised the Consul General and Foreign Office that 'in view of the wording of section four of the Vagrancy Act, 1824, there is some difficulty in the way in dealing with fortune-tellers who confine their advertisements to foreign newspapers'. The key sticking point was that section 4 was limited to 'H. M. subjects' and so did not cover overseas citizens. Clifton was presumably well aware of this.[42] The police finally got him in 1923. Now aged 52, Clifton had continued his mail-order business, branching out into advertising globally, employing five typists to process his correspondence with clients. They found thousands of letters from across the world.[43]

British police carried out regular surveillance of fortune tellers, some-times in response to complaints from upset clients and sometimes as proactive campaigns to deter the trade, in some cases spurred on by press calls for action. The common modus operandi was entrapment. The police would stake out and monitor the fortune tellers' premises or houses, sometimes over a period of days, monitoring the number and gender of the clients who visited. Female detectives, usually policemen's wives and female relatives, were then employed to consult the fortune tellers so that they could act as witnesses to the fact that money had changed hands, thereby enabling successful prosecution under the Vagrancy Act. The tactic did not pass without some criticism. In April 1916 the socialist Welsh newspaper *The Pioneer*, edited by the pacifist and founder of the Labour Party Keir Hardie, criticized the Merthyr Tydfil police for employing it: 'We have little sympathy with "fortune telling",' an editorial observed, 'but we do not like this habit of deliberately using policemen's wives as stalking horses for the local police prosecutions. It looks too much like connivance to us.'[44] The police also occasionally dressed up as soldiers. When the Aberystwyth constabulary investigated Madame Smith Evans (alias Madame May) and her accomplice partner, a male clairvoyant and herbalist, in May 1918, Police Sergeant Thomas put on a major's uniform. He told the court, 'I have acted the amateur detective before.' The prosecuting lawyer said it was 'a role which Sergeant Thomas played with great success, as excitable ladies who rushed to have their fortunes told would not come forward to give evidence'. His colleague PC Evans dressed up as a collier when he paid a follow-up visit to the Evans's.[45]

Urban police forces conducted periodic crackdowns in areas with high concentrations of fortune tellers.[46] In August 1915 the police visited and arrested five fortune tellers in the seaside resort of Morecambe. The Metropolitan Police raided a number of female fortune tellers in the Edgeware Road, north-west London in February 1917, and followed up with raids in Barking and Ilford in east London. The chairman of the magistrates' court said these were the first prosecutions of their kind in the district, and that future cases would be dealt with severely.[47] The periodical for the magistracy, *Justice of the Peace*, praised the initiative: 'the effort has been one of unusual thoroughness, no doubt because the extent to which the evil had grown within the past two or three years called for stringent measures if it were to be successfully grappled with'.[48]

The northern newspaper the *Burnley Express* also voiced its support for the London police's crackdown, and said that the magistracy and the police in the provinces now 'have a special duty stopping such folly'.[49] As a result, there were considerably more prosecutions in 1917 than any other year of the war. The actions of the Metropolitan Police were also noted in Australia, where the press praised the raids. That year the law against fortune tellers was tightened up in Tasmania in light of what was seen as the inadequacy of the British Vagrancy Act to deal with the problem, and the police in several states launched their own campaigns in response to a directive from the prime minister's office to tackle those 'preying' on soldiers' relatives. As a consequence, of the 247 prosecutions for fortune-telling in Australia between 1900 and 1918, eighty-three were in 1917 alone.[50]

No matter how rigorously they were conducted, raids and prosecutions against practitioners were never going to stop or even dampen the fortune-telling trade. The demand was too great. In Paris, Émile Marie Laurent suggested to the Minister of the Interior that the most effective way of dealing with the problem was to ban newspapers from taking advertisements from fortune tellers. Yet the press bureau of the Ministry of War rejected the idea, saying that there was no appropriate law to enact such suppression. 'The exploitation of credulity' did not, for example, constitute a 'disaster' as defined in Article 8 of a law of 1849, which authorized the military suppression of publications. The press bureau concluded that the best extra measure that could be taken was to encourage newspapers to insert warnings to the public.[51] As we have seen, newspapers across the combatant countries took up this task with some vigour—even while, in Britain and in France, continuing to take the advertising revenue from fortune tellers. Editorials and thought pieces adopted a general tone of understanding about the wartime stresses that led people to resort to the diviners, while also chastising the gullibility of people and the perniciousness of those who enticed them. In the winter of 1916 the *Daily Mail*'s war correspondent Harold Ashton launched a mini-crusade, reporting on his visits to fortune tellers, exposing them, and giving evidence against them in court. Newspaper reports of prosecutions also often highlighted the condemnatory statements made by prosecution lawyers and magistrates as another means of getting the message across. At the trial of the London clairvoyant Elizabeth Mary Porter, for instance, the presiding magistrate stated: 'nothing could be more cruel at a time like this. People went to fortune-tellers, and were told that their relatives were in danger or were going to be killed. They exploited nervous feeling, and made money out of it.'[52] The prosecution against the Exeter medium and fortune teller Clementina Norton described the resort of large numbers of the public, including soldiers, to such people at such a time was 'a danger to the community'.[53] Personal stories of psychological damage caused by the fortune tellers helped illustrate the problem. In April 1915 London newspapers reported that a woman charged with drunkenness at Tottenham police court complained that her daughter kept visiting a fortune teller regarding her four sons who had gone to war. One had already been killed and another seriously wounded. The fortune teller had warned of misfortune to the family, and the mother complained that 'the fortune-teller's tales have undermined the health of us all'.[54]

A Women's Problem

The fortune-telling 'problem' was widely seen as a female problem. Women had long been stereotyped as more 'superstitious' and gullible when it came to popular magic and divination. By the First World War the influence and language of psychiatry had seeped into the educated idiom, and so this supposed female predilection for divination was now being couched in terms of flawed female psychology rather than the old familiar line of women's 'superstitious' ignorance and lack of education. So, in 1915 a Dublin newspaper, grumbling at the wartime popularity of fortune tellers, explained that as women were 'more highly strung and imaginative than men', they were 'more easily gulled'.[55] It was also suggested that women, however well educated, coped less easily with the stresses of wartime conditions. At the National Union of Women Workers conference in the autumn of 1915, Professor Gilbert Murray, Regius Professor of Greek at Oxford University, a public figure who was also President of the Society for Psychical Research (1915–16), gave a paper on 'What women will be asked to do in the future', in which he expressed concern at the worrying tendency during wartime of common-sense people, mostly women, to act foolishly by seeking out fortune tellers and actually doing what they were told by them.[56] This view was echoed in the *Yorkshire Evening Post*, in an article headed

'Simple-Minded Patrons of Fortune-Tellers: Soldiers' Wives and their Curiosity'. It opined that 'a marked revival in fortune-telling is one of the accompaniments of the war. There is an anxiety felt nowadays which drives many women to seek comfort in the vain visions of a new and motley tribe of charlatans.'[57] Prosecution reports certainly confirm that women made up a significant majority of the clientele of fortune tellers during the war. To give just a couple of examples, at the prosecution of the Edgeware Road fortune teller Beatrice Mary Smith, aka Madame Zenobie, in 1916, police reported that twenty to thirty women went to her during the day, nearly all of whom were relatives of men serving in the war.[58] At the trial of two Barnsley fortune tellers, Miriam Vaughan and Mary Ann Yates, in June 1916, police described the constant traffic of women, especially soldiers' wives, going to the defendants' houses day and night.[59] When police officers analysed the clients' letters found in the office of the mail-order astrologer William J. Harrison, 1,786 were from women and 247 from men.[60]

The First World War generated numerous expressions of masculine anxiety regarding the influence of women on the home front. This focused most obviously on concerns about the sexual and moral corruption of fighting-age men through prostitution and the transmission of venereal disease. But the concerns were manifest in more subtle ways regarding the disorder that might ensue in factories and the civil service due to perceived female frivolity and thoughtlessness. The 'new woman' might inappropriately adopt male traits, furthermore, and thereby undermine masculine authority and professionalism.[61] We can locate the concerns over fortune tellers in the same gendered context. Fortune-telling might undermine patriarchal control in the domestic sphere. Oral history interviews with elderly women recalling life in south London prior to the Second World War confirm the hostility of male members of households to their wives, sisters, and daughters visiting local fortune tellers. 'Mustn't let father know' was no doubt a frequent refrain, and one can imagine that for women in repressive households there was a modest thrill in venturing forth to hear of and fantasize about a future life of happiness and prosperity.[62] For some husbands the concerns were merely financial, annoyance that their wives wasted money on having their fortunes told on a regular basis. But as the oral histories suggest, there was also a decided masculine adherence to fate, which was also prevalent in the trenches. Fate was not to be interfered with or predicted. 'If it's going to happen it will happen,' and visiting fortune tellers was meddling. In other words, this was not a domestic conflict between female 'superstition' and male rationality. It was about women drawing upon intimations of the future to build confidence in their prospects, and this was unsettling to male authority and the order of things.

Patriarchal concerns about the domestic disruption caused by fortune tellers spilled into the courtroom. At the trial of three Preston women for fortune-telling in September 1915, the chief constable told the court that the police had received frequent complaints from the husbands of women resorting to fortune tellers, 'with the result that there had afterward been much domestic unhappiness at home'.[63] This is borne out by several domestic abuse cases. In September 1915 a 30-year-old soldier named Patrick Welsh, of Hebburn, was summoned for giving his wife a black eye during a quarrel. He said in his defence that she was going to fortune tellers. When George Webley, of Coventry, was charged with assaulting his wife, he said they had been 'having bothers' year in and year out, and it all arose, he said, after his wife visited a fortune teller. In November 1916 William West of Fulham was summoned by his wife for persistent cruelty, as a result of which she requested a separation order. William West's lawyer asked her in his defence, 'Hasn't he complained about you going to fortune-tellers?' He then produced a discoloured sheet that turned out to be an old mail-order horoscope she had purchased some twenty years before, which predicted that her married life would be very comfortable. The poor woman had to endure mocking laughter when this was read out in court.[64]

It is clear that both before and during the war a significant majority of fortune tellers were women. A survey of fortune-telling prosecutions between 1900 and 1950 reveals that 76 per cent were women, compared to 62 per cent in the period 1849–99.[65] It is likely that the war years saw an increase in female practitioners. The author of an article in the *Yorkshire Evening Post* certainly reckoned there had been a decided gender shift amongst the practitioners in Leeds. Prior to the war, the writer suggested, male fortune tellers in the city practised openly from premises, but nearly all of them had ceased trading due to the efforts of the authorities. Now, it told its readers in a disapproving tone, the new wave of practitioners was predominantly women operating from their own homes, charging modest sixpenny consultations. Any woman with 'a ready tongue and a lively imagination' could quickly have twenty women waiting to consult her.[66] Fortune-telling had always been an aspect of the female makeshift economy, and with many husbands in the armed services, it provided an independent, low-cost line of work for numerous working-class women, such as Frances Wilson, who was fined £7 in a Liverpool court in October 1917. She pleaded in mitigation that her husband had left her and her son was fighting in the war.[67]

If women were thought to be the problem, then maybe they were also essential to the solution. In December 1916 the *Dundee Evening Telegraph* reported its concern about the wartime boom in fortune tellers, and suggested the creation of an advice or guidance bureau to combat the problem: 'if experienced women volunteered to give advice and guidance to puzzled and worried women large numbers of the women who crowd the waiting-rooms of the self-styled fortune-teller would go to the bureaus'.[68] The idea never came to fruition. At the National Union of Women Workers conference in the autumn of 1915 it was urged that more women be recruited to the police force as constables with the same powers and pay as the men. One of the advantages cited was that the number of women going to fortune tellers was far greater during the war and female constables could better help in their detection and suppression.[69] This plan had a little more traction. That same year Edith Smith became the first female police officer in the country with full power of arrest. She was based in Grantham, a northern garrison town, where the military authorities had already requested support from the Women Police Volunteers, founded in September 1914, to deal with 'disorderly women' in the area. In 1917 Edith submitted her first annual report to the chief constable of Grantham. She noted that all her police time had been confined to matters of women and children, including 'wayward girls', prostitution, female drunkenness, illegitimate children, and disorderly houses. She also reported on a fortune teller she had charged and convicted.[70] Some Australian states also recognized the value of allowing wartime women constables in order to suppress fortune-telling and other crimes typically considered as female misdemeanours during the war. Lillian Armfield, one of the first plain-clothes female detectives with powers of arrest in the New South Wales police, recalled that she was generally requested to keep quiet about her police work, except with regard to successful fortune-telling cases.[71]

Who Do You Think You Are?

The most contested aspects of the crackdown on wartime fortune-telling concerned the legal status of spiritualist mediumship and the practice of psychical sciences. In wartime Germany some of those prosecuted under the *Gaukelei* laws argued that they were students of science and religion, and certainly not common fortune tellers or charlatans. In May 1917 the Bavarian police put a hypnotist and spiritualist named Adolbert Haugg under surveillance due to suspected offences under Article 54. One policeman reported that Haugg would use any loophole to evade official control. Haugg, aware of the police attention, and angry that he had been forbidden to use the term 'experiment' in his advertisements, used his public lectures to rail against the religious, medical, and judicial author-ities for trying to suppress the hypnotic mediumship he espoused. A year later a spiritualist named Hanna Vogt-Vilseck, founder of a spiritualist club called Die Sucher ('The Seekers'), went on the offensive when the military authorities forbade her to put on any public events with occult or spiritualist content. Vogt-Vilseck wrote back to the authorities repudi-ating the accusation that she caused public harm, and expressing a hope that a future new government would be more enlightened.[72] But an article in the German occult periodical *Zentralblatt für Okkultismus* made the point that while it thought the Bavarian laws harsh, there were fraudulent and inferior occultists who needed to be suppressed to protect the reputation of the occult sciences and mystical arts.[73]

In Britain phrenology was one of the pseudo-sciences that repeatedly came into question. From its controversial heyday in the first half of the nineteenth century, phrenology was a pale shadow of its former self by the First World War, but still retained a hold in working-class culture.[74] The notion that the character and morality of individuals was encoded in the shape of the skull had long been weeded out of scientific ortho-doxy, though its influence lingered in early criminology and the eugen-ics movement. It was not an occult science per se, and there was little reference to it in the leading occult periodicals of the war years, such as *Light* and the *Occult Review*. Still, some esotericists considered phren-ology, like palmistry, as the 'mental science' of character-reading, and during the war the short-lived occult journals *Man* and *Superman* included phrenology in their remits. Although the venerable organ of phrenology, the *Phrenological Journal and Science of Health*, had folded in 1911, the British Phrenological Society, which had been established in 1881, continued in to the war years and beyond, and had its own journal, *The Phrenologist*.

While maligned and mocked, the phrenologists felt they had a significant contribution to make to the war effort. Several days before the signing of the armistice the British Phrenological Society held its annual meeting, at which several speakers referred to the war. One urged that the recruiting authorities should examine the heads as well as the bodies of conscripted soldiers to assign them more effective military roles. The society's president, Alderman D. J. Davis, who was a Justice of the Peace, told members that, from an educational perspective, phrenology would play a very prominent part in the post-war reconstruction.[75] Some supporters of phrenology also used their 'science' to promote the inferiority of the German race. A correspondent to the *Hastings and St Leonards Observer* claimed in 1917, for instance, that the average German skull was phrenologically quite different from the English one, with a telltale more sloping forehead and smaller chin. He thought that the English were consequently not predominantly Anglo-Saxon in origin like the enemy, but Anglo-Latin, as a consequence of the Roman occupation of Britain.[76]

There were quite a few self-styled phrenologists dotted around the country who advertised their services during the war. Phrenological institutes could be found in Eastbourne and Cardiff. Stephen Langham, of Rushden, was a well-known phrenologist and instructor in physical culture in Northamptonshire who served at the front. His wartime whereabouts were repeatedly reported in the local press, first as missing in action, and then as alive in a prisoner of war camp in the summer of 1918. Each time his status as a phrenologist was reported without comment.[77] John Baxter, of the Hood Battalion, recalled finding himself and Langham in a 'caboosh' or hole in the side of a trench in the Cambrai sector in February 1918. German shells were falling thick and fast and the pair felt they were in great danger. Langham turned to him and said, 'Jack, let me give you a head-reading to take our minds off this business, if only for a few minutes.' Baxter was impressed by Langham's character-reading 'under such nerve strain and in such a crude "consulting room"'. Langham continued to advertise his services into the 1930s.[78]

But phrenology was considered a problem by the police, and although, unlike palmistry, it was not explicitly mentioned in the Vagrancy Act, the constabulary clearly sometimes considered it as a divinatory practice. This lack of understanding about phrenology meant the police could waste a lot of time and effort bringing prosecutions under section 4. On 13 October 1917, for example, a Rumanian, Abraham Aarononitch, of Blackfriars, London, pitched himself in the market-place of Aylesbury exhibiting a phrenological chart and examining people's heads for 1 penny. A plain-clothed policeman observed him for some time before going up to him and asking to have his fortune told. Aarononitch looked him up and down and replied that he did not tell fortunes; he was a phrenologist who delineated character. The policeman had his head read and then arrested him for 'pretending to tell fortunes by means of phrenology'. The magistrates subsequently found Aarononitch not guilty, however.[79] The substance of the arguments in such a case was detailed in the prosecution, in February 1918, of the Bath phrenologist 'Professor' Gustave William Wack, a former shell stamper aged 32, who was investigated by the police and charged under section 4 for having deceived three women who were paid by the police to consult him. In his defence Wack argued that phrenology was a science of the brain and his procedures akin to medical diagnosis, and certainly nothing to do with foretelling the future. He had clients among the great and the good in the town, he claimed, including one who was on the War Savings Committee. In their summing up the magistrates concluded that some of Professor Wack's advertisements and business cards were misleading but that the prosecution had not sufficiently proven the case under section 4.[80]

Still, police suspicions of those offering their services as phrenologists were sometimes correct. It is clear that the title of 'phrenologist' was used as a respectable cover for straightforward fortune-telling. G. A. Morley Wright, of Ferndale, described himself as a 'Phrenological Lecturer and Physiognomist' but advertised in the Welsh press in 1915 that he practised palmistry and offered private advice on journeys, marriage, prospects in life, and lucky months. The Cardiff Phrenological Institute operating in Queen Street Arcade in 1917 turns out to be the consulting room of Madame Eugenia, an expert in 'giving Advice on health, business speculation, marriage, &c.'. In July 1918 Jules Audiger Tovey and his wife Alexandra ran what they called a Phrenological Institute in west London, but were fined the considerable sum of £57 12s under section 4 for telling fortunes with the cards and by palmistry.[81] The palmist Gertrude Garrett's desperate last plea rather summed up the empty basis behind some of the claims of phrenological practice. After being fined 50 shillings she asked the court clerk whether she could carry on selling her books and giving palm readings for free. The clerk replied, 'You must not tell fortunes.' Gertude asked in desperation, 'Phrenology, sir?' 'That will do Mrs Garrett,' he replied.

As we have seen, perusing astrological predictions was a considerable preoccupation during the war, and the newspapers regularly contained advertisements from astrologers offering their personal services, but it was potentially a crime under the Vagrancy Act. Alan Leo's extensive publications, public profile, and good reputation did not prevent his prosecution for selling mass-produced mail-order horoscopes during the Metropolitan Police's crackdown in 1917. Leo's defence lawyer argued that his client had no intention to deceive or impose. He and others practised a science that millions believed in. It was argued, furthermore, that Leo, unlike some astrologers, did not avow to predict the future. It was true that he had long argued that 'the stars incline, they do not compel' and that free will or character and character alone was destiny. Leo was, nevertheless, found guilty. As a consequence, he determined to rethink how he wrote about and promoted his horoscopes, avoiding any statements that intimated 'inevitable destiny' and focusing instead on 'character reading'.[82]

'I'm a psychometrist not a fortune teller' was a refrain heard fairly frequently in prosecutions under section 4. Unlike phrenology and astrology, however, it was not a term widely recognized in popular culture. When Emma Mary Davis, aged 41, was prosecuted in Birmingham for fortune-telling, the journalist reporting the case clearly misheard her husband (a phrenologist) describe his wife as a 'psychomistress'.[83] When the prosecution lawyer asked Madame May to explain the meaning of psychometry, she asked whether he had read the works of Conan Doyle, Oliver Lodge, and W. T. Stead: 'It is a science which everyone possesses and can be developed. It is believed in the highest society.'[84] There were, indeed, popular guides available during the war on how to hone the necessary psychic skills, such as O. Hashnu

Hara's *Practical Psychometry: Its Value and How it is Mastered* (1906), and James Coates's *Seeing the Invisible: Practical Studies in Psychometry* (1906). The term was coined in the mid-nineteenth century to describe the notion that objects, particularly personal items like clothing and jewellery, were imbued with an aura of their history, place, or owner, which certain mediums could psychically envision by touching them. In essence it was a form of clairvoyance, and most psychometrists also advertised themselves as clairvoyants. Spirit mediums also employed the method to make contact with the other world. As long as practitioners kept their remarks to the current state of the owners of the objects, then they were technically on the right side of the Vagrancy Act. But some clearly were engaged in telling their clients about what would happen in the future. When the police informer Jenny Macdonald visited an Ilford clairvoyant, Emma Neville, she was asked for something she had worn a long time. Macdonald handed over a silver locket, which Neville placed on her forehead, before pronouncing: 'there are two boys who take an interest in you; one will be wounded. You'll hear in a few days' time. He will be fetched home to England and placed in hospital. You will go to see him, and you will say, "This is like heaven."'[85] As a critique of the law observed, 'the very moment a psychic delineator makes the smallest reference to *future* happenings the mischief is done'.[86]

While some appealed to the validity of psychical experimentation, others appealed to religious inspiration. Consider the Exeter diviner Edgar Marshall, a fitter by trade, who had told one client that her husband would return safely from the firing lines. He claimed in court in November 1915 that 'he was called by the inspiration of God to explain things given him from on high. He belonged to the ministry of spiritualism, and must go forward with it, spreading his knowledge as far as the east was from the west.' He further claimed that man had the gift of prophecy as much as any Old Testament prophet, and that he was himself a seer and definitely not a fortune teller.[87] The Chester fortune teller Martha Dodd similarly told the court that her gift was from God and her mission was to comfort everybody in his name. It was 'spirit work' and not fortune-telling.[88] As these two instances suggest, the umbrella of spiritualism proved a popular defence in court, but what exactly was it sheltering? Harriett Ford Baxter and her husband James ran a 'Spiritual Temple' from a shop and premises in Stokes Croft, Bristol, with some two hundred members. People were charged sixpence at the door and received a session with Harriett and some prayers and spiritual advice from James, who was described as the temple speaker and adviser. Police put the place under surveillance and counted fifty-four women and seven men entering one evening. Harriett conducted her sessions with members in an inner room, where she employed psychometry. Those attending placed an item in a basket and then Harriett would take each item and provide information about its owner. She told one client, for example, that she could see a little boy but that he would be the last she would have. The prosecution claimed the Baxters were operating a fortune-telling business under the cloak of religion, and despite the defence going on at length about the serious scientific interest in psychic studies, the couple were found guilty of fortune-telling and fined £5 and £2 expenses. A man at the back of the court shouted 'It is an injustice!' and had to be ejected from the room.[89] A few months earlier, in the autumn of 1915, John Henry Thomas, a painter and paperhanger, along with his partner Bertha Pixton, rented the Spiritual Hall in Every Street, Ancoats, Manchester. They charged twopence entry, and around sixty or seventy women, mostly soldiers' wives, attended. Hymn books were handed out and singing took place. Money was collected during this service, though Thomas admitted he sometimes took money at the door from people who turned up late. The women sat in a circle and handed Bertha an item that belonged to the person whose fortune they desired to be told, and Bertha drew upon her psychometric powers and her communications with the 'angel people'. One of those who attended regularly was asked in court, 'Is it part of your religion to hand such articles as a matchbox and rings to Mrs Pixton for information about the future of persons not present?' She replied, 'I do nor call it religion; I call it far-seeing.' They were fined with an extra guinea for costs under section 4, and Thomas stated that he intended to close down the room for good as the police had been around day after day.[90]

Were they conscientious spiritualists practising their faith or were they cynically exploiting the respectability of spiritualism as a cover for commercial fortune-telling, as the magistrates concluded? As far as I can tell, neither the Baxters nor Thomas and Pixton were operating under the auspices of a registered spiritualist church according to the Places of Worship Registration Act of 1855, or were members of the Spiritualists' National Union. Then again, the difference between Baxter's Spiritual

Temple, say, and a registered spiritualist church would not have been obvious in the local community, as many of the latter in the early twentieth century were also merely rented rooms rather than buildings dedicated to worship.[91] But it was not usual practice to charge entry fees at bona fide spiritualist church seances. From the perspective of the clients these issues were probably irrelevant, though. As the statement above about 'far-seeing' suggests, it is likely that most clients of Baxter and Pixton and the like were not at all interested in the religious tenets of spiritualism.

There was a big difference between contacting the spirit world for the comfort of the bereaved and asking the spirits to predict the future. The view that the spirits had prophetic powers was not spiritualist ortho-doxy at the time. Departed spirits did not have any more knowledge of the future than that available to the living. When James Hall, honorary president of the Edinburgh Association of Spiritualists, gave a lecture on spiritualism at the Abbey Church, Arbroath, in 1918, he noted the association between spiritualism and fortune-telling, and admitted that 'advice upon physical and moral matters are [sic] frequently given from the platform, that no more constituted spiritualism than what might be given by the man in the street'.[92] Even if the spirits did have prophetic powers, some argued that, just like the living in this world, they could not necessarily be trusted, and mediums could err in their choice of spirit guides.[93]

These issues were highlighted during the prosecution of Annie Brittain. She and four others were charged under the Vagrancy Act in October 1915. All but one were members of local spiritualist churches, and their congregations turned up to support them in court. Brittain was the most well-known medium in the Potteries, and a long-time member of spiritualist churches in Langton and Hanley, Staffordshire. She had recently been consulted by Oliver Lodge following the death of his son, and Conan Doyle held her in high regard. From 1917 onward he regularly sent her contact details to mourners who had written to him asking for advice on how to find a good spirit medium. He reported in 1922 that out of the first hundred such cases he referred to Brittain 'eighty were quite successful in establishing touch with the object of their inquiry'.[94] The police, as usual, sent in their female detectives with spurious questions about their husbands in the army. One reported that Brittain requested that she give her a glove, which she then placed in a drawer under a crystal ball. She looked at the crystal and said that the client's husband was not wounded, fortunately, but he was having a nervous breakdown due to the dreadful things he had seen. So far this was straightforward clairvoyance, and there was no divining the future, but another police informant, Mrs Fanny Pickford, said that Brittain predicted her husband would be wounded in France. She also told a policeman disguised as a farmer that his 'nephew' in the navy had been wounded, and he would receive news shortly. On such evidence Brittain and the others were found guilty of fortune-telling, with Brittain charged £5 5s and the others £3 3s each with costs.[95] Oliver Lodge was deeply annoyed about this. He was principal of Birmingham University at the time, and so this suppression of mediums was going on in his backyard, so to speak.

The Witchcraft Act

In November 1915 Lodge wrote to the private secretary of Arthur Balfour, who was then First Lord of the Admiralty in Asquith's coalition government, expressing his concerns about the persecution of mediums:

> The fact is there have been rather senseless prosecutions of 'Mediums' lately. Those I know of having been in North Staffordshire (the Potteries), but I am told that that [sic] there is an Anti-occult League afoot, anxious to put in force an antique Act against necromancy of all kinds. Now, I know that many of these people are genuine, and some of them are giving much comfort at the present time to bereaved folk. It is not a time for wasting the energies of the Police or the Law on prosecutions of this character which I believe moreover to be completely out of date.

Lodge went on to request that Balfour speak to the Home Secretary Sir John Simon about his concerns. With regard to the latter, Lodge wrote: 'I have no inkling of his views on this matter. He may, for all I know, be hostile to any cultivation of occult faculties, and may wish to have them put down.' There is nothing to suggest Simon had any particular views on spiritualism.[96] An internal Home Office memorandum confirms that Lodge's concerns were investigated, but reported back that officials were unaware of any recent prosecutions of spiritualists, and if there had been any, they had certainly not been instigated by the Home Office. Still, it stated, 'there is a great tendency on the part of relatives of killed or missing soldiers to resort to clairvoyants and mediums; and very possibly this may have led to an increase of prosecutions'. The Home Office rightly guessed that the 'antique Act' referred to by Lodge was the Witchcraft Act of 1736. As to the suspension of future prosecutions of mediums under the Vagrancy Act, it concluded that the Secretary of State would be potentially liable to impeachment under the Bill of Rights if he were to issue instructions to the police that no proceedings were to be taken against spiritualists at all.[97]

It was the Witchcraft Act of 1736 more than the Vagrancy Act that most exercised the spiritualist movement during the First World War. It was, at the time, an enlightened piece of legislation that formally ended the witch trials in Britain. It repealed the 1604 Act against Conjuration and Witchcraft, under which death was the punishment for consulting evil and wicked spirits, and redefined witchcraft as a fraudulent pretence rather than a satanic crime. The Act also sought to suppress all those who defrauded the public by practising magic and divination:

> And for the more effectual preventing and punishing of any Pretences to such Arts or Powers as are before mentioned, whereby ignorant Persons are frequently deluded and defrauded; be it further enacted by the Authority aforesaid, That if any Person shall, from and after the said Twenty-fourth Day of June, pretend to exercise or use any kind of Witchcraft, Sorcery, Inchantment, or Conjuration, or undertake to tell Fortunes, or pretend, from his or her Skill or Knowledge in any occult or crafty Science, to discover where or in what manner any Goods or Chattels, supposed to have been stolen or lost, may be found, every Person, so offending, being thereof lawfully convicted on Indictment.

So it covered similar ground to the Vagrancy Act, though more explicit in its reference to the types of magical activity condemned, but allowed for more severe punishment, up to one year's imprisonment and a stint in the pillory. Over the next two centuries, the law was rarely employed, with magistrates preferring the Vagrancy Act. The pillory was abolished as a punishment in 1837, and there was sense of embarrassment about invoking a law that contained reference to witchcraft. There was a flurry of concern in the spiritualist community about its potential use against them in the 1870s and 1880s, as there was in the astrological fraternity as well, but the mediums who were prosecuted at this period were generally charged under the Vagrancy Act.[98]

While Lodge's concerns over an 'Anti-occult League' were unfounded, there were, as we have seen earlier in this book, numerous voices decrying the popularity of spiritualist mediums during the war. But it had been over a decade since the Witchcraft Act had last been invoked, and there had been little open expression of support for its employment by the critics of spiritualism. The Home Office was clear that it was not machinating in this respect. One rare endorsement of the Witchcraft Act, but against fortune tellers, came from the professional magazine for the magistracy, *Justice of the Peace*. In January 1917 it opined that while the concerted enforcement of the Act against fortune tellers would not stop the trade, the publicity it would arouse might prove 'more valuable than the punishment'.[99] It is somewhat surprising, then, that in 1916 the Spiritualists' National Union decided to launch its 'Parliamentary Fund (Witchcraft Acts Amendment)', thereby resurrecting a battle fought by spiritualists several decades earlier. An announcement in the spiritualist press explained the issue:

> The incidence of the penalties expressed in certain Acts of Parliament, passed in other and quite different times to those of to-day, has for long been an oppressive burden upon the legitimate practice, professionally, of mediumship as understood by Spiritualists. Such Acts were placed on the Statute Book of the realm at a time when the world knew little of the orderly and scientific examination of evidences afforded by the use of psychic faculties, which prove that man can hold a perfectly natural communication with the world of discarnate humanity. At a time, indeed, when such communion was ascribed to the Devil, and its practice was bitterly denounced as necromancy or witchcraft of the most reprehensible kind.
>
> The action of the law has been supported by appeals to the Old and New Testaments, from which it has been sought to gather religious sanction for the persecution of all who are mediums by denouncing them as witches, and as such to be put under pains and penalties cited in the Jewish law of the past, or to-day dealt with as rogues and vagabonds by the civil power instead of the ecclesiastical courts.[100]

The SNU's president, the tireless spiritualist, socialist, and lecturer Ernest Walter Oaten (1875–1952), was at the forefront of the campaign. During his trial for refusing military service at Sheffield West Riding police court, the activities of the Witchcraft Act Amendment Committee were brought up by the prosecution. In answer to a question about what the Amendment Committee did, Oaten explained: 'The Committee was formed for the purpose of approaching Parliament for the revision and amendment of a certain Act which implies that there are no spirit entities in existence, which Act certain interested individuals have been trying to stretch and use against us.'

Q. And you are doing your best, as a Spiritualist body, to get rid of these Acts?
A. Most emphatically we are not trying to get rid of them.
Q. Well, you put it upon your notepaper.
A. We want them amended in order that they may become stronger.
Q. What, stronger against you, or what?
A. Stronger against the practice which they were passed against.[101]

In June 1917 a further initiative was set up in London with the creation of the London and Provincial Mediums' Union, the aim of which was to protect the interests of all reputable professional mediums within a 25-mile radius of London. This included supporting the SNU's campaign and the legal defence of spiritualists facing prosecution.[102]

Not all in the spiritualist community agreed with the campaign. Lieutenant W. J. McIntosh, a spiritualist recovering from shell shock, wrote in a letter to *Light* that there was a 'rising tide' of tricksters and charlatans performing spurious imitations of psychic and spiritual phenomena for commercial gain. 'I have come to the conclusion that the law is not opposed to the private practice of Spiritualism,' he said, 'but only to the gallery playing of the fortune-tellers, and to the counter-jumping tactics of the would-be prophets. Therefore I regard the law as a potential friend and ally.'[103] If the Witchcraft and Vagrancy Acts were to protect more effectively the spiritualist community, then they would have to create clear blue water between themselves and the fringe mediums, fortune tellers, and downright charlatans. A lawyer and King's Council advised on the matter in 1918, suggesting that the offence of fortune-telling would be difficult for a magistrate to uphold if mediums read to their clients a statement such as 'From the messages which reach me it would appear that what I am going to tell you will happen. But I do not say that it will in fact happen. It is very possible that the messages may be incorrect.' With regard to protecting palmists, he suggested the following line: 'I do not *know*, and I may be quite wrong, but according to my studies, the lines on your hand would appear to indicate the following as likely to happen.'[104] But the best way for spiritualists to distance themselves from the possibility of prosecution was to cease conducting mediumistic seership, full stop. An entry in the committee minutes of the York Spiritualist Society for May 1916 records that a formal request was, indeed, made that 'all mediums both local and national should refrain from forecasting the future at all public meetings'.[105] But there is little evidence that this wise caution was adhered to across the movement.

War Stories

The Blackpool fortune teller Elizabeth Ann Musgrave, otherwise known as Madame Vane, defended herself in court by saying she had foretold what had taken place in the trenches of the Dardanelles. In occupied north-eastern France, in 1916, the German authorities sentenced the medium Mme Juana to sixty days in prison and banishment to Switzerland for predicting the complete rout of the German forces. In March 1917 the Ilford fortune teller Emma Neville told a client that her son would be wounded but that she should not worry, as the war would be over in three months.[106] Despite these examples, most fortune tellers refrained from statements pertaining to the outcomes of battles, military strategy, or the duration of the war, leaving such sensitive national predictions to the astrologers and almanac compilers. Their focus was on the fate of the individual, and whether they were mediums, phrenologists, clair-voyants, psychometrists, palmists, cartomancers, or crystal scryers, when one reads through enough prosecution reports, clear patterns emerge as to what they told their clients and why. Their pronounce-ments were often more guided by basic psychological assessment than by the application of their psychic powers or divinatory sciences.

Many women resorted to fortune tellers, fearing the worst after a drought of communications from their husbands, sons, brothers, or other family members in service. In such cases, it was usual for the fortune teller to divine that the absent were, happily, still alive. The fortune teller might then opt to provide further comforting news regarding their return home from the battlefields. A Kenilworth servant girl, Maggie Ruddleston, testified that the itinerant gypsy fortune teller Amy Smith had divined that 'I had got a young man abroad in uniform, that he was coming home before April, and that I was going to marry him and go abroad with him.'[107] A recurring explanation for the lack of letters from the front was that their loved ones had been taken prisoner. In January 1917 a Glasgow police court heard how the palmist Mary Spence was consulted by one woman who explained that her husband had been missing for some time and she had not received any official information. Spence looked at her palm and divined that he was a prisoner of war in Germany.[108] When the French police investigated a clairvoyant and fortune teller in the town of Tours in early 1917, they found she was running three 'seances' a week exclusively dealing with missing soldiers. She confessed that she hardly ever gave bad news and generally told her clients that their husbands, brothers, or sons were German prisoners of war.[109] Another common refrain was to state that soldiers were alive but wounded and in hospital. The London card reader and newsagent Elizabeth Mary Porter told one of her clients, 'You have not had a letter from your husband lately. He is wounded. I can see a change of beds. He may be sent to England. Your son in the army is all right.' The Chester fortune teller Martha Dodd told a client that 'she would receive a letter from him. It would be news from a hospital, but he would not be wounded, but would have something which would cause him to be sent home out of danger.' Eliza Ann Bryant, from Torquay, had harsher news for one of her clients. She was sentenced to a couple of months in prison after, among other things, telling one customer that she would have 'a cripple in the family', either a nephew or brother who would return from the war wounded.[110]

Fortune tellers shied away from forecasting the deaths of sons, but were sometimes prepared, whether by the honest deployment of their divinatory techniques or as a carefully observed assessment of clients' hopes and anxieties, to give married women terrible news about their husbands. The London crystal gazer Madame Charles told one female client at a society function, whose army officer husband had returned from Egypt and was about to be sent to France, that he would never return to her and he would be killed in action. The officer was informed of this prediction by his wife, and he wrote a letter of complaint to Scotland Yard.[111] At the other end of the social scale, a caravan dweller,

Mary Ann Lowther, was prosecuted at Crewe for telling a soldier's wife that he would never return from the war. The Sheffield fortune teller Bertha Hawksley told a client that her 'husband was a soldier who had been wounded once and would be wounded again, and that this time he "would go under"'.[112] The reason why fortune tellers found it more acceptable to divine the deaths of husbands was because some married women perhaps secretly welcomed the prospect. In the early twentieth century the divorce laws discriminated against working-class women due to prohibitive legal costs. In 1914 aid was made available to poor petitioners, but uptake only began in the decades after the war. Until the grounds for divorce were equalized in 1923, women also had to prove both adultery and another fault such as cruelty or sexual abuse, whereas men only had to prove adultery. Furthermore, before 1925 custody of children over the age of 7 belonged to the husband.[113] As harsh as it may sound, for some married women the prospect of the death of an unloved or hated husband fuelled fantasies and dreams of a new life. Fortune tellers tapped into this female angst and unhappiness, just as they had long fed the marital dreams of servant girls. So, in April 1916 the Lancashire fortune teller Madame Neilson, who received many relatives of soldiers, told one client that her husband was dead and that she could marry again. When, in May 1917, the wife of a soldier serving in Mesopotamia consulted Rupert de Montmorency (on behalf of the police) in Birmingham, he told her that she would be a widow and marry someone else who had plenty of money. When one of the clients of Madame Val, from Southport, told her that her husband had been killed in Flanders, Val comforted her by saying 'it happened for the best and she would be much happier in the future'. She would meet a man named Ernest while playing tennis or bowls.[114]

While most of the wartime visitors to fortune tellers were women, many soldiers of all ranks also consulted them before heading to the front or going to sea, and it is likely that the war saw a significantly greater recourse of men to diviners than in peace time. In late 1917, for instance, the Metropolitan Police noticed that the palmist Louise Hutchinson, who operated from the Oriental Restaurant, Brompton Road, London, seemed to be particularly popular amongst army officers. They sent two policemen dressed as lieutenants to entrap her. When the Edgware Road palmist Madame Vox was arrested, she was busy examining the palm of a wounded officer with the aid of a magnifying glass and an electric torch. When it came to such military clients, fortune tellers were, again, usually careful to calibrate their predictions accordingly. I have not, for example, come across any cases where a fortune teller told a soldier that he would die in battle. At her trial in April 1917, the Bayswater palmist Olive Starl was asked, 'you tell officers only good news and not the bad?' She replied, 'Yes.' Starl was also asked, 'Do you tell officers what is going to happen to them when they go abroad?' She replied, 'Not so far as accidents are concerned, but as to the places where they will go.'[115] Starl was not alone in adopting this strategy. After going into a trance and apparently communicating with the spirit of a captain, the Exeter medium and fortune teller Clementina Norton told a private in the Army Pay Corps that 'he might be going abroad shortly to Serbia or Gallipoli'. She then changed her mind and said that 'she could picture him in a little town just outside Brussels'. Another strategy was that of predicting a light injury that would enable the soldier to return home, perhaps for good. The Luton palmist Gertrude Garrett told Edward Timothy Allen, of the Army Service Corps, that he would go to the front, and would be slightly wounded in the hand.[116]

Another set of clients sought to know whether they or their loved ones would be going to war at all. We have to remember that, following the introduction of conscription in 1916, military tribunal reports reveal that a significant minority of men in Britain sought exemption from military service on the basis of their occupation.[117] Many were clearly reluctant soldiers, and one can understand their hope that fate would intervene on their behalf. So, when PC Evans visited Madam May disguised as a collier he asked whether, if he was sent to France, he would come back alive. She took his gloves and divined that he need not worry, as he would not be going to France in the first place. In September 1915 the Preston card reader Mary Hunter told Rose Anne Livesey that her 'young man will have a change of work, but you must tell him not to enlist, as there will be better use for him other ways. He will do better as he is.'[118] A mother and daughter visited the Lincoln fortune teller Elizabeth Harrison no fewer than twenty-four times in 1917, paying between 1 and 5 shillings each session. Harrison was a cartomancer and used a crystal ball but claimed she 'worked by the spirits'. On one occasion, she produced her cards, shuffled them, and then handed them over to the mother to shuffle and cut into three. Harrison then laid them out on a table, read them, and observed that they indicated something 'not particularly good, not really bad'. Her husband in the army would be moved farther away from home, but his legs would give way, preventing him from being sent to France. Harrison then asked her to hold the crystal ball for a minute, before she then looked into it. It was a psychometric procedure. She said she could see her client's husband in the company of other men, and also a coffin that suggested there would shortly be a funeral of a near relative. The reason the mother and daughter were paying repeat visits, and up to 5 shillings a time, was that Harrison said she could ensure, 'by working with the spirit', that the daughter's fiancé would be brought out of the army and returned to her. When she looked into the crystal ball, she could see him sitting on his kitbag playing a mouth organ, with five or six soldiers around him singing, but she foretold that she would be married to him within five months.[119]

As well as practising divination, several clairvoyants claimed to channel psychically the physical experiences of soldiers past, present, and future, constructing brief but startling narratives of the fear and pain of combat for their clients. The Aberystwyth psychometrist Madame Smith Evans was one such. When consulted by a disguised police sergeant, she held his hand and went into a self-induced trance:

> 'I am you now.' She went through a number of convulsions, coughed, and at last vomited and said to me, 'you have been gassed.' She again put her hands to her head and said, 'Oh, what terrible pains. You have had terrible pains in the head.' She appeared to be suffering pains and said, 'You have had dysentery and pains in the bladder. You have seen very tight corners. You did not know which way to turn—whether to go this way or that way.' She suddenly put her fingers to her ears and said, 'Oh, what terrible noise. Have you had shell shock?'[120]

At Pontypridd she went into a similar trance before some grieving clients, mimicking their son's terrible final moments of life on the battlefield. The spiritualist medium Arthur Whyman, who was prosecuted along with Annie Brittain, went one step further by claiming to feel, through clairvoyance, the experiences that would befall soldiers. When a client consulted him about a brother, he replied, 'Oh, dear! Is he a soldier? I feel such a stab as though I had been bayoneted in the stomach.' When she told him her brother was currently in a training camp, Whyman said, 'He won't be long before he is at the front. I felt a proper stab.'[121]

As the reader will have gathered, the fortune tellers were regularly proved wrong in their forecasts. The London diviner Madam Jacques told a client that her husband was a prisoner of war, for instance, when in fact her husband was at home and not in the army at all. The Rotherham fortune teller Sarah Ann Flint unfortunately told a client that she could expect a letter from her brother at the front, not knowing he had already been reported killed.[122] The bogus nature of such predictions was all the more starkly revealed by the police practice of entrapment, with fortune tellers blithely forecasting the future of detectives' relatives. This does not necessarily mean that most fortune tellers were outright frauds. Some clearly were, but others were earnest but misguided in the application of their divinatory arts. When they are considered as popular therapists, though, the significance of wartime fortune tellers shifts from issues of the deceit, success, or failure of their predictions to their influence on the collective state of mind of each combatant country. Much has been made in histories of the First World War of the comfort provided by mediums in professing to enable contact between grieving parents and their loved ones who had 'passed over' to the spirit world. But relatively few people sought out such Raymond-like conversations. The fortune tellers and clairvoyants discussed here, who undoubtedly saw many more clients than did spiritualist mediums, provided similar psychological reassurance, but with regard to the living and not the dead. And it is equally clear that some operated on the basis that their role as therapists was paramount and worthy of their fees, above and beyond any predictions they provided. Along with the soothing promises and predictions, the feedback given by fortune tellers also exhibited a perfect awareness of the horrors of the trenches, the egregious loss of life, the trauma of gas attacks and shell shock. Indeed, the honesty of the myriad wartime fortune tellers was as of much concern to the authorities as their mendacity.

5

BATTLEFIELD LUCK

A soldier of the 1st Cavalry Brigade remembered how, in a lull during the second Battle of Ypres, in May 1915, a Cockney trooper dropped a bit of looking-glass while shaving. He casually remarked to the trooper, 'Bad luck for seven years.' The reply came back, 'If I live seven years to 'ave bad luck it'll be blinking good luck.'[1]

In the histories of the First World War much has been made of the profound fatalism of the soldiery, expressed in terms of the regrowth of 'superstition', the psychology of coping strategies, and the renewed adherence to divine providence.[2] There is no doubt from memoirs, diaries, and letters that notions of fate were a common talking point amongst soldiers on all sides. A Serbian infantryman related, for instance, how on the front line facing the Bulgarian army he and his comrades would talk together about fate and the possibility of being killed or not killed. The war correspondent Philip Gibbs recalled in 1920 that 'most of the men became fatalists', mentioning what became a defining First World War motto, 'if your name is written on a German shell you can't escape it, and if it isn't written, nothing can touch you'.[3] Indeed, in terms of First World War history, the notion of fate has almost been elevated to a military faith in its own right. But the notion of a widespread 'what will be be will be' attitude amongst the soldiery is somewhat undermined by their resort to fortune tellers, as we saw in the previous chapter. And the equally pervasive concept of luck in the trenches raises philosophical and psychological issues around expression, perception, belief, and action when it comes to soldiers' attitudes toward and investment in the future.

A private in the British Army wrote on Christmas Day 1916, 'after the manner of fatalists, we come to regard being alive and well as merely luck'.[4] But fate and luck are not interchangeable or even compatible notions. There can be a fundamental tension between them.[5] Adherence to luck rather than fate allowed the possibility to change one's future through action or engineer the intervention of providence through belief. Indeed, luck more than fate pervades the written experiences of combat. The French First World War flying ace Georges Guynemer, who was often referred to as 'a lucky dog', reflected on the matter: 'If we talk this way, every person alive to-day is lucky, for he might have died yesterday.' Guynemer was shot down seven times. So surely he was lucky? 'I know that they will rejoin that this was really luck, for I managed to escape death,' he responded. 'But we could continue the discussions eternally on the same subject and I prefer to abstain from it.' Ultimately he felt that such talk would encourage others to assume undue confidence and commit foolish errors. He was killed in action in September 1917.[6] The rest of this chapter explores the myriad and pervasive ways in which military personnel sought to subvert fate and ensure they survived the war, and how the forces of commerce as much as faith, popular tradition, and personal sentiment played key roles in defining how luck was expressed.

Averting Bad Luck

The number thirteen was traditionally considered a lucky number in France. It was represented on numerous First World War good fortune or *porte-bonheur* postcards and was popular as a charm in pendant form.[7] In Britain and North America, however, triskaidekaphobia, or fear of thirteen, was taken quite seriously. In June 1915 charitable donors presented to the city of Liverpool seventeen ambulances to ferry the sick and wounded from the port and railway station to military hospitals in the area. They were numbered one to eighteen, with number thirteen omitted 'out of respect to a rather common superstition among sailors, soldiers, and others'.[8] The fighter ace Charles Parsons recalled how, during his squadron Christmas meal in 1916, they were all sat down when fellow American aviator James R. McConnell breezed in late. Halfway through the meal James looked around carefully and suddenly turned white. 'My God!,' he exclaimed in a serious tone. 'Thirteen of us here. That's sure death. Wonder who'll be the next to get it.' They tried to make a joke of the circumstance, but everyone was now uncomfortable. James was the next in the squadron to be killed in action, shot down on 19 March 1917.[9] The belief was fostered by the wartime newspapers in Britain, which were ever ready to print instances of unlucky thirteen. The *Coventry Evening Telegraph* reported in July 1915, for instance, on how thirteen convalescing soldiers had been struck by lightning while walking on Hampstead Heath, and in August the same year the *Leeds Mercury* printed a letter sent home from the front by Bombardier Naylor, who was a carter at Leeds railway station before the war, in which he complains to his brother about his unlucky thirteen encounters: 'The 13th of the month has been a trying time. On April 13th we sailed for France, on May 13th I was in hospital, on June 13th we were shelled out of our position, on July 13th the Germans sent over gas shells, which stink awful and make your eyes smart worse than a bonfire, and on August 13th they fired "Jack Johnsons" at us.'[10]

Averting bad luck by the avoidance of certain actions, symbols, or numbers was also the basis of one of the iconic First World War trench 'superstitions', namely that it was unlucky to light three cigarettes or pipes from the same match and that one of the three smokers would die as a consequence. The notion seems have been born on the battlefields of the Second Boer War (1899–1902). But it only became pervasive and well known during the First World War. A story even did the rounds in the spring of 1918 that army head-quarters in France had decided to try and extinguish the 'superstition' in order to save on matches. The belief spread rapidly and widely amongst the military of other countries. Apollinaire observed the pervasive grip of *Jamais trois cigarettes!* on the French soldiery, and after the war American folklorists began to notice its presence there in civilian life.[11] For one battalion of the Durham Light Infantry the number three was also to be avoided when serving out spirit rations. When it was poured into small 'dixeys', each tot would be counted with three missed out.[12]

Wearing dead men's boots or clothing was avoided as much as possible, as this had long been considered unlucky amongst sailors. This became quite a challenge for the army quartermaster's department when second-hand clothing began to be issued, with soldiers finding all sorts of stratagems to try and obtain new footwear and clothing and avoid the potential of wearing dead men's hand-me-downs. The plus side for the quartermasters was that soldiers had to prove how badly worn their own apparel was to get brand new replacements.[13]

Despite widespread adherence to such broad cultural folklore, people's personal experience and assessment of coincidences led to idiosyncratic decisions as to what was or was not lucky, perhaps sometimes influenced by exposure to other traditions encountered in wartime. This led some British and Americans to adopt the number thirteen, for example. The aviator Allen Peck wrote home on 1 July 1918 to announce that he finally had his own plane: 'Guess what it is? Number 13.' His flight commander asked if he was superstitious about it, but Peck was not bothered: 'I always felt 13 more or less lucky. So the first time I go over the lines I will carry a great big "13" on my plane.' What with his black cat mascot and the big '13', he reckoned it would give 'something for the Bosche to think about'.[14] Lance-Corporal Henry Beaumont of the West Riding Regiment wrote to his wife in the autumn of 1914, 'What about this for lucky 13? I belong to No. 13 Battalion, D Company, No. 1 Section, with 13 men to start with. We had 13s. pay, and we sailed from Ireland on the 13th, so that you can tell the number is lucky for me. I was at the battle of Mons also the Aisne. In fact, we have been at it ever since we came out here.' News was subsequently received that he had been killed in action on 11 November.[15] As in close-knit village life, the reporting of repeated coincidences also led to the generation of new, short-lived, group-avoidance observances that had no prior basis in popular custom or tradition. In one British battalion, for instance, it was noticed that whenever one of the men went home with a German helmet as a trophy, he would be killed by a sniper on returning to the front line. As a consequence, men of the battalion came to refuse any requests for helmets. Similarly, the rumour went along the British line in 1916 that German bullets were drawn to rum ration jars, after several reports of stray bullets shattering them. The soldiers who carried the rum ration bottles were consequently considered to have double the chance of being shot, and so both the task and proximity to those engaged in it were avoided as much as possible.[16]

Individuals could also gain repute for attracting luck and bad luck. Reputations for invincibility and repeated miraculous survivals in the army led to comrades sticking close to certain people in the hope that they would be protected under their aura. Bad luck in the army usually meant death, but in the navy there was the tradition of the 'Jonah', a sailor whose ships repeatedly sank while he managed to survive. In early 1916 a seaman named Charles Dunn was brought before a Liverpool court charged with failing to join an Admiralty transport ship. It transpired that Dunn had served on four ships that had sunk while he was serving on board, namely the *Titanic*, the *Empress of Ireland*, and the torpedoed *Lusitania* and *Florizan*. He was something of a minor celebrity because of this, with his likeness appearing on music-hall cinematograph images. To his fellow mariners, though, he was considered a Jonah who jinxed the ships he was on. Those on the Admiralty transport ship had threatened to throw him overboard if he dared join the crew. So he joined the Royal Navy Reserve instead.[17]

Notions of luck, fate, and jinxes, and the rituals to influence them, were neither timeless nor vestigial. Emergent technologies during the early twentieth century generated novel hazards and environments that accrued their own folklore and rituals. The rise of the motor car led to the creation of new genres of mascots for protecting machine and occupant. The submarine provided a novel environment for adapting old seafaring practices as well as generating new beliefs and rituals amongst U-boat crews. The advent of aerial warfare during the First World War, the awareness of imminent death once up in the air, and the solitary nature of the combat duel created an intense psycho-culture of protective ritual.[18]

Fashioning Protection

The pervasive desire for emotional comfort and physical protection generated by the war opened up new commercial opportunities for the burgeoning global market in mass-produced trinkets, charms, and talismans. The town of Attleboro, Massachusetts, known at the time as the 'Jewellery Capital of the World', was a major beneficiary. Companies based there first started large-scale importation of cheap trinkets and novelties from Japan in the 1870s, and it then became a major manufacturing centre of costume jewellery and novelties, which were exported to the European market.[19] During the war, wholesalers in Britain purchased job lots of charms from the likes of the Attleboro companies, and sold them on to local shops and street vendors. In September 1915, for instance, one wholesaler advertised in the *Manchester Evening News* for 'Hawkers and Buying Agents for our Lucky Charms'. The folklorist Edward Lovett mentions visiting a shop near Long Acre, in central London, during the war which sold charms along with beads and trinkets. In November 1916 there was even a Good Luck Fair at London's Hotel Cecil in aid of charity, where visitors could peruse numerous stalls selling a range of mascots and charms.[20] Some dealers, as we shall see, developed sophisticated marketing campaigns selling mass-produced charms direct to customers via the thriving mail-order marketplace.

Across the combatant countries many jewellery firms also developed significant sidelines catering for soldiers and their loved ones. An article on the vogue for wearing charms published in 1915 noted that green jade pigs and platinum horseshoes were 'displayed ostentatiously in every jeweller's window in Bond Street, the prospective present of the war-bride to her hero'. It was similarly observed in 1917 that in the galleries

Fig. 5.1. A range of popular French charms worn during the war.

of the Palais-Royal, Paris, numerous jewellers' shops presented window displays of their *porte-bonheurs or* lucky charms.[21] In the run-up to Christmas 1914 Mappin and Webb advertised metal pocket mirrors for soldiers that would neither rust nor break and would deflect bullets. J. C. Vickery of Regent Street offered lucky white heather pendants and horseshoes in gold as 'parting souvenirs'.[22] The 'talisman of Lammermoor' by Alexander Cargill & Co. was designed so that it could be snapped into two interlocking pieces. One piece was to be given to a relative or loved one heading for France as a lucky talisman. Then, when the two people were reunited, the two pieces could be locked together again and 'worn as an everlasting memento and proof that your dear one has "done his bit"'. The company offered to engrave the crest of any regiment on one side of the talisman.[23] German jewellers also conducted a thriving trade in lucky rings and amulets, particularly St Michael rings, such as one showing the archangel in medieval armour, the Iron Cross on his chest, Kaiser Wilhelm II on his shield, lancing a dragon. In 1914 the Austrian War Assistance Bureau, the Kriegshilfsbüro, generated income by working with the mayor of Vienna and its jewellers and metalworkers to produce thousands of cheap *Kreigsglücksringe* or lucky war rings for soldiers going to the front. They were made simply by bending and soldering iron horseshoe nails. On the outer side of the ring was engraved '*Kriegsglück* 1914' or 'War Charm 1914', and a motto ran, 'May it be worn by the soldiers as a visible sign and protect against misery and death.'[24] In England, Iron Cross 'Zepp' charms were made from the aluminium frame of an airship brought down by anti-aircraft guns in Essex in September 1916, the proceeds going to the London and North Western Railways War Seal Fund, and similar charms in the form of a swastika were fashioned from the airship that crashed near Potters Bar the following month.[25]

The production and sale of *porte-bonheur* postcards provided another commercial opportunity. They must have sold in their millions across the combatant countries. Some were humorous, such as the British card with a smiling black cat turning its head to declare, 'I've left the Kaiser, (his luck's out) and I've come to you.' Many depicted the same array of symbols that were represented in lucky jewellery and amulets. Others, particularly German and Italian ones, portrayed religious scenes of providential interventions on the battlefield by Jesus, Mary, or angels. Silk embroidered postcards, some bearing good luck symbols,

Fig. 5.2. Protective symbols depicted on a 'Good Luck' postcard, including the Hand of Fatima and the Alpine Edelweiss.

as well as the flags of the Allied countries, and floral scenes, were manufactured in considerable numbers, mostly in France, but also in England and Switzerland. Nearly every shop in the French ports of Calais, Boulogne, and Dieppe sold them to the soldiers passing through.[26]

The *American Journal of Nursing* reported in 1916, 'hospital nurses find many strange charms and mascots on the persons of wounded soldiers'.[27] As we shall see in Chapter 6, many of these were religious in nature. The focus here, though, is on the wide range of 'strange' secular objects given and carried for protection. Some had long roots in folk tradition, such as touching wood. Soldiers carried a range of little wooden charms for this purpose. The British war correspondent Philip Gibbs found himself eating one day with some gunner officers in a ruined farmhouse near Kemmel Hill, an important strategic salient on the Flanders battlefront. He asked, 'Have the Huns found you out?' 'Not yet,' said one of them. They then 'all left the table at which we were eating lunch, and, making a rush for some oak beams, embraced them ardently. They were touching wood.'[28] Each country and culture had its numerous familiar objects and symbols that were thought to bring luck or had protective properties. Irish soldiers, for example, carried a range of talismans carved from green Connemara marble, such as the four-leaf shamrock, heart, and boot in the collections of the Imperial War Museum.[29] The museum also possesses a lucky lump of coal carried by a soldier of the City of London Yeomanry. It had been sent to him by his sister in 1917. This tradition, which had become popular by the early twentieth century, derives from the growth of coal as the staple hearth fuel of the industrial poor. Philip Gibbs wrote how, just prior to leaving for Ypres, an Irish officer took a little lump of coal out of his tunic and said in earnest, 'It will help you as it helped me. It's my lucky charm.'[30] One Private Matthews of the Devonshire Regiment carried a naturally perforated pebble, an item which had long been considered potent against witchcraft and was hung up or worn for protection more generally.[31] Lucky silver sixpences were widespread among the British military, with a mascot dealer reporting in August 1917 that he was doing a thriving trade in crooked silver coins amongst soldiers and their loved ones. Sapper Jim Cross kept a lucky silver threepence on his identification disc.[32] Edward Lovett found the practice of sewing a farthing into the left brace over the heart was widespread amongst soldiers, and that it was a tradition of long standing in the military. The farthing bore the profile of the king, who was a representative of God, and so imbued it with royal and divine protection.[33]

Italian soldiers resorted to several ancient types of protective charm, such as red coral pendants, sometimes in the form of a hand making a horn sign with the little finger and index finger, and the widespread Mediterranean charm against the evil eye known as the Hand of Fatima, named after the daughter of the prophet Mohammed. Benito Mussolini recorded in his war diary for November 1915 that he wore on his little finger a ring made from a horseshoe nail. Italian soldiers also wore rings crafted from the nails of coffins of soldiers who had survived the wars of independence against the Austrians (1848–9, 1859).[34] The historian of First World War Italian soldier folklore Agostino Gemelli recorded a variety of other rituals and charms. The names of the three wise men, Caspar, Melchior and Balthazar, were written on three different pieces of paper and kept in three different pockets—three being a venerable magical number in religious and secular ritual. A variation on this concerned carrying three pieces of three garden peas kept in three sachets in three different pockets, with the sachets needing to be changed around each day. Soldiers from the Abruzzo region carried a little sachet of earth from their birth place, and just before battle would throw a pinch over their shoulders. A tooth of a soldier that had survived a war and had been encased in silver foil was much prized.[35] In the early months of the war an Italian doctor observed that a lot of the wounded Serbians he treated wore chains and belts of dinars on their chest, and he was told by one wounded soldier that they were talismans for protection against enemy projectiles.[36]

German soldiers carried lucky coins and horseshoe charms, and also had pieces of silver sewn into their uniforms to protect against bullets. More unusually, they also carried carp scales, the fish being a traditional Christmas meal in parts of Germany, and hence reflective of domestic sentiments and good fortune.[37] Amongst the arsenal of charms carried by French soldiers were little trinkets representing a man with a hunch back, it being thought that touching the hunch of a person with a hunchback brought luck. This belief was not unknown in Britain. When, on 3 September 1914, Lord Torrington and companions were waiting at Paddington Station to set off for the front, he called for a newspaper boy named Walter Evans, who had a hunchback. They all rubbed his hunch for luck, and paid him for the privilege before getting on the train to France. Torrington was stated as missing in action in the Balkans some months later.[38] The French poet and *poilu* Guillaume Apollinaire wrote of the widespread practice of carrying a cold coin over the heart, despite the French government request that soldiers should not carry any gold that could end up in enemy coffers. It was generally thought to protect from bullets, but Apollinaire also heard it said that if the wearer was killed, it would halt the putrefaction of his body until it was returned to his birthplace.[39]

Horseshoes, which had long been considered potent against witches, were widely represented on lucky postcards in Britain and France, and appeared in a variety of talisman forms and sweetheart brooches. One German horseshoe amulet worn by soldiers bore the words 'Bring you happiness, Come back safely.' A Royal Flying Corp pilot, Henry Devlin, who was shot down and killed on 19 September 1917, was found to have a small metal horseshoe hidden beneath one of his pilot's wings.[40] In 1918 the American Brill Brothers clothing company gave away good luck Victory tokens to returning soldiers and sailors bearing a horseshoe symbol with the words 'May the good luck that brought you safely home be with you always.' The Imperial War Museum possesses a brass horseshoe talisman fabricated from a German shell at Ypres by a

Fig. 5.3. The horseshoe was a widespread symbol of good luck during the war. On the left a British regimental good luck badge, and on the right a French badge with a personalized photograph of a soldier.

wounded Belgian soldier.[41] One of the most unusual protective horse-shoe traditions concerns the Yorkshire village of Catwick, which was one of the fifty-one 'Thankful Villages' in England and Wales where every serving soldier came back alive. At the beginning of the war the village blacksmith, John Hugill, nailed a lucky horseshoe to the door of his forge and each time a man from the village went to join the fighting, he nailed a coin next to the horseshoe to give them good luck.[42]

Rabbits' feet were particularly popular among North American soldiers, though it would seem the tradition of carrying them for luck only became widespread during the early twentieth century. The practice probably derived from the cultural diffusion of African-American magical beliefs, in which the left hind foot was most prized, particularly if the rabbit had been killed at night.[43] Koon Beck, who became known as the 'Rabbit King' of Kansas for becoming wealthy on the back of selling jackrabbits for meat, promised publicly to give a free rabbit's foot, a left hind foot no less, to every black soldier from the state who was going to fight the Germans.[44] He had no shortage of the objects, as Beck had a government contract to supply 1,200,000 dead rabbits to be packed and shipped to military garrisons and camps.[45] A Boston newspaper reported in January 1918 that the American 23rd Company of the Depot Brigade was currently the only company in the battalion not under quarantine, and that Corporal K. H. Brocksieper put it down to the number of his company who wore lucky chicken bones and rabbits' feet. The same year a report about the salvage operation at the Canadian base at Witley Camp, Surrey, England, noted that amongst the objects they regularly dealt with were bones and rabbits' feet carried on watch chain guards for good luck.[46]

Some amulets and talismans were of a personal nature in terms of their origin, creation, and efficacy rather than expressions of familiar folkloric traditions. Some were ancestral keepsakes. A soldier from one Highland regiment carried a little smooth black stone that he believed protected him against fatal wounds. He said it had been used at Waterloo and that one of his uncles had carried it through the Boer War and he had survived without a scratch.[47] Allied soldiers sometimes treasured the simplest of things given to them by French children or women. One British soldier wore a button on a piece of string around his neck given to him by a little girl while he was billeted in a French village. Mundane objects found on the battlefields sometimes accrued special significance, such as buttons from German tunics. In the trenches at Ypres, the *poilu* Auguste Salé found a small earthenware cup that bore his first name, and he carried it as a lucky mascot throughout the rest of the war.[48] The carrying of bullets or pieces of shrapnel that had been removed from the bodies of soldiers who survived was also quite widespread across the combatant countries. They were sometimes turned into pendants, such as the shrapnel ball enclosed in a gold frame fashioned by a French soldier's wife.[49] Part souvenir of death evaded, part protective talisman, it could also serve as a symbol of divine providence. There was often a 'tipping point' when such sentimental mementos turned into potent protective charms, and it usually concerned death evaded. An Australian correspondent wrote in 1918 of a Queensland soldier of Scottish extraction he knew who left for Europe with a silver coin given to him in the spirit of fun. He wore it on a cord around his neck. 'I don't know exactly when it ceased to be a mere keepsake and became a powerful mascot,' wrote the correspondent, 'but I think it must have been after the Gallipoli landing.' His battalion was decimated, but he survived with minor injuries. 'Not serious,' he wrote home. Then, stationed in France in 1916, he was once more wounded in battle, but, once again, 'not seriously', he reported.[50]

An English charm dealer observed in August 1917 that, as well as driving a lively trade amongst soldiers, he sold many to their relatives and loved ones, who then gave them to soldiers as parting presents.[51] The essential quality that turned many mundane, manufactured, or personal items into lucky charms was, indeed, the act of gifting. It did not matter what the item was: the potency was unlocked by the intimate association between the giver and receiver, and the parting words or unspoken sentiments that accompanied the emotional moment of bestowal. This is perfectly illustrated by a woman interviewed by the folklorist Edward Lovett shortly after the outbreak of the war. Her son was setting off to the front, and he asked her whether she could give him anything for luck before he went. When Lovett inquired what she gave him, she answered, 'Oh, it don't matter what you give 'em. I gave 'im a very old metal button, and I ses "Jack, my boy, there's a mascot for you, and I hope God'll take care of you."' She subsequently received a letter from him saying that before an attack he took his mascot from his pocket and said, 'My mother gave me this for luck,' adding, '"May God take care of you," and I believe he will.'[52] Not all such gifts were knowingly bestowed, though. Edward Lovett knew of another old lady, who lived near Stoke Newington, whose only son was called up and was due to set off for France. She wanted to give him a mascot, but he refused to accept it, saying he was opposed to such things. So, unbeknown to her son, she secretly sewed a small orange Carnelian pendant inside the lining of his tunic to keep him safe.[53] When soldiers carried charms and talismans, they also carried the beliefs and hopes of others.

The Trade in Cauls

There had been a long tradition that babies born with the amniotic membrane still enveloping their head or face would make good sailors, as this covering or 'caul' was interpreted as a sign that the person would always be protected from drowning. Anyone who carried a caul on their person would also be saved at sea. This led to a lively trade in dried cauls amongst mariners. Whenever Britain was at war, the price spiked. So the beginning of the war with Revolutionary France in 1793 saw one advertisement appearing in *The Times* offering a caul for 'persons going to sea' for the huge sum of 15 guineas. In 1850 one Bristol vendor asked for 5 guineas from 'Captains of vessels and others', and prices peaked again during the Crimean War, with the *Liverpool Mercury* in 1854 printing an advertisement for one that was going for £10. It was not only periods of war that generated demand. As another Liverpool advertisement a few years later indicated, the flow of British and Irish emigrants through the port provided another source of custom, with one advertisement targeting 'Captains, Emigrants and others'. Demand subsided during the early twentieth century, with Edward Lovett purchasing two cauls in the London docks for the modest sum of 18 pence each.[54]

Prices predictably spiked again during the First World War, and a new development in naval warfare made them all the more desirable. In 1915 the *Liverpool Echo* observed that the proliferation of caul advertisements in the city's press was 'one of the most curious by-products of the German submarine policy'.[55] When Lovett returned to the London docks in 1916, he found the going price for a caul had increased significantly to more than £2. Seeing a notice on a window stating, 'Child's caul for sale, enquire within,' he innocently asked the proprietor why the price had gone up. The shopkeeper replied, 'The submarine has made life at sea so terribly risky and caused such fear that all the old superstitions have revived, and I could sell a lot of cauls if only I had them.'[56] While British naval power was far greater than the Germans', the U-boat fleet proved an effective military asset, causing significant disruption around the British coast and the Mediterranean. The German policy of unrestricted submarine warfare in British waters from January 1917 also led to the targeting of relief ships and merchant shipping. They played a significant propaganda role too, with rumours circulating in Germany about how the British were on their knees with starvation thanks to the blockade by the German 'miracle weapon'. British newspapers regularly reported on the losses inflicted on Allied shipping, meanwhile, no doubt heightening public concern.[57] It is no surprise, then, that the cost of cauls rose further later in the war, with market forces leading to local variations in demand and price in coastal regions. In November 1917 a caul was advertised by a Dublin resident in the *Liverpool Daily Post* for £4, and a caul was advertised for £3 'or near offer' by a Dorset resident in the *Western Gazette* a few months later. But look to the south-east of England and its ports of military disembarkation and, in November 1917, the *Dover Express* carried an advertisement from a caul seller on the Isle of Wight asking for £10 'or best offer', and ten months later someone was asking for £10 10s in the *Hastings and St Leonards Observer*.[58]

While the war was rarely specifically mentioned in English caul advertisements, mirroring the general reluctance of fortune tellers to promote their war business, the protective purpose of cauls was sometimes made explicit. 'Very lucky', ran one pitch, while an Exeter vendor also promised it was a 'lucky mascot'.[59] Most advertisements for cauls were unsurprisingly posted in newspapers that served coastal towns, and were directed explicitly at sailors. 'To seafarers' began advertisements in the Hull, Manchester, and Liverpool press. 'To Captains' or 'Captains and seagoers' announced others. But an advertisement in the *Irish Independent* in September 1918 avoided the usual coyness, with the caul on offer described as an 'infallible mascot against U Boats'.[60]

Clover Wars

Across the combatant countries various plants were kept for their well-known protective properties. The herb rue, traditionally said to have powerful anti-witchcraft qualities, was carried by Italian soldiers to prevent them from being hit by bullets and shrapnel. German soldiers similarly carried pieces of fern for protection.[61] In Britain a sprig of white heather had long been considered lucky. A journalist noted that a soldier friend of his who was about to go to the front carried a piece of white heather in his pocket, noting 'it will be a sad day for his piece of mind when he loses it'. In December 1914 the mother of Sapper Stanley Ellison, Benfleet, Essex sent him a letter asking for 'a line if possible as we are all very anxious about you', and enclosed a piece of 'lucky heather'. It was too late. She was unaware that her son had been an early casualty of the war, killed on 23 August.[62] The Christmas goods supplied to the King's Own Royal Lancaster Regiment 55th Divisional Canteen in 1917 included a box of lucky heather to hand out along with cigars, brandy, meat, and mistletoe crackers. At the expensive end, the Regent Street jewellers J. C. Vickery offered a gold lucky white heather pendant as a 'parting souvenir' for £1 15s.[63] In France the lily of the valley, or *muguet*, a native plant that flowers in May, was traditionally given to friends and family for good fortune, and during the war it was often depicted on *porte-bonheur* postcards. In the archives of Indre-et-Loire there is a touching letter from a *poilu*, sent from the front in May 1915, which contained a sprig of *muguet* he had picked in the woods as a lucky gift for his family.[64] For the Irish, of course, the shamrock or clover had special significance as the country's symbol, and there was huge demand for it. In early 1916 the Irish post office gave notice that due to the huge demand for sending shamrocks to the Irish Expeditionary Force in France, people would have to post them especially early to ensure delivery for St Patrick's Day.[65] But the most desired was the four-leaf shamrock.

It was widely reported in the Allied press during the first couple of months of the war that the Kaiser kept a dried, pressed, and perfumed four-leaf clover in his pocket book for good luck. The story went that it was found by the young daughter of a court official named Louis Schneider in a Prussian royal park in 1870. The girl was allowed to present it to old Kaiser Wilhelm, who, on returning victorious from the Battle of Sedan in the Franco-Prussian War, gave it back to the girl with the words, 'It has brought me luck, and I hope it will bring you luck,

Fig. 5.4. A soldier's amulet collection from France. From left to right: a piece of lucky heather, a four-leaf clover, a scallop shell representing the pilgrim's guide to the right path, a horseshoe, and an old shoe—a symbol of good luck for a new journey in life.

too.' Years later, Miss Schneider told the story to the Countess of Dohna and gave it to her as a gift. Then, in the early weeks of the First World War, the countess related the story to the German empress and gave the clover to her. She then presented it to the Kaiser to give him the good fortune that it had bestowed upon his grandfather forty-four years earlier. And so, said the reports, the Kaiser and his talisman were now inseparable.

When an abbreviated version of this story was published in the *Irish Independent* in September 1914, one reader saw a commercial opportunity, subsequently placing this small advertisement in the paper, as well as in the *Irish Times*: 'The Kaiser's Mascot is a four-leaved shamrock. I could exchange one for a £10 Note.' Ten days later, a rather less shameless and more moving small notice appeared in the *Irish Times*: 'Lucky Mascot, Four-leaved Shamrock; poor widow in difficulties will dispose of.'[66] The private and charitable trade in four-leaf clovers flourished. In July 1916 several Scottish and English newspapers reported that the demand for genuine examples was 'chiefly for the front, where the luck-bringing leaves are removed from their card-board backing by the recipients and placed for safety in the wrist watch case'.[67] The Red Cross seems to have generated some of the trade. At a Red Cross white elephant sale in Great Missenden in October 1916 there was a brisk trade in the sale of four-leaf clovers, for example, and at a Red Cross fete in Selkirk girls under the age of 13 could enter a four-leaf clover hunt.[68]

The Star reported in October 1914 that it had received a four-leaf clover and a letter from an 11-year-old girl named Edith Green, of Slough. 'Will you please send it to one of the English generals, as I have faith in it, and think this war dreadful,' she wrote. The paper expressed its agreement and sent both on to General Sir John French.[69] He was not the only recipient of such public generosity. The following year a French labourer from Nancy named André Krier found a four-leaf clover in the fields and sent it to President Poincaré. In return, he received a letter from the presidential general secretary thanking him for the gift of this *porte-bonheur*.[70] During the abdication crisis in Britain, numerous First World War veterans wrote supportive letters to King Edward VIII out of a sense of comradeship and shared experience due to his war service in the Grenadier Guards. One of them included one of two four-leaf clovers the correspondent had kept preciously during the war. They had been sent to him during his time in the Gallipoli campaign of 1915, and he attributed his survival to them when over two hundred thousand others died. Now he offered one to Edward to share his luck.[71] They did not protect the life of the American aviator Edmond Genet, though. He wrote home in May 1915 that he had found no fewer than twenty-seven four-leaf clovers just behind the lines in France: 'I never could find four-leaf clovers in the States and I'm always picking them up over here.' 'I hope they bring me lots of luck,' he wished. Genet was shot down and killed by German anti-aircraft guns on 17 April 1917.[72]

Swastikas Everywhere

In 1915 an article in the English provincial press observed, 'To find prominently displayed the Swastika, look into the windows of leading tradesmen in our cities and towns.'[73] Indeed, the swastika was as much a symbol of the First World War in Britain as it was of Germany in the Second, but with very different connotations. How could this be? While this ancient global sun symbol is today mostly associated with the Nazi Party, whose founders adopted it in 1920 to represent Aryan origins and superiority, Western interest in the swastika had been widespread during the late nineteenth and early twentieth century thanks to archaeological discoveries of its global depiction and also esoteric interest in Eastern mysticism. The books of the famed novelist Rudyard Kipling contained a swastika image on the cover and copyright page due to his familiarity with it as a Hindu luck symbol. The Scouts also contributed to the swastika's cultural vogue during the war. In 1911 the movement's founder Baden-Powell created the Swastika Thanks Badge as a global sign of fellowship. As Baden-Powell explained in *Scouting for Boys*, 'A Scout on seeing a person wearing this badge will go up, salute, and ask if he can be of any service.' So, in the Netherlands scout groups handed out swastika watch charms to those who supported them, and as a result one observer noted in 1913 that 'you are likely to run across a good many of these swastika charms among the business and professional men of Holland'.[74] Throughout the war the British provincial press also reported the local presentation of the swastika badge of thanks by local scout groups to persons who had helped them.

Numerous European and American companies, including the Danish brewer Carlsberg and the Dublin Swastika Laundry, also adopted the symbol as a logo. While the swastika had been adopted as an Aryan rune by small Austrian and German mystical nationalist groups before

Fig. 5.5. The swastika was one of the most popular lucky symbols in Britain during the First World War. On the left is a charm made from the aluminium of the Zeppelin shot down near Potters Bar in October 1916, and on the right a common image of the swastika key.

and during the First World War, its military use in Germany at the time had nothing to do with its future sinister symbolism.[75] The German ace Werner Voss painted a heart and a white swastika on his plane simply for good luck, and another fighter ace, Paul Billik, painted a black one on his Albatross fighter plane. A black swastika was also briefly adopted as a unit marking on planes in the Jasta 23 squadron.[76] There is no evidence these pilots were demonstrating their *völkisch* or nationalist leanings, and, besides, Billik was Jewish. The Finnish air force also adopted a blue swastika as its logo when it was founded in March 1918, thanks to a plane bearing the symbol that was donated to the newly independent Finnish 'White' government by the Swedish aristocrat Eric von Rosen. Rosen had seen the swastika represented on ancient rune stones in Sweden as a child and adopted it as a protective family sign, sometimes marking it next to his signature. (It is worth noting that von Rosen's sister-in-law married Hermann Göring, a First World War fighter ace and future head of the Nazi Luftwaffe.)

It was in Britain in particular that the swastika was most prominent in everyday life during the war, in part due to commercial trends in the jewellery and fashion business. The Attleboro company Paye & Baker helped promote the trend in 1907 by producing a series of lucky swastika pins, bangles, and leather goods.[77] Soon after, reports appeared in several American newspapers on how 'in everything in the way of jewelry the interesting swastika design is utilized and not in jewelry alone, but in embroidered and stencil borders, carrying always a suggestion of good luck and prosperity'.[78] A range of products began to proliferate in Britain. In 1908 a Sheffield newspaper included an item on the popularity of embroidered swastika cushions that promoted good fortune, while in February 1914 readers of the magazine *Forget-Me-Not* were offered a Valentine's giveaway of one hundred gilt silver swastika charms.[79] During the war it was depicted on numerous lucky postcards, and was sometimes represented as the bit part of a key, as in the key to good fortune. The popularity of swastika amulets is evident from their appearance in the lost property columns of newspapers. In December 1916 a reward was announced for the return of a 'swastika charm keepsake' lost on the streets of Middlesbrough. In October 1917 someone posted in the *Western Mail* that he or she had lost a 'swastika charm' near the hospital in Dynas Powys.[80] Government agencies also caught onto the value of the lucky symbol. The National War Savings Committee adopted the swastika in 1916 as its 'Savings Symbol' on sixpenny coupon stamps to raise public funds. 'One of our most successful schemes', reported an official in December that year. In 1917 a renewed campaign by the committee and its local branches hoped to display its swastika symbol in windows, offices, and shops, with poster stamps affixed to sauce bottles, jam jars, and paper bags.[81] The British government also commissioned a brand of swastika cigarettes for soldiers that were not on general sale.

Animal Magic

While some army and navy animal mascots were formal regimental appointments, so to speak, presented as gifts by royalty or dignitaries, many were adopted informally while on active service or rescued from the battlefields. Sometimes soldiers made appeals in the press. In August 1914 a member of the 6th Royal Highlanders Black Watch (Irish Section) wrote to the *Irish Times* that his section was 'on the look-out for a well-bred Irish terrier, about twelve months old, to bring with them on active service as a mascot'. The following year, the Burnley Company of the 11th East Lancashire 'Pals' Regiment sent a letter to the press back home appealing for a new animal mascot after their beloved monkey had been killed accidentally while on duty. 'We ask you to assist us in our appeal for a lucky substitute. He is missed among us. By doing this you will greatly oblige.'[82]

A journalistic survey of mascots conducted in 1915 confirmed that dogs were the most numerous. A pair of shaggy-haired terriers named Wolf and Floss, for instance, were the 'luck bringers' of the 2nd Battalion of the London Scottish, while the 10th Royal Fusiliers had a pointer named Bob. Cats were particularly popular amongst sailors, such as Togo the Persian cat of HMS *Dreadnought*, which liked to relax in the barrels of the ship's big guns. Welsh regiments had long been known for their goats, and donkeys and pigs were not uncommon. The New Zealand Army Service Company had an Egyptian donkey named Moses while stationed in France in 1918. There was Piggy, the stray pig, kept by the transport section of the Army Service Corps, and also the pig found swimming in the sea following the sinking of the light cruiser *Dresden* in March 1915. A British sailor dived in and rescued the German porker, and it became the lucky mascot for his warship.[83] Monkeys were quite prized. As well as the ill-fated Burnley Company mascot, there was Jacko the Monkey of torpedo-boat destroyer HMS *Loyal*, who drowned in December 1914 after having distinguished himself previously during the Battle of the Heligoland Bight. The first African-American pilot to serve in the war, Eugene Bullard, who was with the largely American, but French-led Lafayette Escadrille, also had a monkey as his pet mascot.[84] Foxes, birds, and a range of other wild animals were also adopted. Allied soldiers from Canada, Australia, and New Zealand brought over bear cubs, tortoises, and parrots. Australian soldiers even brought a kangaroo that overwintered with them in Egypt.

Animals as lucky mascots were also represented widely on postcards and in the form of amulets and ornaments. Each combatant country had its own traditions regarding which animals were thought to bring fortune and prosperity. In Germanic folklore the stork had long been considered a good omen, particularly if it nested on your roof, and so we find it represented on sets of wartime lucky spoons. The celebrated French No. 3 Squadron, which included Georges Guynemer, was known as *Les Cigognes* or 'The Storks' due to the images of a stork painted on each plane's fuselage. When, in the summer of 1915, it was reported that German artillery had shot down a stork flying over the Alsatian town of Colmar in mistake for a French aeroplane, the inhabitants feared that it would bring bad luck upon them.[85] The ladybird was considered a bringer of good luck in France, and it adorned numerous lucky postcards and jewellery.

In Ireland little pig talismans of bog oak and Connemara marble were popular before and during the war. The pig was quite widely used as a symbol of good luck on French *porte-bonheur* postcards. Lucky pig pins were also sold at a fete for prisoners of war held in Chedworth, England, in 1916.[86] In sailors' traditions having a pig tattooed on the foot or knee protected them from drowning—'Pig on the knee, safety at sea.' One English tattooist told the *Daily Mirror* in 1914 that it was a common request to have a lucky pig tattooed on the arm. 'Both men and women come to me to have lucky pigs designed for them,' he observed.[87] In contrast to the mariners' tattooing tradition, pigs were taboo amongst fishermen, and there was a widespread and long-standing belief that one should never set out to sea if one encountered a pig. The word 'pig' should never be uttered either. One Yorkshire fishing family used to refer to pigs as 'grecians' to avoid the taboo. As a Scottish newspaper reported, however, the war years helped undermine the old aversion to pigs in fishing communities, with it becoming a more common practice on steam drifters and large trawlers to keep pigs on board to economize on waste and feed the crews.[88]

The European adoption of the elephant as a good luck symbol during and after the war derived from Asian rather than African colonial influence. The various merits of elephants, including their luck-bringing, were discussed in ancient Sanskrit manuscripts, and the tradition continues to this day, with white or pale elephants being particularly revered in Thailand and Burma. It was not, however, the British colonial experience that generated its popularity in the European war zone. An item in the British press in 1913 noted that the charm most in demand in Paris during the early months of the year was a little white elephant in rock crystal, enamel, or ivory. Its fashionable status was, the press reported, due to a 'woman oracle' having asserted its luck-bringing powers.[89] The unnamed oracle was none other than Madame de Thèbes, whose adherence to lucky elephants was widely reported at the time.

Her consulting room was full of small porcelain and bronze elephant ornaments, and the cover of her popular almanac bore an image of an elephant with its trunk up. In a private interview she explained, 'My elephants? Yes, they are my *porte-bonheur*, indeed...the animal most sensible, most wise, the most prudent.' Jewellers began to capitalize on the interest, and in 1917 the *Thé de l'Éléphant* brand of teas even offered a free good luck elephant charm with some purchases.[90] While the trunk-up elephant was predominantly a French talisman, it also became popular in post-war Britain, with returning soldiers no doubt influencing the vogue. It was reported in 1921 to be 'the mascot of the moment', and advertisements appeared in the press for charms such as the 'Elephant Hair Ring, made from guaranteed real Elephant Hair and Solid Gold'. Elephant ornaments, like those that graced Madame de Thèbes's consulting room, also became popular on British and American mantelpieces.[91]

The British Bublldog was emblematic of the country's spirit, and it was depicted on numerous patriotic postcards, where the bulldog was shown biting or threatening the Kaiser. In 1915 the 'Bow Wow' 'empire mascot' was marketed in the British national press. Produced by the jewellers Badcoe & Hanks, Holborn, London, it was a small silver or gold bulldog, but if you turned it upside down the base resembled the German eagle. So, when standing, the charm represented the bulldog crushing the eagle. Described as a 'wonderful luck bringer', the advertisement declared it 'had been graciously received by leading members of society, officers, and men of his Majesty's Army and Navy', and presented the following jingle:

> I am your faithful friend;
> 'Good Luck' I bring you now;
> From evil I'll defend
> All those who trust Bow! Wow!![92]

Larger metal paperweight versions were also produced. There were other bulldog charms as well. In September 1917 the French newspaper *L'Intransigeant* reported that the little *tou tou* or 'bow-wow' dog mascot, a little velvet black and white form with a silk scarf around its neck, was currently the most sought after talisman in London.[93]

While the black cat is commonly thought to be a bad omen today, the folklore of the last century and a half shows a confused picture, with as many references to black cats being lucky.[94] During the war, fortune definitely favoured the black cat, though, and it became one of the most important charm motifs in North America, Britain, and France. The real thing was also a popular ship's mascot. Commodore Sir Reginald Tyrwhitt, commander of the Harwich Force, kept a black cat with him on his flagship during the war, while HMS *Neptune* kept one called Sideboy, which enjoyed sleeping in his own miniature hammock.[95] Cats were less at home in planes for obvious reasons, so aviators made do with cuddly toy versions. The American First World War ace Allan Peck wrote home shortly after completing his flight training in November 1917:

> I want you to get me a black cat, one of those stuffed animals with the bead eyes and kind of cloth fur, and about six inches high. You know what I mean. Then put a red ribbon around his neck with a little brass bell on it. I want it to hang with wires on the front of my machine at the front. They are wonderful luck, and I know a black cat would keep anything from hitting me. Remember, though, it must be very sturdily put together and not too large, as it will have to tear through the air at way over a hundred miles an hour. Get the animal to me at once.[96]

A fellow American fighter ace, Charles Parsons, joined the French-led Lafayette Escadrille in early 1917, but met with no combat success for five months. Then, on a visit to Paris, a female acquaintance gave him a life-size velvet cat with typical arched back and tail standing straight up. He brought it back to the front and had it wired to the centre strut of his right wing. 'Whiskers streaming back in the slipstream, he or she (I never could decide) kept an eagle eye on everything,' he recalled. 'It always gave me a lot of courage in a tight place to see the very placid, untroubled expression on her or his face. If the cat wasn't worried, why should I be?' Within four days he had downed his first German plane, which he attributed to his 'feline fetish'. He was distraught, however, when, in late September 1917, the hangar housing his plane received a direct hit. He searched in vain for his cat, but not a whisker remained. He refused to fly until he returned from Paris with a new gift of a cat even cockier-looking than the first. He brought it with him when he joined the Storks, and later asserted that it saved his life during a dogfight in the summer of 1918.[97]

Back on the home front in Britain and lucky black cats were ubiquitous. Peruse the papers and the Black Cat brand of cigarettes was

I'VE LEFT THE KAISER,
(HIS LUCK'S OUT)
AND I'VE COME TO YOU

Fig. 5.6. One of numerous British lucky postcards from the First World War that represented the black cat as a good luck symbol.

widely advertised with the slogan 'BLACK CATS are lucky for you,' depicting a black cat smoking one of the cigarettes.[98] When elementary schoolchildren in Baildon, Yorkshire, sent letters to soldiers at the front, some embellished them with drawings of black cats for luck.[99] Charity fundraisers commonly sold buttons and badges bearing an image of dark felines. In 1916 Florence Parbury sold lucky black china cats to raise funds for her Jacobean Studios, where wounded officers could take tea in cosy surroundings.[100] The Red Cross sold for six pence little black cat mascots attached to a card bearing the following verse:

> Wear this Pussy, and you'll find
> Fortune will be very kind,
> For as sure as she is black,
> You good luck shall never lack.

Manufacturing Little Gods

In the years before the war there was a craze in Britain for placing mascots on the bonnets or radiator caps of motor cars for good luck and as a bit of jollity. Along with teddy bears, black cats, and policeman figurines with hand outstretched and bearing the words 'Propitiate the fates!!', one of the most popular items was a golliwog.[101] It was a competitive market. In 1914 the vendor of a popular 'touchwood' charm advertised to all car owners that he sold an extra-large bonnet version of his mascot 'to take the place of the senseless and useless golliwog, Teddybear, and billiken'.[102] Indeed, it was concern over the sullying of their limousines with such objects that led the directors of Rolls-Royce to commission the iconic Spirit of Ecstasy bonnet ornament in 1911. During the war the sale of woollen and paper gollywogs as personal mascots for servicemen was a staple of the charitable effort in Ireland and Britain. In 1917 the 'E.C-s', a charity supporting the Ecclesall Infirmary for wounded soldiers, set themselves the task of making 16,000 golliwogs to be sold on 27 October, which they designated 'Golliwog Day'.[103] The Red Cross also held similar such Golliwog Days up and down the country. But the war also generated new mass-produced commercialized genres of humanoid mascots that were promoted through extensive national and international marketing campaigns. In 1917 an English newspaper article on soldiers' mascots referred in passing to the recent appearance of 'small black gods, of the "touch-wood" type'.[104] What where these little gods?

The touchwood talisman has usually been attributed to an East End trinket seller named Henry Brandon. Brandon, whose real name was Hyman Pokrasse, was a German Jewish Ukrainian who, along with his family, and many others at the time, fled the pogroms in Ukraine, and settled in the East End of London in the 1890s. His father made a living as a barrow lender, which was someone who rented out barrows to costermongers on a daily or weekly basis, while the youthful Pokrasse worked as a street vendor. Then, several years prior to 1911, while in his mid-twenties, he left home and spent some time in America, where he became a US citizen. He was back with his wife and family by 1911, when he is recorded in the census as working in advertising. It was in early 1914 that he began to offer for sale in the daily press 'The Wonderful

Eastern Charm known as "Touchwood"'. The advertisements stated of this little trinket that 'the Eastern people call him their Holy Charm, because his little head is made of sacred oak, with arms and legs either in gold or silver, with most curious brilliant eyes, which seem to follow and stare at one until almost out of sight'. Brandon claimed he had received three repeat orders for touchwoods from Buckingham Palace in one week alone, with Queen Alexandria being particularly taken with the wonderful charm.[105]

Brandon was not the first to advertise touchwoods for sale, though. In November 1913 the Incorporated Association for Promoting the General Welfare of the Blind had posted advertisements for touchwoods, the 'mysterious little eastern mascot that brings you good luck!'. 'It is the new society fashion to wear this quaint little oddity,' the charity declared, and marketed them as a Christmas gift, with the touchwood mounted on a Christmas card on which touchwood was depicted peeping out from a hollow tree trunk. Corroborating Brandon's reference to his Buckingham Palace customers, the charity noted in the advertisement that its patrons included Queen Alexandria.[106]

Fig. 5.7. Two variants of the touchwood charm marketed in Britain by Henry Brandon in 1915.

Perhaps Brandon had been employed by the charity for fund raising purposes or perhaps he had been inspired by the advertisements, but, whatever the case, he clearly saw touchwood's potential. So did others, with the likes of the Aberdeen stationer Thomas Lamb also advertising them for sale in March 1914. Their presence on the streets grew. In May that year someone felt the urge to send a letter to the periodical *Notes and Queries*, having seen 'a tiny gnome of wood called "touchwood"' in a shop window. A verse on the backing card to which it was attached began, 'Eastern wisdom gave me birth'. The correspondent asked, 'can any of your readers give authority for the first line?'[107] The French actress Jeanne Provost also purchased a touchwood on a trip to London around this time, and told a journalist she religiously gave it a kiss for luck.[108] But where were these charms coming from? The Incorporated Association for the Blind merely mentioned they had 'secured' a number of the charms for sale. It transpires, not surprisingly, that the touchwood charm derived from the global trinket capital of Attleboro, Massachusetts. Its maker was the Attleboro Manufacturing Company, with its promotion and sales handled by one of its divisions, the Baer & Wilde Company, which had been set up in 1908 to specialize in men's jewellery. With America's entry into the war the Attleboro Manufacturing Company also became a leading manufacturer of military dog tags.[109]

In the autumn of 1914 the company added a new 'Mrs Touchwood' to their range, and Brandon, clearly clued up to the trade catalogues from American jewellers and trinket makers, ordered a batch, advertising them in some London dailies in November, providing a nice wartime touch by offering them appended to an enamelled brooch of the Allied flags.[110] In January 1915 the trade journal for American advertisers, *Printers' Ink*, ran a two-page feature on how Baer & Wilde Company were setting about an innovative national campaign to boost sales of Mr and Mrs Touchwood lucky jewellery across America. 'Though the work with jobbers and dealers has been going on aggressively for three months past,' it reported, 'and the campaign has been worked out in all its details, not an inkling of the subject has reached consumers except where, here and there, a wide-awake dealer has displayed the goods in his window.'[111] Baer & Wilde's trade promotional material stated, '"Touchwood for luck" is a slogan that will go round the world and on the wave of its popularity, Touchwood Jewelry will sell.' It further declared that its advertisements in magazines and periodicals would reach 74 million Americans. Another trade journal, the *Manufacturing Jeweler*, described how the campaign began at the national trade convention in Providence:

'Touchwood' first appeared on a bulletin board facing the Union Station, the most prominent location in Providence, directly in the path of every visiting jewelry and novelty buyer. 'Touchwood for Luck—Ask Your Jeweler' was all it said. But it started everyone wondering what on earth Touchwood was. When the jewelry buyer arrived at his hotel, he saw in the rotunda a big colored card staring him in the face. This also bore the mystic legend, 'Touchwood for Luck.' In the elevator the same message was repeated and not until he had closed the door of his room did he cease to see Touchwood cards.

The first fruits of the March launch can be seen in the American newspapers from that month, with one brief advertisement for Mrs Touchwood in a Maryland paper stating bluntly that she could be purchased in McCleery's Jewelry Store to 'pass up your bum jinx'.[112]

In Britain, by early 1915 Brandon had cornered the trade in touchwoods and was putting together his own ambitious marketing campaign explicitly directed at soldiers and their families. There was an Easter edition packed in an egg, and then a flattened pendant version mounted with a silver gurkha knife, and also a line of the same with a photograph of the King, Queen, Lord Kitchener, Admiral Jellicoe, General French, or President Poincaré on the reverse side. At some point around this time he also started promoting them as 'Touch*wuds*'. Brandon put out advertisements in May addressed 'to all Members of His Majesty's Forces and to their relatives and personal friends', offering to provide a free touchwood with every regimental badge bought fromhim. The next advertisement ran, 'Mr Touchwud has joined the Army... Everyone is buying them to give to the Boys and Friends at the Front as well as at home.'[113] New editions appeared, with a 'Tommy Touchwud' wearing a khaki army cap and 'Jack Touchwud' with a sailor's cap.

The climax of Brandon's ambitious media campaign occurred on 14 August, when the French actor and singer Alice Delysia, a big star in the West End, was hired to present 1,200 touchwuds to the officers and men of the 6th Battalion of the City of London Rifles in Regent's Park. It took over an hour for the soldiers to file past the actress as she

Fig. 5.8. Two variants of the touchwood charm. On the left Mrs Touchwood (produced in the USA), and on the right Tommy Touchwood.

handed out a touchwud to each man from her motor car. Wounded men from other battalions were also able to queue up for the gift. Officers received a gold version, while a 9-inch-high mascot was also presented to the whole regiment.[114] Pathé News was there to film the event, and *The Times* was inspired to commission an article. It noted that Brandon boasted he had sold 1,250,000 touchwoods since the beginning of the war, and claimed to have received numerous thank-you letters from soldiers at the front, including this endorsement: 'We have been out here for five months fighting in the trenches, and have not had a scratch. We put our great good fortune down to your lucky charm, which we treasure highly.'[115] While Brandon undoubtedly exaggerated the numbers he sold, he was certainly selling them in their tens of thousands, and no doubt many lie buried in the battlefields with their owners.

The summer of 1915 was the high tide for touchwud, and it vanished soon after. The reason why it went out of vogue so quickly is simply that stock dried up. There is no evidence that, despite the big marketing campaign, the touchwood range was a raging success in the USA, and so the company probably ceased production. It was not long, though, before a new little god captured the public imagination, and his name was Fumsup. The Fumsup baby—a naked baby making a thumbs up sign—had been around for several decades as a decorative motif on cards and represented in china.[116] In December 1915 a Staffordshire china version was advertised in three sizes, for instance, and sold as a 'quaint' lucky mascot ornament for mantelpieces.[117] It had a four-leaf shamrock on its forehead for good fortune and cupid's wings on its heels to speed true love. At the same time, another small silver model was advertised that borrowed from the success of touchwud. The venerable jewellery firm Gourdel, Vales & Co., which was based in Birmingham and London, stated they were the sole manufacturers for the wholesale and export trade. It came with its own jingle:

> This charm, just born,
> MUST bring Good Luck;
> It's head's 'TOUCHWOOD';
> It's name's 'FUMS UP'.[118]

This wooden-headed silver version with moveable arms appeared in late December 1915 as part of the Christmas sales push, and was explicitly targeted at the armed forces. The *Daily Mirror* and other papers carried advertisements for it that explained they were 'for Fighting Men at Home & Abroad'.[119] Fumsup was also available from the likes of Harrods and Asprey the jewellers. It also went global. In March 1916 an advertisement appeared in the Canadian press stating 'London's very latest novelty has arrived in Victoria.' Then, in December 1916, advertisements with the same little rhyme appeared in Australian newspapers. Silver and gold versions were being advertised in at least one Italian periodical in 1917.[120] The Fumsup image was also adopted by other companies and placed on lucky products. When a journalist visited a newly founded doll factory in Sheffield in December 1916, he found workers busy moulding horseshoes on which Fumsup was depicted under the words 'Good Luck!'[121].

In December 1916 Gourdel, Vales & Co. put out an advertising puff that included a journalistic piece entitled 'Good Luck! The Romance of a "Fumsup"' written by the experienced hack writer Arthur Lawrence.

This consisted of an interview with an Afrikaner soldier in the South African Brigade named Chris Fourie who was convalescing in a Surrey hospital. He recounted his various adventures and misfortunes. During his stint in the Egyptian campaign he was involved in the Duke of Westminster's pursuit of the Arab forces following their abandonment of the post at Sollum in March 1916. Just before the expedition set out, Furie lost his Fumsup in the sand, but amazingly a comrade found it and returned it within two days. 'It was with me in that wild dash,' he said, 'and was around my neck when the Union Jack was hoisted amidst a very mixed crowd.' While on his way to France, two transport ships in front of his were sunk by torpedoes. Then on 9 July, while in the trenches, a coal box exploded, burying him and numerous others and killing seven of his mates. He was hauled out and on that same day was hit in the foot by shrapnel, which is how he found himself in the

Fig. 5.9. Early examples of the British Fumsup mascots, with their moveable arms, touchwood heads, silver for luck, and cupid's wings on their feet for a swift return to loved ones.

Surrey hospital. 'When he spoke of "Fumsup" his face lit up with a smile,' wrote Lawrence.[122]

Aviators seem to have also been particularly fond of Fumsup. In 1918 the author Jacques Boulenger wrote of the archetypal French aviator: 'he has on him several good luck charms; he lifts the moveable arms of the dwarf god Thumbs up and puts it back in his wallet'.[123] A Fumsup baby was also painted on a Sopwith Camel flown by Second Lieutenant John Raymond Chisman of No. 204 Squadron RAF.[124] He was inspired by his sister, who always ended her letters to him with the cheering words 'Fums Up!'[125] The tradition continued after the war. When the British R34 airship made the first east–west air crossing of the Atlantic in July 1919, the captain, Major George Scott, explained to a journalist that, although they were not superstitious, each member of the crew had been given a Fumsup mascot, gold for officers and silver for the rest of the crew. '"Here is mine," said the Major, laughing, and he produced a small leather case and extracted a "fums up" baby, wrought in gold, the head made of West African bean.'[126]

Touchwud and Fumsup were the most commercially successful manufactured touchwood charms, but they were by no means the only ones circulating during the war. The Horniman Museum and Bristol Museum, in London, possess examples of a gold crescent moon amulet bearing an embossed man in the moon face, with a wooden touchwood bead pinned between the horns of the crescent. These two examples were worn by men of the Yorkshire regiment around 1916–17. I have come across no other literary reference to them and the charm was presumably produced by a jeweller in the county.[127] Across the channel, in 1916 Paris newspapers printed an item that the touchwood amulet was so internationally popular that it was rapidly becoming impossible to obtain. Fortunately, the puff announced, the jewellers Van Cleef and Arpels, jewellers in the place Vendôme, were making their own models, for which they were the sole vendors.[128] Their own distinctive range of touchwood wooden jewellery swiftly became desirable in fashionable female Parisian society, and would prove to be a mainstay of the company's business for decades.[129] Soldiers also carved their own personal touchwood figures. One example, now in private hands but formerly from the Whitehall Theatre of War Museum in London, consists of a roughly carved wooden head peeping out of a shell casing. It bore the inscription:

WAR IS OVER
TOUCH WOOD
NOV 1918
CAPT ROACH
BLACK WATCH

The famed French poet Guillaume Apollinaire (1880–1918), who fought at the front and never fully recovered from a shrapnel wound, wrote of his interest in the 'superstitions of war' and was particularly taken with the popularity during the summer of 1918 of a pair of little woollen mascots named Nénette and Rintintin. They were, he said, 'the first gods born in the twentieth century'.[130] The American poet Adolphe E. Smylie published a poem in honour of them in a collection entitled *The Marines, and Other War Verse* (1919).

> But *I'm* safe; I wear amulets!
> I'm bomb-proof now inside;
> I smoke and sing on night patrol,
> The parapet's my daily stroll;
> Snipe on, you Boche! No bullet hole
> Can Ventilate my hide
> Thanks to wee maid and man,—
> Nenette and Rintintin!
> Henceforth back on my bayonet
> Dead Huns I'll daily bring;
> These worsted, good-luck Belgian twins
> Protect the wearers' precious skins.[131]

What was it about this pair of simple little woollen mascots, which sold for a mere franc, that so captured the imagination?

Part of the mystique of the mascots was that multiple explanations circulated as to their origin. One story was that Nénette and Rintintin were a boy and girl found on an abandoned farm by French soldiers on their way to the front. They adopted the pair, looking after them as they headed for the battlefields. The little girl made two dolls of wool and silk to thank them for their kindness, and the *poilus* named them after the boy and girl. Ever since, the regiment had met with continuous success in battle. Another legend explained that Nénette and Rintintin were twins born prematurely as a consequence of the terrifying bombing raids on Paris by the Gothas (German bomber planes), and as a result they possessed a protective aura against them. Another more prosaic explanation was that they were inspired by the little golliwog dolls British soldiers brought with them to France.[132] Others traced their inspiration to the Parisian illustrator Francisque Poulbot (1879–1946), who often depicted street urchins, and who produced numerous patriotic posters and postcards during the war. In 1913 he had produced two porcelain dolls of a girl and boy called Nénette and Rintintin, which led him to declare publicly he had inspired the woollen twins. But in June 1918 the political and cultural digest *Le Carnet de la Semaine* expressed its disagreement with the claim, concluding 'Poulbot is not the father of Nénette and Rintintin, but he could be their godfather.' Besides, the nicknames Nénette and Rintintin had long been used among Parisians as affectionate terms for young children, puppies, and kittens.[133] In short, Nénette and Rintintin were the collective creation of the war, and not of one man.

Nénette and Rintintin were everywhere in Paris during that spring and summer. The newspapers and periodicals were full of references to them, their image was used on numerous *porte-bonheur* postcards, and they were the topic of songs and ballads. The July edition of the weekly wartime satirical magazine *La Baïonnette* was devoted to humorous cartoons portraying the pair.[134] As well as the ubiquitous woollen charms, they were produced in Bakelite and silver. Writing home from a US hospital for French soldiers in Limoges in July 1918, Elizabeth Cabot Putnam mentioned that a 'touch-on-wood' version of the woollen dolls had also appeared—'they will protect you against Gothas and their American equivalent'.[135] While they became a fashion craze in Paris, there were many worn at the front and in the skies. Charles Parsons noted that his fellow aviators attached small ivory and porcelain versions to their lucky wrist chains. The dolls were only considered efficacious if given as gifts, though. 'The fond one must waft them into existence and her devoted fingers must tie them securely together and get them to the trenches by the fastest post!,' wrote one correspondent. An American journalist in France complained that American soldiers without French sweethearts or girlfriends were accordingly handicapped in obtaining the good luck charms.[136]

French clergymen shook their heads and wrote disparagingly of the sudden popularity of such ungodly and frivolous fripperies at such a

Fig. 5.10. Cartoon from the French satirical magazine *La Baïonnette* (4 July 1918) poking fun at the Parisian craze for Nénette and Rintintin.

grave moment for the country.[137] But the press of the Central Powers looked on with a mix of satisfaction, amusement, and bemusement. A Budapest newspaper reported on this 'latest gimmick of French superstition', while a Vienna newspaper saw the increased wearing of talismans in the capital, and the 'fetish' dolls in particular, as an insight into the fragile state of Parisian minds since the German offensive on the capital. One Prague newspaper described them as the new 'protective gods' that had appeared 'in the midst of the bloodiest misery' of the French, and pondered how Nénette and Rintintin would fare once the bombardment of Paris resumed.[138]

It is possible, and perhaps ironic, that the dolls had more cultural influence overseas than in the distant regions of western and southern France—far from Paris and the battlefields. The fad was reported in the British press, for example, and during the morale-boosting 'France Day' organized by the Mayoress of Exeter in July 1918 golliwogs representing the Paris charms were on sale.[139] Cinemagoers might have caught the brief Pathé report 'Paris: Latest Mascots', which showed a woman playing with the two dolls suspended from her neck.[140] But it seems the Americans took Nénette and Rintintin to their hearts more than the British. Perhaps this was because the British already had their Fumsups, but also because of the American interest in Paris fashions. Several American magazines commissioned pieces from their Paris correspondents exploring why Parisians had so taken to these simple little dolls. One was entitled 'French Fashions: The Spirit of Nenette and Rintintin Help Parisians to Hold Out for Victory En Route'. It was written in July 1918 by the Marquise de Ravenel, who opined: 'The Parisian is a born tease—he or she is first and last a "taquin"—and what greater joy could they have than to "tease" the Boche and keep the beast at bay with a silken string! This is what Nenette and Rintintin are doing just now.'[141] Another reporter contrasted Parisian gaiety and *joie de vivre* in the face of the German artillery with the Teutonic dourness of the oppressor: 'Compare it if you like with the grim and heavy Boche gravity, hammering big nails into the gigantic wooden statue of Hindenburg. The profound soul-difference of Berlin and Paris will thus appear in a strange manner.'[142]

It was not only through the press that Americans were introduced to Nénette and Rintintin. In 1918 the New York Mayor's Women's Committee set up an information booth at the intersection of Broadway and Seventh Avenue, plumb in the city's theatre district, to help the many soldiers passing through on their way to France who had never before been to the city. Free sightseeing tickets were distributed, and a collection box was on display to pay for theatre tickets for soldiers and sailors. One of the committee had been sent Nénette and Rintintin lucky dolls by her son stationed in France, and she made a number of her own which she gave to those charitable passers-by who put 25 cents in the box.[143] Returning soldiers also brought them home with them. The Marquise de Ravenel described the following encounter in the Paris Metro with a 6-foot-2 Californian soldier and his friend, who had been trained at Camp Fremont and were on their way to the battlefields:

> I could not resist the temptation to talk to them and I told the nearest to me that I was pleased to see that he was under *'devine'* [*sic*] protection! He said, 'oh, Nénette (and he pronounced it Nanette quite correctly) never leaves me, I am going to take her back to the coast!' His friend laughed, so did I. But, I ventured again and asked if she were alone! He replied, 'no, indeed, but Rintintin (and he pronounced it 'Ran-tan-tan,' with the ease of an old Boulevardier) is ashamed to come out in the daylight!'[144]

In October 1918 an American draper's shop advertised in the regional press that it sold 'the newest good luck charms', tiny hand-painted Nénette and Rintintin dolls 'worn by all Paris, many of the Allied soldiers, and hundreds of others as protecting charms'.[145] Such was the cultural reach in America that by early 1919 one American fabric manufacturer, Mallinson & Co., introduced a Nénette and Rintintin pattern, with the company donating a percentage of the profits on each yard sold to the Belgian widows' and orphans' fund. A bathing suit cut from the material was garlanded with small woollen Nénette and Rintintin dolls hanging from the shoulders.[146]

From the horrors of the front to the beach fashions of America, the migration of this Parisian cultural phenomenon is best exemplified by the story of the canine film star Rin Tin Tin, one of the most celebrated Hollywood actors of the 1920s. During the last months of the war, an American army corporal, Lee Duncan, was tasked with scouting for a suitable landing strip near the village of Flirey, to the south-west of Metz. He came across an abandoned German Army kennel, where he found a malnourished Alsatian and her litter of puppies. Duncan brought them back to his unit and gave the dogs away, keeping two puppies as lucky mascots, which he named Rin Tin Tin and Nanette. He managed to smuggle them back to the States in July 1919 and gave them obedience training. Nanette died not long after, but Rin Tin Tin went on to star in the first of many films in 1922. Duncan had purchased his lucky woollen dolls from a little girl in Toul, and when he became rich from his dog's acting career, he had solid gold versions of the dolls made, which he wore every day for the rest of his life.[147]

Before the war was at an end another pair of little gods, Yerri and Suzel, briefly challenged the supremacy of Nénette and Rintintin. The rosy-cheeked girl and boy dressed in traditional Alsatian dress were, for some, representative of the two lost provinces of Alsace and Lorraine, annexed by Germany in 1871 as a result of the Franco-Prussian War. One French postcard welcoming the arrival of the Americans showed the pair next to a house bearing a lucky horseshoe with the Statue of Liberty presiding over them, while another depicted storks. Represented in porcelain versions, they also featured in a puppet show. Their rise to stardom owed much to the French propaganda campaign for 'hearts and minds' in the strongly Germanic region. This was led by the Bureau d'Études d'Alsace-Lorraine, created as part of the Ministry of War in July 1917, which devised the creation of a range of pamphlets, posters, postcards, and enticing commercial products that reinforced the ties between France and the eastern provinces. Their primary target was the *poilus*, amongst whom there was evidently considerable ambivalence about whether they should be risking their lives for the Germanic territories. It was hoped that, once enthused, they would then transmit the positive messages of historic and cultural unity back home when on leave. It was also recognized by the French government that Allied soldiers might equally need convincing of the cause of Alsace-Lorraine's liberation as an integral part of the struggle.[148] The invention of Yerri and Suzel was a significant aspect of this Allied propaganda campaign, and in September 1918 the women's pages of *Les Annales politiques et littéraires* advised that Yerri and Suzel was *le fétiche à la mode*, and had 'the advantage of evoking a sense of patriotism and of having a quasi-official patronage'.[149] The London French lingerie shop, Labise Company, Bond Street, even imported woolly mascot versions for sale to fashionable clients, the proceeds going to the French Red Cross. It also sold lucky Yerri and Suzel garters and ties. *Tatler* described them as 'the greatest luck bringers of the times'.[150]

The pair seems to have briefly caught the imagination of the military, though by no means to the same extent as Nénette and Rintintin. In the autumn of 1918 a French newspaper observed how wool and silk Yerri and Suzel mascots had become something of a cult among American and British soldiers, and the French aviator Charles Delacommune wrote of his profound feelings for the 'little Alsatian doll' which he kept in his cockpit. 'You always laughed, holding out your small arms, when the shells exploded near us or the bullets passed, menacingly,' he recalled of his porcelain friend. And then a piece of shrapnel struck it full in the face. He cursed the German artillery for destroying his mascot, 'which was like the link between the "old" crate and the "new" . . . the Past and the Future!' 'She sleeps at present in a cardboard box, her coffin!'[151]

The widespread resort to mascots, talismans, and charms attracted public criticism across the warring parties, most of it from a religious perspective. It has already been noted that the vogue for Nénette and Rintintin excited the disapprobation of the Catholic clergy. After all, as we shall see in Chapter 6, the Catholic Church drove its own thriving trade in protective medals and blessed paraphernalia. In Britain some Church of England clergy also noted the popularity of lucky and protective items with disdain. During a public lecture on the history of 'superstition' in December 1917, one bishop said that 'he could forgive a certain recrudescence of that sort of things in these times of strain and excitement, but, of course, it was all rubbish'. Another, the rector of Guiseley, Yorkshire, described mascots and charms as 'all part of witch-craft', and noted the Bible's condemnation of such things.[152] On the evangelical fringe, there were strident criticisms that the authorities were conniving at a return to idol worship, expressed as either anti-Catholic tirades or concerns over the revival of pagan tendencies in the population. In August 1915 *The Times* printed a letter headed 'Idols' from 'A soldier's mother'. She complained, 'Will no one in authority point out this crying evil?' 'What have we to do with "lucky" horseshoes, stuffed monkeys, goats, dogs, and other "charms"?', she asked despairingly. 'Let the very name of mascot be forgotten; and let us turn in all humility to the God and Father who will brook no other gods, and who is now pleased to afflict His children.'[153] The following day an approving correspondent, signed 'PROTESTANT', thanked the soldier's mother. This angry letter writer was also incensed and motivated by the reports the previous week of Henry Brandon's Regent's Park touchwud stunt. A 'PROTESTANT' asked, 'What must our soldiers think of this proceeding?' and concluded, 'I do trust this form of idolatry will be abolished in our Army and Navy at any rate.'[154] The military authorities had no such intention, though. They were deeply concerned with maintaining morale, and it was obvious that no matter how seriously they were considered or not by soldiers and sailors, any attempt to ban charms and talismans, as the German military had tried, would be counterproductive. A thought piece in the provincial press, responding to the concerns of 'A soldier's mother' and 'PROTESTANT', summed up the more general moderate view. There was a big difference between worshipping graven idols and wearing amulets in the vague hope they would bring luck. Such 'superstition' might be foolish and wrong, it suggested, but 'one yet sees at work the better part of man's nature. If it should happen, then, that our fighting men begin to attach transcendental properties to charms, there is no harm done, and good may result.'[155]

Interest in the psychology and psychiatry of warfare generated observations on how the wearing of talismans and mascots was symptomatic of male infantilization when under extreme conditions. One journalistic report in 1915 noted, for instance, 'In St Thomas's Hospital every man had some mascot. It might be a baby doll with "thumbs up", a woolly cat, a Teddy bear, or perhaps a "Chilly Billy!", but some sort of toy every man had in bed with him. And no baby in the children's ward played more assiduously with its gifts than did these huge, bandaged fellows.' Similarly, an Australian wrote to the press in October 1918, 'we are not going to laugh at our soldiers if, setting out into the Great Unknown of Warfare, they, like little children, adopt the old charms of childhood. If little childish things can interest and amuse them in the short respites from their dreadful task who is going to scoff? Not I.'[156] The Welsh psychoanalyst Ernest Jones, who saw sexual symbolism everywhere, could not help but find Freudian significance in all this. In a 1918 paper on 'The Theory of Symbolism' he claimed that in earlier ages charms, talismans, and amulets were almost exclusively based on Oedipal genital symbolism, and that over the millennia the preoccupation with the protection of sexual organs became a concern with safety more generally, 'as is pathetically shown on a large scale in the present war'. For Jones, the war brought out atavistic tendencies in the psyche. 'Anxious relatives who press a horseshoe or a "fums up" on their man when he leaves for the front have not the faintest idea of the meaning of their superstitious act,' he wrote, 'but that this meaning is not simply a historical one can often be shown by analysis of their dreams, when the true symbolism becomes apparent.'[157]

But some argued that there was a positive psychological function and purpose in the masculine carrying of protective devices, even if it appeared regressive in behavioural terms. Charles Parsons, looking back a couple of decades on from the war, reflected that 'probably we were wrong in being superstitious. But we believed in our talismans and charms and, since they brought us through, who can say that we weren't right?' Writing in the journal *Folklore* in 1930, H. W. Howes similarly spoke from personal experience of the war when he questioned if it really mattered whether luck rituals in the trenches were 'some remote belief altered to suit the circumstances'. 'Is it not more important to discover whether it served any function between 1914–1918?,' he asked. In answer to his own question, he noted that it 'had the psychological effect of bracing the nerve under the terrible strain'.[158] One recent study on the psychology of 'superstition' echoes his thoughts. It questions the evidence behind the common assumption in psychological litera-ture that 'superstitions' such as triskaidekaphobia signify poor psycho-logical adjustment in individuals, linked to anxiety and obsessive behaviour. Its authors point out that most of the testing conducted in the past focused on negative 'superstitions' concerning *avoidance* of bad luck as distinct from those positive 'superstitions' that sought the *promotion* of good luck, such as keeping fingers crossed and wearing lucky charms. A survey of the latter revealed that people engaging with these types of activity seemed to exhibit greater levels of optimism, emotional balance, and self-efficacy.[159] But to understand further the relationship between fear, fate, and faith in wartime, we need to move on and see how people drew upon religion as a form of protection as well.

6

TRENCH FAITH AND PROTECTION

Has he not witnessed strange things away in that unimaginable world called 'The Front'? Things that one does not refer to in broad daylight, but which nevertheless obtrude themselves and haunt the mind when shadows fall. Orthodox religion does not attract him. It is too comfortable, too respectful, too self-satisfied, but he feels acutely the nearness of the Unknown and the strange, unaccountable chances of war.

(*The Globe*, 18 November 1916)

On both sides of the conflict there were religious voices couching it as a crusade, whether French and Italian Catholics, Russian Orthodox priests, American evangelicals, or German Lutherans. It was a modern-day Christian struggle against evil, and national destinies were portrayed in apocalyptic terms. Each side argued they were divinely tasked to purify a degraded Christian Europe.[1] The British were denounced as puffed up with empire and wallowing in the sin of arrogance, while the German state was portrayed as faithless and anti-Christian. One French commentator confidently predicted victory against 'the armies of the Devil, against the hordes of Luther'. American evangelists preached about the 'demonic Hun'. In 1915 the outspoken bishop of London, Arthur Winnington-Ingram, said the task of the Church of England was to 'mobilise the nation for a holy war'. Similar crusading rhetoric was common amongst Catholic and Protestant German clergy early on. Calvinist conceptions of predestination fuelled nationalist rhetoric. In August 1914 one pastor preached in Leipzig, 'this gigantic episode in world history we are living through is an act of the divine world judgement. We, however, salute the world judge as our nation's saviour.'[2] Christianity was not the only major religion concerned, of course. The Ottoman state issued a formal declaration of 'holy war' in November

1914 for political and propagandist purposes to mobilize popular support in the Muslim world.[3]

A Church of England committee report on religion in the British Army published in 1919 observed, 'the idea of salvation by death in battle for one's country has been widely prevalent, and is one of those points in which the religion of the trenches has rather a Moslem than a Christian colour'.[4] It was referring to the representation in word and image of the Tommies as Christian soldiers marching onward, as 'holy warriors' sacrificing themselves for God and country, doing their duty in honour of Christ. The same report made clear, though, that in the face of the rhetoric and the work of army chaplains, few soldiers thought of themselves in this way. And, despite the keen hopes of the churches, there was, furthermore, no great renewal or revival of organized Christian devotion in the trenches or, indeed, on the home front. The vicar of St Thomas, Dudley, was not alone in bemoaning in 1916 that the wives and mothers of men at war were failing to turn up and pray for them in church.[5] Instead, the war engendered a greater degree of national religious consciousness.[6] It also reinforced the ardour of already strong communities of faith, such as Catholicism in Brittany and the Welsh evangelical revival movement that had begun in 1904.[7] There is no doubt, furthermore, that the war created a theatre for religious devotion where the notions of fate and luck we explored in Chapter 5 significantly shaped the ways in which faith and religiosity were expressed.

The terms 'diffuse Christianity' and 'emergency religion' were used at the time in English clerical literature to describe what was defined as a pervasive adherence to a non-dogmatic form of faith, which was concerned more with a personal moral code for daily life and succour in the face of fear than a guide to devotion in honour of God. Soldiers' religious understanding and practices were, furthermore, considered ill-defined or unstable depending on circumstances.[8] These terms are essentially period-specific formulations for what historians, sociologists, and ethnographers have variously called vernacular, folk, or popular religion.[9] Whatever term is used, and there is a scholarly debate about their relative value, they all attempt to encapsulate the ways in which people borrowed from orthodox religious practice and liturgy, and used and adapted official texts and sacraments for practical rather than spiritual ends. In this sense, faith was rooted in pragmatic personal need rather than in spiritual attainment or atonement, though its individual expressions were usually understood and shared by whole communities. The result of such popular acts of faith, if positive, still often ended with thanks to God, and bolstered the pertinence of religion to the experience and survival of war.

Bible Protection

The war presented unprecedented evangelical opportunities. The battle-fields of Europe contained the most intense concentration of biblical literature there had ever been. British agencies such as the SPCK, YMCA, and the British and Foreign Bible Society distributed millions of bibles during the war. In October 1914 alone the evangelical Chaplain-General of the armed forces, Bishop John Taylor Smith, received half a million copies donated by the Scripture Gift Mission for distribution amongst the troops. It has been estimated that some 40 million bibles, prayer books, and other items of religious literature were distributed amongst British military personnel between 1914 and 1916. In 1917 the Canadian Bible Society reported it had distributed 300,000 khaki pocket New Testaments to Canadian soldiers before they left for Europe. The Bible Society of Ireland distributed 200,000 volumes in sixty languages.[10] When America joined the war, the floodgates opened further. Various American organizations such as the World's Sunday School Associ-ation, American Bible Society, and American Tract Society raised funds to send large numbers. It was estimated at the beginning of 1918 that some 1,200,000 Testaments and Gospels had been shipped from America up to that point. During the entirety of the conflict the Ameri-can Bible Society and the American YMCA distributed 4,558,871 pocket bibles and New Testaments to soldiers and sailors.[11] And this was just the Allied side. Consider, now, the vast flows of similar religious litera-ture that poured onto the battlefields from the presses of France, Germany, Belgium, the Austro-Hungarian Empire, Italy, and Russia.

How many people in the past carried bibles on their person all the time? Very few, because of their size and weight in the first few centuries of printing, and then because clothing styles did not make it easy. When print production techniques allowed miniaturization and clothing was designed with pockets to carry small books, then the meaning of and relationship with the Bible and related literature changed. In this respect the Bible was more than Holy Writ in First World War battlefield life:

it was an intimate object that was used to store cards and letters from loved ones, and a place to write personal reflections. There were also those who carried a bible but held no reverence for it or any sentimental value. An American Bible Society member reported that on one occasion, in 1917, when free pocket Scriptures were being handed out to troops, he overheard a soldier advising all his comrades to accept them. They were printed on nice paper he told them, 'and just the right size with which to roll cigarettes, and that he had already smoked through to II Corinthians'.[12]

The bible as a physical object had long been used in popular magic for divination, healing, and good fortune. Not having a bible in the house was considered unlucky at the time, and people kept bibles under their pillows to prevent night-time restlessness and snoring.[13] It is no surprise, then, that for many soldiers these pocket bibles came to have talismanic value. A correspondent of the *Manchester Guardian* observed in May 1918 that pocket New Testaments were in huge demand by soldiers who had absolutely no intention of reading them. They were desired as talismans, and the complete New Testament was favoured for this purpose, as penny pocket Gospels were not considered to be as effective.[14]

One of the iconic artefacts of the Great War is the bible pierced by an enemy bullet or piece of shrapnel. Dozens survive today in private hands and collections across the old warring countries. During the 2014 centenary commemorations numerous examples were reported in the media and displayed by museums.[15] It was a morale-boosting public narrative at the time of the war, with regional and local newspapers reporting or showcasing numerous instances. In 1915 the Bible House of the Bible Society of Ireland in Sackville Street (now O'Connell Street), Dublin displayed a bible with a piece of shrapnel lodged in it. The owner, a sapper in the Royal Engineers, sent it to the society with a letter explaining: 'I want another Bible; this one you gave me was absolutely ruined by a piece of shell which pierced almost half way through it. Without doubt it saved my life.' The same year, another example was on public display amongst a range of British and German artefacts in a free exhibition in Coventry organized by the *Birmingham Gazette* to illustrate life in the trenches.[16] In the spring of 1918 19-year-old William R. Wilson of New Castle, Pennsylvania, was recovering in a Picardy hospital after having been picked out by a German sniper.

The bullet hit him in the arm, but another was deflected by the New Testament and trench mirror he carried in his breast pocket. Wilson became a minor American newspaper sensation for apparently being the first American of the war to be so saved. According to his friends, Wilson was a daily reader of the Bible, and he told a journalist, 'I have always been fond of the Bible. I certainly will never go without one after this.'[17]

Wartime stories of the Bible stopping bullets and so saving lives were nothing new. They were reported during the English Civil War of the mid-seventeenth century, and also circulated after major American Civil War battles.[18] But considering the sheer number of combatants, the amount of munitions whizzing about, and the tens of millions of bibles carried in breast pockets during the First World War, it is statistically likely that hundreds of lives were saved in this manner. Those soldiers who had the experience obviously considered themselves extremely lucky, but was something more than chance involved? Was it providential? In other words, had God interceded and protected them?

The Anglican evangelist the Reverend John Stuart Holden, whose pulpit in St Paul's Church, Portman Square, London, was draped with the Union Jack during the war, told an audience at an American religious conference in 1916 how one of his parishioners had been saved after a bullet lodged in a bible kept in his hip pocket. A general told the soldier, 'It must be very precious to you if it saved your life.' 'Oh, sir,' he replied, 'it saved my soul long ago.' 'So many are the cases in which a Testament in the pocket has stopped a bit of shrapnel from reaching a vital organ', Holden observed, 'that the men have become almost superstitious about carrying one.'[19] Holden's own sense of providence had been informed by the fact that in 1912 he was booked on the fateful voyage of the *Titanic*, but pulled out of the trip the day before because his wife had fallen ill. For the rest of his life Holden kept the ticket above his desk in an envelope on which he wrote 'Who Redeemeth Thy Life from Destruction'. When the Reverend J. M. Richardson, Queen Anne Street, United Free Church, Dunfermline, reported on his experiences in France working among the troops in connection with the YMCA, he noted several accounts of bullets being stopped by the New Testament, including that of Private William Milne, of Shepherd's Loan, Dundee. The bullet passed through a package of letters and a pay book before lodging in his New Testament. It stopped at the 8th Psalm, which tells of God's kindness.

Richardson concluded that 'it was not hard to let the soldier know that God had been kind to him in this rare experience'.[20]

As this anecdote suggests, the providential message was further reinforced by accounts of bullets stopping at prophetic passages in the Bible. When Private Bailey, 11th Manchesters, was shot by a sniper in Gallipoli on 14 September 1915, the bible he carried in his breast pocket shielded his heart. The bullet passed through a passage in chapter 8 of Esther, on the page which Bailey had bookmarked: 'For how can I endure to see the evil that shall come unto my people? Or how can I endure to see the destruction of my kindred?' Two days later Bailey was shot in the hand and shipped back to England.[21] In August 1915 an account was published of the experience of Lance Corporal Duckworth of the Lancashire Fusiliers, 7th Salford Battalion, son of W. A. Duckworth, director of Bury Football Club. On one occasion Duckworth had met an Australian in hospital who was the last of his section surviving from the Dardanelles campaign. The Australian related that, having seen his mate shot dead in a bayonet charge, he had, in the heat of battle, stopped to retrieve his pocket Old Testament from his body, knowing that his father had given it to him. Placing the Old Testament in his own left breast pocket, the Australian continued in the charge and was shot through his left arm, the bullet lodging in the bible. It stopped at Jeremiah 38:2 and 3, with verse 2 tellingly stating: 'Whoever stays in this city will die by the sword, famine or plague, but whoever goes over to the Babylonians will live. They will escape with their lives; they will live.' Duckworth said, 'we were all amazed when we found this out. It seemed like something supernatural.'[22] There seemed to be a further divine message in the case of Private Tom Fox, 2nd Battalion Cameron Highlanders. Not only did the bullet stop at St John's Gospel, piercing some personal letters en route, but it was noteworthy that the bullet did not spoil the two photos of Her Royal Highness that Fox also kept in his breast pocket.[23]

For all those promoting such providential stories, there were other clerical and lay voices that decried and rubbished them as 'superstition' and not religion. The chaplain Edmund Banks Smith recalled in 1917: 'I presented a Bible to a soldier on one occasion and he accepted it in rather a grouchy sort of way, and said, "Well, Chaplain, this may stop a bullet." I replied, "Yes, my man, it may stop a bullet, but do you realize that a pack of cards will stop a bullet better than the Bible?... Now, don't take the Bible for that sort of life preserver." [24] The New Zealand travel writer and First World War soldier Hector Macquarrie also touched on the matter in his 1917 guide for American soldiers about preparing for life at the front. Macquarrie had served at Ypres, was invalided to Britain in mid-1916, and was subsequently sent to Pennsylvania to oversee munitions production for the British war effort:

> I might advise you to take a bible with you and read it. Your mother will give you one. You have all read of bibles stopping bullets as all that sort of thing pleases certain people, and the clergy are able to make use of such instances in their sermons. But there is little that is romantic about it, for a bullet is a funny thing, and can be affected in strange ways...A bullet will take the way of least resistance; when it knocks against anything hard or tough, it will not merely stop, but will tend to go aside, and therefore a bible in a man's breast pocket will tend to turn it aside and make it continue in a circle away from the man's body—but it might easily hurt the next fellow! It always seems wrong to suggest the interference of God in warfare. [25]

The satirical trench newspaper the *B.E.F. Times* made fun of the religious and media preoccupation, producing a spoof advertisement offering 'bullets carefully fixed in Bibles'. [26]

Letters from Heaven

Known as *Himmelsbriefe* in Germany, *lettres du ciel* in France, and Saviour's Letters in Britain, these missives from the skies were venerable pieces of apocrypha that began circulating in the early medieval period. They purported to be copies of letters sent by Christ in heaven for the benefit of humankind. The Sunday Epistle was one example of the genre, which stated that Christ wrote it in his own blood or in gold, and let it fall to earth. It exhorted people to observe the Sabbath strictly and warned backsliders of the dire consequences if they did not. Another claimed to be a correspondence between Christ and King Abgarus of Edessa, who, legend had it, was one of the first kings to convert to Christianity. This letter was purportedly found under a stone centuries later. [27] In the eighteenth and nineteenth centuries these letters were still popular and being sold in large numbers across northern and western Europe in cheap broadside formats. Some versions claimed to be letters found

Fig. 6.1. A fine example of a protective *Himmelsbrief*, popular among German soldiers during the First World War.

in the recent past, with eighteenth-century German examples claiming the letter floated from heaven and appeared in Holstein in variously 1724, 1728, and 1791. Sometimes they also included quotes from biblical texts such as the Epistles, along with a list of Christ's cures. They were pasted on cottage walls to protect the dwelling from fire, stuck above the bed, or folded and kept on the person to avert misfortunes in childbirth, as often explicitly directed in the letters. They also served a more general protective function against witchcraft and evil spirits.[28]

During the First World War such Letters from Heaven were repurposed for military needs. Russian soldiers fixed copies to their rifles, and they were carried quite widely by American soldiers of German extraction. One Pennsylvanian printer recalled how, shortly after America declared war on Germany, he received a small print order from a local village for one to two hundred copies of a sheet bearing 'A Letter for Protection'. It was a *Himmelsbrief* which began, 'Whoever carries this letter with him he shall not be damaged through the enemy's guns or weapons.' They were to be distributed to soldiers from several Pennsylvanian counties.[29] The tradition was strongest in Germany, where numerous printed examples from the nineteenth and early twentieth century show a reduced emphasis on Sunday observance and a greater concern with protection from bleeding, enemy artillery, guns, and bullets. A transcript of a *Himmelsbrief* from 1915 confirms the emphasis on 'stilling' guns and weapons.[30] The following example belonged to a Berlin member of the *Landwehr* or reservist force:

Letter, written by my own hands
If you refrain from sin with good deeds, keep the Sabbath and live in awe of God, you will receive eternal salvation; yet if not I will punish you with fire, plague, hunger, war and eternal punishment. I will cause war one against the other, one master against the other, the daughter against her mother. One brother against the other, one sister against the other, one city against another and I will withdraw my hand from you because of your injustice and will grab you and devour you; and afterwards I will come down to earth with thunder and lightning and double-bladed swords, so that you recognize my wrath in the divine justice, because you are working on Sundays. Out of fatherly love have I so far preserved you, otherwise you would long have been condemned because of your injustice.

I command you, young as well as old, that you attend church more eagerly and confess your sins, during your confession you will have to be insulted by your neighbour. Beware the suppression of the poor, but help those in need.

Whoever does not believe in this letter, shall not attain eternal salvation, but whoever carries this letter with him and lets others read and copy this letter, shall have his sins [forgiven], even if he has sins onto him like stars in the sky or sand corns in the sea.

Yet, those who read the letter and do not copy it and do not keep it in their house, have no blessing, those who do not pass it on to be read and copied shall be damned. Now, I order you that you keep my commandments, as Jesus Christ has taught. In the name of God (✠), the Father (✠), the Son (✠), and the Holy Spirit (✠). Amen. Those who carry the blessing, which is said below, with them, will not come to any harm, will not be wounded by any loaded gun, because these are the words of God, which reinforce the Divine and that you need not fear. This letter protects against everything: bullets, enemies, thieves, robbers, and all ailments; through the following words and through the name of our Lord Jesus Christ and with God all ailments, swords, guns, and artillery can be protected.

1) Stand still all visible and invisible guns, so that you won't attack me, by the command of our Lord Jesus Christ, who was baptized by John in the river Jordan.

2) Stand still, all visible and invisible guns and weapons, through Holy Baptism, God, who suffered and died for us, have mercy on us as our almighty God.

3) Stand still all visible and invisible guns and weapons, so that you won't attack me, by the command of the Holy Spirit.

In the name of the Father (✠), the Son (✠) and the Holy Spirit (✠).

This *Himmelsbrief* has the following addition attached to it:

Those who may not believe these aforesaid words, may write them on a notepaper and attach this to a dog, then try and shoot him and you will see you won't hit him.

In the name of Jesus, as true as this is written, as true as Christ has died and is risen, can those who believe in this letter not suffer physical harm. I pray that all guns and arms will not kill me today, in the name of the Father (✠), the Son (✠) and the Holy Spirit (✠) and all the saints. God the Father should come between all bullets. Amen.

Those who carry this prayer from house to house will be blessed, but those who mock it will be cursed. Also the house, in which he resides, will not be hit by thunder and lightning, also at last, those who say or hear this prayer will see a sign in the sky 3 days before their deaths.

Amen[31]

Himmelsbriefe were an aspect of a broader German *Schutzbriefe* ('protection letters') tradition. The *Schutzbriefe* usually included a mix of prayers, quotes from pertinent Bible passages, and magical formulas tailored to the protection of the individual or the home; in wartime they were often *Kugelsegen* or 'bullet blessings' to prevent being shot. Many examples of *Schutzbriefe* were found on dead Prussian soldiers on the battlefields of the German-Danish War of 1864, the Austro-Prussian War of 1866, and the Franco-Prussian War of 1870. When, in July 1900, German troops were to set sail for China to suppress the Boxer rebellion it was reported that a patriotic craftsman from Silesia sent Kaiser Wilhelm his *Schutzbrief* to be copied for the benefit of the departing soldiers.[32] There was considerable scholarly and public interest in the continued vitality of this tradition. In 1917 the folklorist Oskar Ebermann, known for his study of blood and wound blessings in legend and tradition, gave a talk to German colleagues which discussed the letters and prayers of protection carried by the *poilus*.[33] From the other side, French newspaper articles on the literature found in the possession of dead and wounded German soldiers noted the ubiquity of *Himmelsbriefe*, and in January 1915 the press reported that one German general had banned his troops from possessing *Himmelsbriefe*, in part to stop people profiting from exploiting his soldiers.[34]

The German Protestant clergy were particularly critical of people's misplaced faith in what they saw as pernicious pseudo-pious talismans that perverted true piety. The eminent German theologian and future American professor Paul Tillich, who was a Lutheran chaplain in the German Army throughout the war, wrote in a sermon in 1914: 'Our strength? A splinter from a grenade, and the strongest is gone! Death is

Fig. 6.2. An example of a protective *Schutzbrief* with military imagery worn by German soldiers.

strong. Mysterious powers, *Himmelsbriefe* and charms? Some cling to them. But it gives them no rest.' In June 1915 the Lutheran pastor Karl Schwartzlose gave a sermon in St Catherine's Church, Frankfurt, in which he reflected on why the 'superstitious' continued to resort to

Himmelsbriefe in times of war.[35] There was concern about their popularity on the home front as well as in the trenches. In October 1914 Johannes Meyersieck, pastor of Oetinghausen, wrote of his worries in a letter to his congregation. He was aware that a number of them kept *Schutzbriefe* in their pockets or in a neck pouch. He praised one member for daring to show him a copy. He did not want to scold his brethren, but told them of his sadness that such practices continued to flourish. His cautious tone was understandable. Another clergyman noted he had received nothing but 'hate and persecution' in 1915 after admonishing from the pulpit a farmer's wife in the parish who had been handing out *Schutzbriefe* to every departing soldier. 'All such incantations have no value,' said Meyersieck to his flock. 'Reliance on *Himmelsbriefe* is folly and sin, but some of the warnings that are at the end inviting you to live as pious, honest German soldiers are good and useful.' Instead, he urged soldiers to keep a copy of Psalm 121, which could be copied from several published hymnals for the military. 'But do not just carry it in your pocket, but in the heart,' he urged. 'This psalm also does not make you "bullet-proof".'[36]

'Heaven letters' were also related to a wider tradition of religious chain letters. Examples of these disseminated widely across the combatant countries, despite condemnation by both Protestant and Catholic churches. French parish magazines repeatedly warned their flocks of the danger. In October 1914 one noted that while lots of good prayers were circulating in the parish at the present time, there were those that were truly 'superstitious'. Parishioners were to beware of such, and only accept those that were signed by a bishop or other holy representative. Another instructed its flock, and also those male parishioners at the front, to 'Watch out', and warned them not to recopy or send such letters to nine people.[37] So what did these chain letters contain? The following example was found circulating amongst Italian troops:

Prayer that must be sent to all the soldiers at the front

Merciful Lord, I implore and beg your pity for us, and to pardon us from our sins by the virtue of your precious blood, to be one day eternally with you.

This prayer to be written for nine days and sent to nine different people, to begin the day it has been received. Whosoever refuses to do it will receive great punishments. Do not break the chain.

A French novena that circulated in 1915 was also overtly written for the war, and came with the instruction that it had to be spread across the whole battlefront:

> Oh! Jesus, I just beseech your aid.
> Heart of Jesus, save France.
> Protect us from German bullets,
> Joanne of Arc, save us.
> Saint Michael, pray for us.[38]

An English example that circulated in October 1914 contained the advice:

> It was said in the time of Jesus that all who wrote it were free from all calamities, and all who passed it by met with misfortune. Please re-copy it during nine days to nine different people and on the 9th you will experience some great joy. Please do not break the chain. Be sure and do it for God's sake.[39]

Something similar, distributed as 'An Ancient Prayer' for victory in the war, was received by the archbishop of Dublin in January 1917. At the opening of a church fund raising sale he described the content of the chain letter, saying the pious words it contained 'were good' but the prayer was not a bit ancient. He told his audience 'that this was a most gross superstition, and he hoped they would not encourage it if they got messages of that kind. Prayer did not depend for efficacy upon its volume or length, but upon its intensity.'[40] When, in the autumn of 1917, residents of Rushville, Indiana, began to receive in their post similar chain letters containing a prayer for soldiers, the local newspaper suspected the enemy was at work, concluding it was a 'typical pro-German scheme' to hamper the war effort by clogging up the American postal system.[41]

There were other vehicles for carrying religious protective words that were overtly talismanic in form and function. British soldiers wore coins made by several British firms that had the head of George V on one side and the Lord's Prayer on the other. An American jeweller even sold the Lord's Prayer engraved on a gold pin that could be read with a magnifying glass.[42] The biblical inscription 'MIZPAH' became popular on American and British lockets, rings, and brooches during the second half of the nineteenth century. The Mizpah (meaning a watch post) referred to the line in Genesis 31:49, 'The Lord watch between me and thee, when we are absent, one from another.' As this passage suggests, such items were generally given to loved ones as protective mementos, and they were popular amongst soldiers and their loved ones during the Boer War and the 1914–18 conflict.[43] In August 1918, for instance, the American company D. M. Read advertised a 'Good Luck Charm for Soldiers', which was a metal pocket piece with a four-leaf clover on one side and the Mizpah benediction on the other side.[44]

The carrying of religious words and texts was not only integral to popular religious devotion, but was also central to overtly magical practices. The boundary between magic and religion was often open and malleable in popular culture, and depended on the context in which religious verses or words were used and for what. The following German verse, which was written down and placed on soldiers' wounds to heal them instantly, was, in practice and purpose, a charm rather than a prayer: 'Bin nostensbenstens, nomen, Sebusch, Heronewent, Jesus, Marie, Joseph.'[45] The clergyman Charles Calippe collected several similar unofficial 'prayers' that circulated widely amongst the French soldiery. One used 'to guard against firearms' consisted of the following nonsensical mix of Latin and French: 'Prière. Eccé, Crucem, donini, fugité, parlès, adversé, vicis, l'eodé, Tribu, Juda + faire le signe de la croix, radix, clavo.' It came with the instructions that if the owner recited it three times in the morning, he would be preserved from all peril and death, and ensure all enemies would be vanquished.[46] This charm is similar to the sort of garbled mix of holy, magical, and mundane words and symbols that often made up the arsenal of protective charms supplied by cunning folk, or could be found in popular printed and manuscript manuals of magic that had circulated since the eighteenth century. There is very little evidence that these popular grimoires, which contained written charms for protection, wounds, and ensuring a good shot, were carried and used by soldiers during the First World War, but there was certainly a long tradition of their usage in the German, Swiss, Scandinavian, and Russian military for protection against bullets. *The Sixth and Seventh Books of Moses* was particularly popular in early twentieth-century Germany, while a common American manual of charms with German origins, Hohman's *Long Lost Friend*, was also reprinted in cheap formats at the time, and contained charms for guns and a good shot.[47]

One tantalizing hint that magic books circulated in the trenches, as they did in the French and German countryside at the time, comes from the

Swiss folklorist Hanns Bächtold-Stäubli. In his work as a military censor, he was informed in September 1915 that a regimental commander had confiscated a copy of the *Clavicula Salomonis*, one of the most venerable grimoires, from one of his soldiers and handed it over to the authorities. It contained various magical circles for protection against thunder and lightning, enemies, and death.[48] After having consulted cartomancers as well as an old wise woman, a farmer's wife named Minna Falkenhain of Saxony-Anhalt wrote to her husband at the front in October 1915, stating that she would send him some ashes, which he was instructed to throw towards the morning sun while saying a charm that began:

> O great Adonay, Eloim, Ariel and Jehovah!
> I honour the value and glory of thy power
> I shed the blood of this sacrifice
> and scatter the ashes thereof into the air.
> Be gracious o great Adonay.
> Take me under your protection.[49]

Adonay and Elohim are Hebraic names for Lord or God and Ariel is an angel. These were words of power, magical terms one finds rarely in official Christian prayers but frequently in grimoires and the conjurations and charms of learned magicians and cunning folk. Magic clearly was going on in the trenches.

The Catholic Armoury

It was not just words that could protect or heal. The Catholic Church had an arsenal of sacramental objects that acted as a religious insurance policy against harm. In April 1915 the army chaplain the Reverend P. O'Farrell delivered a sermon to the 5th Battalion, Royal Irish Regiment, in St Mel's Cathedral, Longford. They were soon to depart for the war, and he 'appealed to them to procure medals, scapulars, and, above all, that each man provide himself with Rosary Beads'. He then related miraculous instances of survival in the trenches due to confidence in and prayers to the Virgin Mary.[50] The French military tried to maintain a degree of separation between church and military affairs, and some public tensions arose over the wearing of such religious emblems in the army. In August 1917 General Pétain reminded officers of the religious neutrality of the French State and that 'they must abstain from any act of a religious nature'.[51] Other Catholic countries, however, embraced the motivational potential of the union of sacred and martial purpose.

Across the Catholic combatant countries, if soldiers did not already wear crosses from civilian life, then they were given wartime ones from one source or another. During a Catholic parade at Locre (Loker), Belgium, in 1917, for instance, the 6th Connaught Rangers were given miniature crucifixes that had been blessed by the Pope.[52] Most crucifixes were given by loved ones rather than through such official ceremonies, though. They were one of the common gifts that French and Belgian women gave to soldiers in gratitude. Private J. Moore of the Cheshire Regiment, a member of the Protestant Reformers' Memorial Church, told how he had helped some abused Belgian women and had been given a small crucifix in return, while Private Frederick Edwards of the 2nd Essex Regiment related being given one by a little Belgian girl, who was killed by a shell blast a few minutes later. While some were kept as souvenirs, others were imbued with talismanic potency. A driver of the Royal Field Artillery wrote, 'I think I owe all my luck to a mascot which I carry in my knapsack.' It was a silver and enamel crucifix given to him by a Frenchwoman he had helped out of danger. It is noteworthy that he did not carry it on his person, and one suspects that it was common for non-Catholics to carry such items in their sacks rather than visibly around their necks or in their tunics.[53] There were the inevitable accounts of crucifixes saving lives, like pocket bibles. In March 1917 it was reported that a Catholic soldier, Corporal Goulden, Royal Engineers, had his life saved when a German bullet struck the crucifix he kept in his breast pocket, breaking it in two.[54]

There were numerous marvelling reports from British soldiers of the miraculous way in which crucifixes remained standing in the battle zone while all else had been obliterated. In May 1915, for example, Sergeant G. Forrest, Hampshires, wrote to a friend about his experiences while recovering in an English hospital. 'A most astonishing thing to me was to see the life-size crucifixes all over the country,' he remarked. 'Now it may be a coincidence, but it is strange that however bad a place had been shelled, the Crucifix with the figure of the Saviour looking mutely down, stood intact, though in many cases pitted with rifle bullets.'[55]

Such experiences of the Catholic landscapes of France and Belgium, and the personal value placed on crucifixes gifted to Protestant soldiers, helped feed a revival of the cross in Anglican iconography and practice. This led to concerns by some in the Church. In September 1915 the Reverend F. E. d'A. Willis, vicar of St Stephen's Church, Burnley, wrote in his parish magazine why he had abandoned his intention to have a large cross carried at a recent parish procession. The idea had been criticized as being 'too Roman'. But Willis countered, it is 'the Christian Banner, the symbol and sign of our faith', and 'we are surely not so stupid as to worship the cross'.[56] The Reverend H. Cotton-Smith, vicar of Bourne Abbey Church, Lincolnshire, displayed no such caution. In January 1916 he gave a marketplace address in which he declared the cross was 'now their torch, other lights being restricted'. He talked of the reports of the wonderful instances of wayside crucifixes surviving intact, of a soldier returned from the Dardanelles who had shown him a little crucifix he carried that had 'been through it all everywhere with him'. Cotton-Smith had personally given about three hundred small crosses to soldiers and sailors, which some fastened to their identification discs, and he received letters from others requesting them for their friends. The crosses were, he said, 'reminders to the men of their religion, their home, their Church', but went so far as to say that 'they might even turn a bullet and save a life'.[57]

By no means all crucifixes and crosses were mass-produced or officially blessed objects. One Italian officer from Calabria, for instance, carried a crudely cut cross made from a branch of holly.[58] Numerous examples exist of amulet crosses made by soldiers out of bullet cartridges serving either artistic, devotional, or protective functions.[59] A first-hand account of the fabrication of one such cross was reported in *The Scotsman* in 1916. The author explained how he was passing by the camp kitchen one day when he saw a man sharpening what he thought was a pencil. 'Getting ready to cheer them up at home?,' he asked.

> 'No, sir,' answered the lad. 'I'm doing a little fancy work,' and he held up a copper-coloured object just like the stump of a pencil. 'It's a French bullet without the cartridge,' he explained, and, reversing it, showed how he had pared away the blunt end till it assumed the form of a little cross on a double pedestal. The sharp point remained to prove its original character and purpose.

He had learned to make it by studying one given to him by a French soldier, and gladly gave the one he was just finishing to the author, who considered it a treasured possession. The object fascinated him. 'Its strangeness seems to challenge mind and soul,' he reflected. 'Two worlds meet here—the spiritual and the material, religion and war.'[60]

Sapper Clifford Perry wrote home to a friend in Cardiff, 'Rosaries are very popular here. I think I can safely say that four out of every ten men one meets wear them around their necks.' On the other side, southern Bavarian soldiers were particularly fond of their Marian rosaries, with one German army chaplain describing them as one of 'the best pastoral gifts for soldiers in the field'.[61] Many Italian soldiers also carried them, and rosaries taken from the coffins of the dead were particularly prized for their protective power. As this suggests, rosaries were not always used in the appropriate orthodox way, with some soldiers also twisting them around rifle barrels for luck. When a British soldier who had purchased a rosary in the streets of Ypres had his leg fractured in two places by a mortar shell, he refused to be taken to the dressing station until he had hold of his rosary from his pack. 'If I don't take it with me,' he said, 'I'd get hit again on the way down.'[62] As well as rosaries, Irish and Italian soldiers carried the Agnus Dei (Lamb of God), which was a small disc of wax with the figure of a lamb supporting a cross impressed upon it. One Irish soldier wrote home to say that he was 'well guarded' as he wore his father's Agnus Dei around his neck along with a pair of rosary beads and three medals.[63]

Catholic medals were undoubtedly even more ubiquitous than rosaries. In 1917 the London-based Irish journalist Michael MacDonagh included a substantive chapter on the religious emblems worn by Irish soldiers in his book *The Irish on the Somme*. Amongst the most popular items were the Medal of Our Lady of Perpetual Succour, and the French Our Lady of the Miraculous Medal revealed by the Immaculate Virgin to Catherine Labouré. The latter was offered by the Parisian pilgrimage chapel where a Marian vision appeared in 1830.[64] In his war diary Mussolini wrote in November 1915 of how nearly all his fellow Italian soldiers wore on their wrists medals of the Holy Virgin Mary, deemed efficacious again all evil and harm. As with secular amulets and mascots, Catholic medals were also usually a gift. The American fighter ace Charles Parsons explained how he and his fellow pilots were regularly given religiously blessed *médailles* by French women on visits to Paris, the most popular being those depicting various virgin saints and St Elijah, the patron saint of aviators. All aviators wore such talismans,

Fig. 6.3. These figurines of Joan of Arc (on the left) and the Virgin Mary (on the right) kept in little lead capsules were very popular among French soldiers, and no doubt found their way into the pockets of other Allied soldiers.

to the extent that 'a man's length of service could be approximated by the number of medals he had jangling on his wrist. Some of the old-timers had to wear chains on each wrist to hold them.'[65] In a letter thanking a Glasgow Convent School for sending 1,200 religious medals to his men, an officer from a Scottish regiment explained that they wore them on the same cord to which their identitfication discs were tied.[66] The Italian Lieutenant Antonio Parma wrote home in 1916 how his captain's wife had sent a box of religious medals which the captain distributed amongst his men. The next day three companies were involved in heavy fighting at the cost of fifty lives, but in his company only one person was killed and ten wounded thanks to the medals. The captain had been sceptical, but subsequently placed a cross and a medal around his own neck. Parma added that even the most cynical wore medals, if sometimes only in memory of the wives and children who had given them. They were not only worn for protection from death and bullets: medals of St Benedict were carried to protect from the rain, and those of St Vitus against animal bites.[67]

One hears little, though, of the wearing of St Christopher medals for safe journeys until toward the end of the war, though they had already become popular among the small but growing band of early automobilists. One of the first 'lucky piece' St Christopher talismans struck in America explicitly for the war effort was produced in the summer of 1918 by Karl H. Martin of Buffalo, New York. It was designed to be carried in the pocket or on the instrument board of aeroplanes. Struck in bronze, it bore the verse:

> He who owns this talisman
> Shall protected be
> From all perils of the air,
> Of the land, and sea.

Around the edge was the inscription in French *Invoque Saint Christophe Il Sera Ta Sauvegarde* ('Trust in Saint Christopher he will be thy safeguard'), and on the face was the typical image of the saint wading through water with his staff, but now with his right hand pointing to aircraft and torpedo boat destroyers in the background.[68] It would become a much more popular military amulet during and after the Second World War.[69]

Amongst the Irish and Italian soldiery, the brown scapular of St Mary of Mount Carmel was very popular.[70] These devotional objects usually consisted of two rectangular pieces of cloth bearing religious images or texts, connected by two lengths of cloth or cord. They were worn over the shoulder so that one rectangle rested against the chest and the other the back. While some scapulars, like the brown scapular of St Mary of Mount Carmel, have medieval origins, they became increasingly in demand in popular Catholic piety during the nineteenth and early twentieth centuries. The Pope approved a range of new ones in response, and a few years before the war the papacy also granted that scapular medals could be worn instead of cloth scapulars. One explanation for the advent of scapular medals was so that devout, high-society Catholic ladies could wear décolleté gowns. But apparently their creation was due to a petition in 1909 by the Vicar Apostolic of the Belgian Congo. He wrote to the Pope complaining that cloth scapulars quickly became soiled and dirty rags due to the dirt and heat of African life and the fact that converted natives wore them on their bare chests.[71] The mud and sweat of trench life likewise made scapular badges hugely popular amongst soldiers. They were handed out in their hundreds of thousands. When the international Catholic magazine *The Tablet* launched its Rosary and Prayer Book Fund in October 1914, for instance, every sixpence received funded a devotional pack for a wounded Catholic in the French field hospitals, containing a scapular medal, rosary, and a Sacred Heart badge.[72] For much of the war the Reverend Patrick Boyle, priest of Hednesford Our Lady of Lourdes Church, Staffordshire, England, put notices in the Irish press promoting his fund raising and offering to send a Lourdes scapular medal to every Catholic soldier and sailor whose name and address was sent to him on stamped envelope.[73]

The sheer demand for Catholic sacramentals, or blessed objects, inevitably opened up new commercial possibilities. Michael MacDonagh, writing in 1917, observed that rosaries, once the monopoly of religious institutions and repositories, were now for sale in every shop window. The London palmist Louise Hutchinson offered to obtain medals blessed by a Catholic priest from the London Oratory for her soldier clients. Retailers such as the 'Catholic Depot' in Motherwell, Scotland, did a lively trade. In 1918 it advertised that it sold wholesale and retail a 'Large Assortment of Rosary, Beads, Crosses, Badges, Medals, Scapulars, Medallions, Holy Water', while a Liverpool dealer, no doubt targeting Irish soldiers landing at the port, placed a notice in the *Liverpool Echo* stating he sold brown scapulars for a very modest penny.[74]

One of the reasons for the bonanza was that the Catholic armoury achieved popularity far beyond the Catholic faithful. MacDonagh

Fig. 6.4. A scapular medal from the First World War. These were hugely popular among Catholic soldiers on both sides of the conflict, and were also purchased and given to Protestants. The figure of the infant Jesus is represented handing a scapular to a worshipper.

collected evidence of how Protestant soldiers warmed to the message of ritual, miracle, and protection. He interviewed nuns at London convents who said they frequently received Protestant soldiers requesting medals and badges. One nun reported that she had, that very day, given fifty badges of the Sacred Heart to a private from the Royal Welsh Fusiliers for distribution amongst his regiment.[75] In November 1917, in preparation for the Feast of the Immaculate Conception at Lourdes, Patrick Boyle put out notices in the press that he would be conducting a double novena of Masses and prayers. It included a telling postscript. He now offered a Christmas letter and a Lourdes scapular medal to 'every soldier and sailor' and not just Catholics.[76] The French clergyman Charles Calippe observed how, when the British soldiers first arrived in the town of Albert, they readily accepted the ten to twelve dozen medals handed out by the local nuns, as well as the crucifixes and pocket rosaries they had, with demand soon outstripping supply.[77] A sapper named Clifford Perry, writing about the popularity of rosaries, observed that 'those who are not Catholics do not wear them as curios or ornaments either, as upon cases of inquiry they attach some religious value to them even though they cannot explain what it is. Still, no one could convince them to part with them.'[78]

Saints and Cults

Marian shrines boomed in France, Belgium, Italy, and Catholic Germany during the war as soldiers and their families sought the intercession of the Virgin. The Vatican approved novel forms of Marian devotion in Bavaria to boost popular enthusiasm, including a special blessing.[79] Pilgrimage sites produced their own promotional devotional publications to cash in financially and spiritually. Catholic soldiers created little shrines of their own on the battlefield and, while on leave, offered prayers at the nearest local sanctuary or embarked on pilgrimages to the main Marian or other shrines. Ex-votos were offered to the Virgin both during and after the war in thanks for evading death. These often took the form of a depiction of a miraculous escape during combat accompanied by a photo of the soldier concerned, an expression of thanks, and the inevitable donation. After surviving a battle, Italian soldiers sometimes clubbed together to send substantial sums of money along with a letter in gratitude to ensure continued divine protection.[80] The letters sometimes described their recent experiences of the war, such as that of Carlo Spagnolini in December 1915, who told of how had recently been involved in combat with Austrian troops and had prayed to St Damian, before requesting the saint not to forget him and ensure he came home healthy.[81]

Allied soldiers, sailors, aviators, and their relatives wrote hundreds of letters to the Carmelite religious establishment in Lisieux, Normandy, to give thanks to Sister Thérèse, who was referred to variously as 'their little sister of the trenches', 'their godmother of war', 'the saint of the *poilus*', and 'the shield of the soldiers'. Marie Françoise-Thérèse Martin died in 1897, and by the First World War she had a huge and international following, with Lisieux second only to Lourdes in terms of French pilgrimage destinations. Her beatification process had begun just before the outbreak of war, but was halted due to it. In 1920 a book of these letters, which ran to over 230 pages, was published as part of a renewed propaganda campaign for her beatification.[82] Hence the book contained the rather disingenuous proviso that any mention of miracles, her sainthood, and visions in the letters was not intended to influence the papal decision-making. The letters show the widespread wearing of her medals and images, and provide numerous examples of their protective power and the miraculous recovery of their wearers from serious or life-threatening injuries. Artilleryman Paul Dugast wrote in December 1914 of how, at the Battle of the Marne, he was nearly crushed by his cannon after falling over. But his 'little relic of Sister Thérèse' saved him, and just after his miraculous escape he took out of his pocket a white crayon and wrote in big letters on his cannon, 'Batterie Sr Thérèse de l'Enfant-Jésus'. Louis Tangay told how his feet had become so frozen in the trenches of Argonne that his toes had turned black. He was sent to a hospital, where a doctor gave him an image of Sister Thérèse and instructed him to say a novena. Four days later he took off the bandages to find his feet were completely healed. Camille Moranges related that, while at the front, a piece of shrapnel tore through his clothes, wallet, and papers, and was stopped only by the image he carried of Thérèse. A heavy artillery officer wrote in August 1916 to request medals and images for his regiment, which was composed of men from Brittany and the Vendee. They had been through some terrible times since the beginning of the war, but attributed their protection to the sister.[83] There were several second-hand accounts concerning North African Muslim soldiers. One concerned a doctor who noticed a devotional image of Thérèse on the chest of an injured Algerian rifleman named Djelida. 'What would Mohammed say to see that?,' asked the doctor. Djelida replied that Mohammed would say that he should keep it all his life. The superior of a hospice in Argentan wrote to tell of the conversion of a Moroccan soldier badly injured by a dumdum bullet at the Battle of the Marne. He was restored to health at the hospice after saying novenas to Sister Thérèse.[84]

The main wartime challenger to the cult of Sister Thérèse in the hearts and minds of Allied soldiers was that of the Sacred Heart. It had its origins in the medieval period, but was revived in popular devotion in seventeenth-century France, and became an important focus for popular Catholic revivals over the ensuing centuries.[85] Worshippers expressed devotion to the wounded physical heart of Jesus, depicted flaming and surmounted with the crown of thorns and a cross, as a symbol of divine love for humanity, Christian sacrifice, and redemption. On the eve of the First World War its popularity was greatest in France, but its worship was also encouraged in Ireland and Catholic Germany. The war undoubtedly gave a boost to this quasi-official cult, and the Church became keen to promote the relevance of its symbolism, with German bishops considering it approvingly as a 'specific cult for dealing with the war'.[86] A French newspaper reported in November 1914 that the following prayer had been found written on a scrap of paper in the packs of dead Westphalian troops: 'Sacred Heart of Jesus, I have faith in you; Holy Mother of God, come to my aid; Saint Joseph, sustain me.'[87] Karl Dalvai from the Tyrol copied something similar in his diary on 4 December 1914, which he recited every day to protect his two sons in the army.[88]

In Ireland the Sacred Heart was vigorously promoted by the Jesuits based in Dublin through their monthly magazine, *The Irish Messenger*. The Irish military were encouraged to wear badges depicting the flaming, pierced heart, which were either obtained before leaving Ireland, were sent by relatives to those already on the battlefield, or could be obtained from convents in London on the way to the front. Sacred Heart scapulars were also approved by the papacy in 1900–1 and again proved popular. In wartime France the cult was most rigorously and controversially promoted by a young convent sister and mystic named Claire Ferchaud, who had been educated in a Sacred Heart school and claimed to have received appearances from Christ. Supported by her bishop, she became a national celebrity as she pushed the cause of the Sacred Heart at the highest levels of authority, causing considerable irritation in political and religious circles. She wrote to fifteen generals in May 1917, for instance, urging that the Sacred Heart be included in the national colours of the French Army.[89]

Letters printed in Irish and French religious publications reported how their authors had been saved by the Sacred Heart. Private Edward Sheeran, Royal Irish Rifles, wrote how 'Every time I heard a shell approaching I said, "O Sacred Heart of Jesus, have mercy on us!"' While the man next to him was blown to bits on one occasion, Sheeran escaped with a very light wound to his shoulder. 'Thanks to the mercy of the Sacred Heart I was able to rejoin my battalion two days afterwards.'[90] The *Irish Messenger* and the Irish press periodically printed examples of how the badges had miraculously stopped or deflected bullets. In August 1915 an Irish newspaper reported that at the Dardanelles landings one Thomas Kelly, Royal Munster Fusiliers, was neck-deep in water as the bullets whizzed all around him. He put his left hand on the Sacred Heart badge sewn inside his tunic above his heart when a bullet hit the emblem and glanced across his chest, passing through his right shoulder. The story was promoted by the Sisters of Mercy, Dungarvon, Waterford.[91] The *Irish Messenger* printed a letter from the brother of an Irish Catholic nurse in a military hospital in France who related how his sister had observed that the Irish and English Catholic soldiers 'put more trust in the Sacred Heart than in surgeons and nurses'. Still, there were boundaries to be maintained, however nominally, between orthodoxy and popular piety. The Irish Jesuits circulated a statement that the Sacred Heart badge should not be worn as a 'charm or talisman to preserve the wearer from bullets and shrapnel'. That was condemned as superstition. Rather, it offered 'for those who wear it in the proper spirit the grace and protection of God'.[92] But the messages coming from the clergy were mixed. One French regimental magazine included a piece from a priest in which he urged, 'come and ask me for a little Sacred Heart. It will advantageously replace the bracelet charm that I have seen on your watch, your little good luck pig charm.'[93]

Rumours circulated of soldiers in France being arrested for overtly wearing Catholic paraphernalia. In June 1915 Canon Maurice Clément issued a communiqué on behalf of the cardinal archbishop of Paris after stories appeared in the Irish press that the French government was hampering Irish soldiers from practising their faith. Clément reported that they were fully at liberty to conduct their acts of worship, and that 'the vast majority of soldiers wear the badge of the Sacred Heart of Jesus and the miraculous medal of the Blessed Virgin'.[94] But there were some genuine obstacles to the supply of devotional protective items. In July 1918 an Irish newspaper reported that a prisoner of war, James Keegan of Ballyshannon, Royal Inniskilling Fusiliers, had written to his mother to send him a badge of the Sacred Heart. Her letter in response, which contained the badge, never got to him, though, because the English censor returned it with a notice stating that letters to prisoners of war must not contain any enclosures or printed matter. The press complained that the soldier was being denied the consolation of his religion.[95]

New Thought and Bullet-Proof Thinking

While the Protestant, Catholic, and Orthodox churches represented the Christian faith of the vast majority of the European armed forces and their loved ones, there were a variety of much smaller nineteenth-century Christian denominations that had a distinct stance on the war. The Jehovah's Witnesses and the Christadelphians attracted attention, for example, due to their pacifism and conscientious objection, while Seventh Day Adventist soldiers were court-martialled for refusing to work on Saturdays. Spiritualists provided a cathartic service for the bereaved. The New Thought movement has received little attention with regard to the First World War, and yet its beliefs and practices proved particularly adaptable to the needs of the soldiery. It was promoted as a scientific religion for a scientific war.

The New Thought religious philosophy was developed by an American clockmaker, mesmerist, and healer named Phineas Quimby (1802–66), and shaped by venerable metaphysical ideas. He taught that God was the only reality and that human selfhood, a true oneness with God, could in itself be divine. Central to the movement's practice was the notion that disease and misfortune were mental in origin and could be overcome with the appropriately pious projection of thought. In short, mind over matter, the spiritual ever conquering the material. Quimby inspired what would become the most influential offshoot of the movement, Christian Science. This was founded by one of his students named Mary Baker Eddy (1821–1910), who emphasized that all matter was illusion rather than merely under the control of the spiritual. The consequences of this for well-being were set out at great length in her foundation text and practical guide to metaphysical healing, *Science and Health with Key to the Scriptures*, which was first published in 1875. Numerous updated and expanded editions appeared subsequently. More to the point, the implications for the outcome of the First World War were mind-blowing to some. If there was no matter, then no physical harm could be wrought as long people only thought of the world as spiritual. Consider, for instance, the advice of the American Christian Scientist W. S. Leake in his 1917 collection of articles entitled *How to Protect our Soldiers*: 'In working against danger the great thing is to get your realization of heaven as clear as you possibly can, and then realize that there can be no danger in that perfect world. Realize that there is no matter, following with the affirmation that all is Spirit and the manifestation of Spirit.' To put it in practical military terms, Leake stated simply, 'In case of danger from submarines and mines realize there are no material submarines or mines, for all God's ideas are spiritual and perfect.'[96]

The Christian Science church grew rapidly during the early twentieth century, with its 635 churches in 1906 increasing to 1,913 by 1926, by which time its membership was over 200,000 in the United States.[97] It also gained a foothold in Britain over the same period, and expanded significantly in wartime and post-war Britain, with the number of churches growing from 65 in 1911 to 169 in 1926. The number of its ministers (called 'practitioners') grew from 219 in 1911 to 346 in 1921—the majority of them women.[98] The Christian Scientists were, therefore, well organized in terms of their war work and also had a physical presence in France. In the autumn of 1917 they began to produce a pocket edition of Eddy's *Science and Health with the Key to the Scriptures* for the troops and sailors. Some forty thousand copies were distributed to the military 'without money and without price'. A Christian Science report recorded letters of thanks from soldiers stationed in France, India, Syria, Greece, and Egypt. Copies of the *Christian Science Monitor* and their other regular publications circulated in their millions.[99] The miraculous battlefield effects of Christian Science teaching seem to have been kept to a minimum in most of these official publications, which focused on material relief and spiritual support rather than metaphysical protection. It was its magazine the *Christian Science Sentinel* that acted as the main forum for proofs of the amazing efficacy of right thinking in combat, with regular 'testimonies of healing' appearing from British and American soldiers.

Lawrence A. Hayter, of Letchworth, England, had his letter published in the *Sentinel* on 24 November 1917. He was an infantryman in the Bedford Regiment, and had been in active service in France for a year. 'One occasion stands out strongly in memory,' he wrote:

the floor of our shallow trench was sensibly heaving with the explosions of shells which dropped close to us on every side but never touched our little band of five. I could tell of many similar experiences; in one recently our trench was battered out of shape by heavy shelling along its whole length, except for the few yards in which I and the comrades in my section were taking shelter.[100]

He went on to relate how he had cured himself of dysentery by resisting 'the temptation to believe in the reality of any seeming material indisposition'. He ended his letter: 'The mists of horror, fear, and misery in which animal magnetism had shrouded the scene of war have proved to have only the supposed substance given them by mortal mind. Most clearly have I proved the healing power of Christian Science, and I am ever grateful to our Leader for her wonderful life and work.' Hayter died on the battlefield a few weeks later on 30 December 1917. His remains lie in Klein-Vierstraat British Cemetery in Belgium.

Sergeant Eric Ericson, M. M., East Surrey Regiment, had his testimony published in July 1918. He had been a Christian Scientist for five years, and his wife, mother, and sister were all 'Scientists'. He expressed his gratitude to them and to his 'practitioner' for their 'right thinking', which helped keep him safe and healthy. Ericson joined one of the first Kitchener battalions, crossing to France in August 1915. He spent the next twenty-six months on active service at the front line in the battles of Loos (1915), the Somme (1916), and Messines-Wytschaete Ridge (1917), and in the third Battle of Ypres (1917). No wonder he felt he had been especially protected. Reflecting on his experiences, he explained:

> I found Christian Science invaluable in enabling me to demonstrate the truth against the false claims of error in the forms of trench feet, frostbite, etc., during the winters of 1915–1916 and 1916–1917, when on several occasions I spent stretches of eighteen days in what is called 'the Salient', thigh deep in mud and icy cold … I just held to the truth knowing that since I was doing my duty I was doing right, and in doing right I could not suffer from erroneous beliefs; since sickness is unlike God and unreal, therefore I, as God's child, could experience only harmony, perfect health … my understanding of Christian Science has enabled me to overcome every form of error found in a front line trench,—shell fire, poison gas, etc., as well as privation and hardship.[101]

He ended his letter saying that he was currently attending Officers Training Camp. From other sources we know he made second lieutenant that summer and joined the Royal Sussex Regiment. He was killed in action at the Battle of Épehy on 18 September, at the age of 27, and is buried in Épehy Wood Farm Cemetery.[102]

While the prayers and right thinking of loved ones and practitioners far away from the battlefields were clearly thought to provide a general level of protection, it was the resort to Christian Science techniques at the moment of danger that helped. A Yorkshire Christian Scientist, Michael J. Fahy, explained how, having to retreat from the front line, he found himself waist-deep in water in a ditch. The warning of a doctor of the fatal consequences of such a position flashed through his mind, but, he explained, 'I immediately corrected this and realized I was in God's care; and so it proved, for no fatal results followed as was prophesied.'[103] The power was such that it also protected those around the Christian Scientist, whatever their faith. One survivor of the war, Donald Southwart, of Halifax, England, marvelled that during the time he was with his platoon they did not suffer a single casualty despite being in reserve, support, and on the front line at three different sectors. It proved to him that 'the real battle we have to fight is mental'.[104]

Other American New Thought movements had their evangelists at the front as well. One such was Mabel Huntley, a member of the Unity School of Christianity based in Kansas City. The Unity movement was founded by Charles and Myrtle Fillmore and was one of the more substantive New Thought ministries, although in 1906 the Fillmores declared themselves separate from the New Thought movement. Its origin lies in the Society of Silent Help, founded by the Fillmores in 1890, which, as the name suggests, was a ministry based around regular silent prayer meetings. Their theology was eclectic, influenced by the Fillmores' engagement with and interest in Christian Science, Quakerism, theosophy, and Hinduism, and centred on the unity of spirit, body, and soul, and the unity of all peoples through truth and love. Through this, one could achieve oneness with God, which brought personal peace and health. Charles wrote his own text, *Christian Healing* (1909), based on his various articles in Unity publications, in which there was a strong emphasis on 'absent treatment'. Indeed, a key part of the school's activity was concerned with processing letters, telegrams, and telephone calls requesting remote treatment for physical ailments.[105]

Mabel Huntley was in Paris when war broke out. She wrote on 2 August 1914 of how she and her sister were stuck: 'We have the chance to leave France today, but we have not the money to do so, nor in fact anywhere to go. We, therefore, for the next three weeks are obliged to remain here, as all railways, etc., are used for troops.' She considered her precarious situation to be God's will. For one moment she 'allowed the horrors of what this all means to overcome me, but then I looked up and saw the sun shining so brightly, so I realized, "There, now you see the sun; it is shining on France, on Germany, on all the world. All this tumult does not change it."'[106] A few months later she wrote another letter from Paris to the movement's periodical, *Unity*, describing the evangelical work she and her sister were carrying out amongst wounded British soldiers. Attending local hospitals, they encouraged the men to read the limited number of copies of *Weekly Unity* and *Unity* they possessed. According to Mabel they were very well received. 'You see, I just read first the small healings at the back', explained one convalescent, 'and then I commenced on articles—they were a bit stiff at first.' This particularly receptive soldier then began to instruct other soldiers. One fellow patient who had just been brought in with frostbite groaned all night, and the receptive soldier said, 'we did have to laugh, for in his pain we heard him saying, "O God, why do you make me suffer like this, when I never even killed one German up at the front?"' He was clearly in need of a dose of silent prayer, and so the convert told Mabel's sister, 'tonight, after supper, I am going to explain this to him. I'll give him a good lesson and then he can commence and read.'[107] The power of this was demonstrated when one soldier, a widower whose wife had died just before the outbreak of war, and whose seven children were not receiving a proper allowance due to some administrative problem, was, after reading a copy of *Unity*, all of a sudden sent back to a hospital in England close to his children and relatives. His dream had come true: 'this man had never expressed any open desire for the wish he thought could never be fulfilled'. Unity literature had, however, apparently unlocked his internal yearnings.

In response to Mabel's letters, the editor of *Unity* set up a 'Unity Foreign Literature Fund' to support her work in France. With America's entry into the war, the Unity School of Christianity also provided a suite of supporting materials for the benefit of soldiers in the trenches. It produced a khaki pocket edition of Huntley's *A Truth Student with the Soldiers*, stating that 'having withstood the practical test of being soaked in water, we know the soldier boys will find the book very serviceable'. For every dollar subscription to *Weekly Unity* it also offered to send a booklet entitled *Bullet-Proof Soldiers* to a named soldier in the trenches. To expedite the reception of this gift the subscriber filled out a coupon with the rank, regiment, division, and camp of the recipient soldier or sailor. As a further gift, the Unity School of Christianity promised to 'take your boy up for protection in the prayers of the Silent Unity Society'.[108]

The intriguingly entitled *Bullet-Proof Soldiers* was a pamphlet edition of an interview conducted with Frederick Laurence Rawson by the *Boston Post*'s London special correspondent in December 1916. It bore the sensational headline: 'London Doctor says he makes soldiers bullet-proof'.[109] We have already encountered Rawson, a British inventor, entrepreneur, and electrical engineer, as an active member of the occult fraternity in London. His father, Sir Rawson Rawson, was an old Etonian who became an influential Board of Trade official, president of the Statistical Society, and vice president of the Geographical Society. Frederick was a shameless self-promoter, to the extent that a rather nauseous autobiographical piece written in the third person tediously listed his many sporting achievements, including such trivia as the fact that, at 50 years of age, he had made more runs and taken more wickets for Epsom cricket club than any other player.[110] What it does not mention is his series of failed ventures in the City. Thousands apparently lost money on his scheme to extract gold from seawater, while another venture to harness the resources of Iceland came to nothing. He was more successful as a design engineer, developing an armoured train and electric floodlighting systems for illuminating battlefields and tennis courts. In the early twentieth century he was heavily involved in airship design, being the consultant engineer for the Barton Airship Company.

What was known as the Barton-Rawson airship was the first dirigible balloon built for the British War Office. Made of silk and bamboo, it made its first ascent from Alexandra Palace on 22 July 1905. Rawson was on board with three others, and piloted the rudder. It sailed for around an hour to much satisfaction, but the descent was disastrous—it crashed into a potato field near Romford. The airship was wrecked but the crew amazingly walked away without injury. It was international news. On the same page as the headline 'German Kaiser is now the boss of all Europe', the *Pittsburgh Press* printed a syndicated eyewitness account of the flight by the American newspaper mogul William Randolph Hearst. He had been travelling around Europe on holiday during the summer of 1905, collecting valuable artworks. Finding himself on the outskirts of London on 22 July, he reported:

> Suddenly I looked up into the summer sky and there I saw a long white boat an immense distance in the air... I recollected how Tennyson in his 'Locksley Hall', had spoken of 'floating armies in the sky', and here right above me was the first of the great airships which are to be, but which I trust may only come to perfection when war shall be no more.[111]

A short time after, in a talk at the Aeronautical Institute, Rawson prophesied that within ten to fifteen years all battles in the world would be fought in the air.[112] But a few years later Rawson would come to claim his greatest contributions to the war effort were psychical and not physical.

Rawson became fascinated with Christian Science healing after being commissioned by the *Daily Mail* to investigate the movement's claims from the perspective of a leading scientist. To the surprise, perhaps, of his employer, Rawson became convinced by Eddy's writings and joined the Third Church of Christ, Scientist in London, which had been founded in 1908, though its physical church was not completed until 1911. He soon chafed at the rigidity of the Church, however, and took issue with some of the rudimentary scientific explanations put forward by Eddy. In return, his forthrightness and healing activities annoyed some fellow members.[113] Rawson was shunned by the Third Church and its members were forbidden to speak to him. He later claimed he was driven out by 'malicious mental malpractice', a reference to Eddy's notion that through 'malicious animal magnetism' rogue Christian Scientists could harm others at a distance by the application of negative thought power.[114] During the war Rawson founded his own New Thought movement, the Society for Spreading the Knowledge of True Prayer, and set up a psychical healing service at 90 Regent Street, London, which dealt with a wide range of problems, from curing gout to diverting Zeppelin bombs through thought power. His 1917 pamphlet *Divine Protection for the Garden and Farm* even made the case for how 'right thinking' could help the war effort by restoring sickly plants.[115]

As was explained in *Bullet-Proof Soldiers*, Rawson claimed to have saved the lives of many soldiers through the power of 'right thinking' applied through his 'audible treatment'. This required him to enter a state of deep contemplation, fix his gaze as though looking into space, concentrate his thought power, and utter aloud: 'There is no danger; man is surrounded by divine love; there is no matter; all is spirit and the manifestation of spirit.' He showed journalists letters from the front demonstrating his miraculous interventions. One explained:

> Have just come out of the 'big push' without a scratch, quite safe and sound. All the other fellows in my company were killed or wounded. I am the only one left. The _____ took all before them and pushed the Huns back for miles. We suffered heavy casualties, but my life seemed to be charmed: shrapnel and bullets whizzed all around me, but did not seem to find a home in my body.[116]

Another testimonial, from a lieutenant colonel in a Midland regiment:

> His battalion was under fire in the front support trenches for eight weeks continuously and during that period not a man was touched. He himself was wounded in the left shoulder. The bullet entered by the collar bone, but when the doctors examined him, though there was no trace of the bullet having passed through and out, no bullet was to be found.[117]

He concluded that the bullet had dematerialized thanks to Rawson's treatment. Whether these letters were real or not is obviously moot, but the war correspondent Philip Gibbs wrote of his encounter with a colonel in the North Staffordshires who clearly believed in the same. 'I have a mystical power,' he said in a quiet matter-of-fact way. 'Nothing will ever hit me as long as I keep that power which comes from faith. I go through any barrage unscathed because my will is strong enough to turn aside explosive shells and machine-gun bullets. As matter, they must obey my intelligence.'[118]

Such reports no doubt brought Rawson more clients, but they also attracted the concerned attention of *Daily Mail* journalist Harold Ashton, who wrote a feature on his undercover visit to Rawson's 'prayer bucket shop', describing him as 'a clever, resourceful man, as wily and as slippery as a monkey'. Ashton explained how the 'prayer shop' operated, with a number of well-dressed young women employed in interviewing people about their loved ones in the war, and explaining to clients how much they would be charged for Rawson's protective services. Ashton caused uproar in the 'shop' when he put Rawson's mind power claims to the test. Rawson had boasted to Ashton that through the power of thought he would be unable to lay a blow upon his person as a demonstration of how bullets could also be stopped. The mystic duly went in to his mesmeric state and said aloud, 'You will not touch me!' Ashton then swung a punch that landed fully under Rawson's collarbone. His disciples were outraged and jumped to Rawson's rescue, including one man who said he had just been cured of blindness by Rawson. The ruffled Rawson explained, 'I – I – don't think that my mind was quite correctly tuned to the occasion. And, besides, there was a spirit of levity.'

The *Daily Mail*'s attacks on Rawson had ramifications beyond his London operation. Just days after the exposés were published, Rawson had been booked to give a talk on 'How to Protect our Soldiers by True Prayer' at the Tunbridge Wells Pump Room. Protests flooded in urging the lecture to be cancelled. Because the YMCA occupied the Pump Room as a soldiers' social centre, they were mistakenly assumed to have organized the talk and so received considerable criticism. In fact, Rawson had been booked by an unnamed lady of substance who lived in the area. In the end she and Rawson agreed to cancel the lecture.[119] The public sensation died down, and later in the year Rawson gave the same talk in Birmingham and elsewhere.[120] Rawson set up operations in Paris and New York after the war. We find him in America in March 1920, where the St Louis authorities threatened to prosecute him for practising medicine without a licence if he did not leave the city immediately. He was giving lectures in New York in 1923 when he died of pneumonia. For four days prior to his cremation, female members of the Society for Spreading the Knowledge of True Prayer prayed for his resurrection, and they continued to do so as his body was incinerated. One follower told a journalist that Rawson had raised two people from the dead a few years before in Spain. Back in London, he was still fresh enough in the popular memory for *The Times* to report on the death of the First World War 'Spiritual Healer'.[121]

In the guise of what was marketed as Pelmanism, self-improvement through New Thought was stripped of its spiritual basis and presented as a secular scientific discovery for personal empowerment. As explained by the Pelman Institute: 'Pelmanism is the science of right thinking, the science of putting right thought into dynamic action.

It will help you to use fully the powers that you know about, and what is even more important, how to discover and use the hidden, unsuspected powers.'[122] It was, in essence, little more than a self-improvement course offering memory enhancement exercises, but it was sold as a way to gain power and get ahead in business, and to enhance military skills by giving a confident edge in combat. The institute created a very successful publicity blitz during the war, with puff pieces appearing regularly in any publications that would take them, including magazines for the soldiery at the front, such as the *London Scottish Regimental Gazette* and *The Dagger, or London in the Line*.[123] In July 1918 *The Tablet* published an endorsement by the former Scottish Free Church minister and newspaper editor Sir William Robertson Nicoll in which he claimed:

> From the battlefields in France and Italy I have received many remarkable accounts of the practical value of Pelmanism to officers and men of our armies. A personal friend—he was a University Professor—who was out lecturing at the Front, found everywhere that the Pelman system was being discussed by officers. And I have been told that in several regiments practically every officer is a Pelmanist.

He included supportive letters, such as one from a flying officer who explained he was a nervous wreck owing to his machine catching fire in the air and crashing. He had been badly injured and was awarded compensation for injuries by the Admiralty. Yet, thanks to Pelmanism, he recovered swiftly and was passed fit for flying again. 'Without the aid of the course to make me put my back into my efforts', he concluded, 'I doubt whether I should have succeeded.'[124]

The branding and advertising of Pelmanism during the First World War helps us to understand how religion was being recast in popular culture at the time.[125] Its promoters deliberately targeted both the religious and military press. An advertisement entitled 'Pelmanism in the Army', for instance, in the French edition of *Stars and Stripes* in 1918, stated, 'Pelmanism is not a magical secret key to success; there is no "mystery" about it.'[126] Yet its commercial potential and degree of popularity were predicated on the way it connected the mystical interstices that opened up between religion and 'mental science' during the war years.

Global Faiths

Despite the pervasive rhetoric of the war as a symbolic struggle of Christian nationalism, millions of the combatants were not Christian. There were 100,000 Jewish soldiers in the German Army, over 500,000 in the Russian forces, and tens of thousands in the Italian, British, French, Belgian, Australian, New Zealand, Canadian, and American armies. Canada sent 6,000 Jewish soldiers, for example. Romania's First World War army contained 38,000 Jews.[127] Some 2 million Muslim soldiers fought in the Ottoman Turkish Army during the war. Well over a million Hindu, Sikh, and Muslim Indian troops were employed on the Western Front as part of the British Expeditionary Force, against the Germans in East Africa, and against the Ottomans in Egypt, Mesopotamia, and at Gallipoli. The French Army deployed around 450,000 troops from its African territories, who fought in France, the Dardanelles, and the Balkans. Most were Muslims, while some followed indigenous African religions. Germany also deployed colonial troops in the African theatre of war, though not in Europe. There were also tens of thousands of Chinese labourers on the Western Front.[128] Regarding these millions of non-Christian combatants, comparatively little has been recorded about how their popular religious devotions and magical rituals were practised on the battlefields. Yet all the religions above, just like Christianity, had similar venerable protective traditions that were adaptable to and purposeful for the conditions of the war.

In Jewish religion, for example, the placing of *mezuzot* on doorposts had long been practised. These consisted of scrolls of parchment bearing two passages from Deuteronomy on one side, and the holy word *Shaddai* (Almighty) on the other, which were then placed in containers that were attached to the doorposts of the main entrance of homes to protect their inhabitants. Writing in 1939, the great scholar of Jewish religion and magic Joshua Trachtenberg observed, 'The *mezuzah* has even come off the doorposts,' noting that during the First World War many Jewish soldiers carried *mezuzot* in their pockets to deflect enemy bullets. One of them was the Jewish *poilu* Pierre Hirsch, whose veteran father gave him his old *mezuzah* 'as he said goodbye and blessed me'.[129] A scrapbook kept by the British Third East Anglian Field Ambulance Officers Corp reflecting their time stationed in Gallipoli, Palestine, and Egypt between 1914 and 1919 contains a *mezuzah*, stuck in upside down, showing, perhaps, that the religious and protective purpose of this memento was not properly understood.[130]

For millions of troops fighting in the First World War, the Koran and not the Bible was the sacred book carried or recited during battle. As with bibles, the Koran accrued talismanic properties for some Muslims. T. E. Lawrence wrote of his fighting companion, the Bedouin Arab leader Auda Abu Tayeh: 'thirteen years before he had bought an amulet Koran for one hundred and twenty pounds and had not since been wounded. Indeed, Death had avoided his face, and gone scurvily about killing brothers, sons and followers.' The book was actually a very cheap edition printed in Glasgow, 'but Auda's deadliness did not let people laugh at his superstition'.[131] For centuries soldiers in Muslim cultures had worn a *taweez* for protection, which is an amulet worn around the neck, attached to the shoulder, or worn around the arm, consisting of a pendant capsule or leather bag containing passages from the Koran. In 1903 it was recorded how among Swahili-speaking Muslims in East Africa, which was a theatre of conflict during the First World War, verse 20:1 of the Koran worn as an amulet was considered to give protection in combat. It was prepared by fumigating it with incense.[132] In light of the Ottoman call for jihad against its enemies, the French military was careful to accommodate the Islamic beliefs, rituals, and practices of its North African troops.[133] This is exemplified in a nuanced report from a journalist accompanying soldiers on their way to the Dardanelles in May 1915. He mixed with Senegalese troops who had already fought in France, and noted their traditional amulets to avert danger. These usually consisted of a small bag containing verses from the Koran, along with other items of ritual or magical significance. The journalist then went on to make the point that French soldiers were no different with their own 'fetishes' for protection, such as Catholic medals.[134]

Amongst Muslim Indians, magic paper squares containing appropriate numbers from the Koran written on paper or birch bark acted as general protective amulets worn in little metal capsules or worn on the upper arm.[135] In December 1917 a Muslim Indian cavalryman, Mahomed Latif Khan, King George's Own Central India Horse, wrote home from France concerning a troublesome servant about whom complaints were being made to the British officers. The substance of the letter, though, was to ask his correspondent, a holy man, why the servant had not received a talisman he had requested from home: 'Your prayers are of great efficacy; but what your servant wanted were such incantations, as he might use by reciting and then exhaling his breath in the direction of his enemies so that their thoughts toward him might become kindly— such incantations, moreover, as would give him prospects of promotion.' The censor commented that 'this letter has psychological interest, and shows how superstitious some of the men are'.[136]

As to indigenous religions amongst African troops, or those in the African fields of conflict, there are some tantalizing references. Amongst the Mwera peoples of Tanzania, for instance, part of German East Africa at the time of the war, the belief developed that men who drank from the hot springs at Kilembero would become invulnerable to German bullets.[137] In West Africa gris-gris bags, already alluded to above, were often purchased from marabouts (holy men and healers) to stop bullets. While they often contained verses from the Koran, they also included a mix of items, such as roots and herbs, which had magical significance in non-Islamic cultural contexts. The Paris-based Russian war correspondent and novelist Ilya Erenburg was given one such bag by a Senegalese soldier that contained three German teeth. Bakary Diallo, the first francophone Senegalese author to write of his First World War experiences, who was badly injured at Sillery, near Reims, wrote of his own arsenal of traditional protective amulets. It included roots, monkey tails, elephant hairs, and snake heads.[138]

While at a national, institutional level there is little evidence that the war led to a great upsurge in church membership or churchgoing, we should not dismiss the myriad impacts the war had on personal faith. The observance of religion in battlefield life was as much a practical as a spiritual exercise. Adherence to the notion of fate, defined as an acceptance of the will of God or the gods, whether in terms of predestination, providence, or inscrutable whim, was not, it would appear, a widespread, abiding tenet amongst the military. Faith was focused strongly on proactive survival techniques that either sought the intercession of divine or supernatural powers or relied on personal control of the environment through mental concentration. In Christian terms, the new age of 'scientific religion' and interest in the psychical and psychological meant that the efficacy of prayer became, for some, as much an exercise in positive thinking as a devotional reflex. The experience of war also encouraged syncretic responses to luck and an accumulative approach to personal protection. This was expressed in the way soldiers curated collections of charms. Italian soldiers, for instance, wore leather belts to which were attached a mix of religious medals and secular talismans. When Jewish soldier Pierre Hirsch went off to the front he wore not only his father's *mezuzah* but also a Catholic 'holy medal' and a medal he had received from a Protestant lady. A hospital nurse noted how, when tending to an Irish soldier with a serious scalp wound, she found a piece of Irish bog oak, a prayer written by a French girl, a withered shamrock, and a piece of wood from a saint's cell.[139] For many, then, faith was an exercise in hedging one's bets in the game of life and death.

7

AFTERMATH

Come to think of it, there's more of that sort of thing now than ever there was when I was a girl. I was brought up not to dabble in that sort of thing, but I don't know as I think the same now. There's things happening in these days makes you wonder where you are.

(London woman, aged 32, interviewed about astrology in 1938)[1]

Historians have described the resort to the supernatural during the war in such much-quoted terms as 'an avalanche of the "unmodern"' and 'a plethora of very un-modern superstitions'.[2] But the idea that the war heralded a brief era of 're-enchantment', so to speak, is problematic. Historians of witchcraft and magic have increasingly rejected the idea of an age of magic that succumbed to science and reason by the nineteenth century, pointing out the false dichotomies that have been generated between science and the supernatural, faith and rationality, modernity and magic.[3] The notion of the First World War as a fundamental, transformative event in everyday life has, in this respect, been further reinforced by the common academic habit, particularly in Britain, of using 1914 as the end point for studies of social history, suggesting that irrevocable change was wrought across societies by the experience of war.[4]

There are valid reasons for choosing the beginning and end of the conflict to define momentous social change. The experience of war was framed in such terms at the time, for instance. With hindsight, we can also identify clear socio-economic turning points, such as the emancipation of women, though these were often shifts that were determined by longer-term developments brought to the fore by the conflict. The visions, apparitions, omens, prophecies, divination, and magical beliefs described in this book were all evident in the decades leading up to the First World War, and they continued to manifest themselves in the years after.[5] The periodization of European social history sometimes masks these broader continuities and trends. So in the post-war era spiritualism and middle-class occultism are considered aspects of the supernatural worthy of academic study, but popular belief in witchcraft, magic, and fortune-telling is considered largely irrelevant to our under-standing of twentieth-century society. One might get the impression that the old supernatural traditions had to die out for the modern, 'educated' interest in occultism and esotericism to take root. What we see during the war, and in the years after, though, is a situation where some aspects of the old and new supernatural continued on separate planes, while in other ways the war experience elided the two and generated new ways of expressing both trends.

Many of the men who went to war grew up in cultures of trad-itional witchcraft and magic, and returned to communities where people continued to fear supernatural powers. Johann Kruse's cam-paign against witchcraft accusations and witch doctors gathered pace, and he accumulated ample evidence. One of the numerous instances in his files was a prosecution in the town of Heide, Holstein, in 1927. A woman who suffered from a leg complaint believed a neighbour had bewitched it. She placed a broom in front of the house door to keep the witch away, and informed other neighbours of the witchery. She was prosecuted for slander. Another trial, this time in Mecklenburg in 1935, concerned an old woman from a farming family accused of witchcraft. Her family could not fetch a good price for their livestock because of the rumours, and in court witnesses were reluctant to testify as they feared she would bewitch them.[6] Similar prosecutions were heard in British and French courts. In 1922 the Spalding Petty Sessions, Lincolnshire, dealt with a case where spinster Rose Ellen Graham, of Whaplode, prosecuted her neighbour Mrs Mitchell after she sprang through a hedge one day and stabbed her on the back of the wrist. She drew blood and exclaimed, 'You won't witch me, you ____, any more.' Several years later a war widow, Florence Bodecott, of Gorleston, prosecuted her neighbour, 43-year-old Aquilla Hewitt, for threatening to cast a spell over her and fill her house with witchcraft.[7] Across the Channel at Niort in France in 1929, a family of seven was arrested for beating a neighbour they accused of bewitching them. Numerous such court cases also occurred in the United States in the period.[8] These were the more violent expressions of witch belief, but gossip, rumour, and muttered accusations of witchcraft continued to be quite widespread across the former warring countries through the 1920s and 1930s.[9]

On another cultural plane, it has recently been argued, furthermore, that the trauma of the war heralded a new wave of fictional witches in literature, and the creation of the thoroughly modern witch figure.[10] She appears, for instance, in Stella Benson's *Living Alone*, published in 1919. This novella is an unusual fantasy set in wartime London, where the lives of several members of a war savings committee are changed by their encounter with a witch who runs a boarding house. Benson was a suffragette and engaged in charitable work supporting the London poor during the conflict. The novel cleverly melds the mundanity of everyday life on the home front, with its war profiteering, poverty, and air raids, with the possibilities of magic in the ether. When one of the characters, a wizard and serving soldier called Richard Higgins, discusses the causes of the war, he complains, 'The worst of this war is that it has nothing whatever to do with magic of any sort. It was made and supported by men who had forgotten magic.' Such magical realism, where witches and aircraft flew above London, was a romantic reaction to the trauma of the conflict, which 'helped to transform terrible realities into empowering magics'.[11]

While neighbourly tensions continued to play out in terms of witchcraft accusations and the resort to cunning folk, the oft-decried 'modern witchcraft' of spiritualism became further entrenched in society, in part as a consequence of the experience of the global conflict. While there was no surge in membership of spiritualist organizations in Britain during the war, there was steady growth through the following two decades. The likes of Arthur Conan Doyle and Oliver Lodge continued to proselytize effectively for the movement through the 1920s. The number of societies affiliated to the Spiritualists' National Union is indicative, although it does not represent the totality of spiritualist groups. In 1919 there were 309 affiliated societies or churches, climbing to 496 in 1934. Enthusiasm for 'home circles' also seems to have grown significantly, with seances being conducted for small groups in front rooms and parlours. A short-lived International Home Circle Federation was founded in 1919, and in 1931 an association called the Link was set up to support and promote home circles. But inflated claims were made at the time about the number of practising spiritualists, and we need to be cautious about over emphasizing popular participation in organized spiritualism in the inter war period. On the outbreak of the Second World War, the SNU had over 500 affiliated churches, but that represented a total membership of only 14,028.[12]

Still, public interest in and acceptance of spiritualism clearly expanded, though it would be an exaggeration to state it grew to have mass appeal. New platforms appeared for its public practice—in urban areas at least. In London large public seances were in vogue, with thousands attending venues such as the Royal Albert Hall to see star mediums speak to the dead.[13] Through such events and home circles a wider section of the population familiarized themselves, at first hand, with the basic idea of contacting the dead as therapy, if not with the wider tenets of spiritualism. On the eve of war, a 42-year-old London woman interviewed about her beliefs said, 'I go sometimes to a spiritualist meeting when things get too bad, I believe in it.' On one occasion she was told that her husband would lose his job, and he did. Another woman of a similar age agreed: 'I've been to lots of Circles. There's a lot of comfort in it, there's nothing to be afraid of, I've talked to my Mother lots of times.'[14] As such comments suggest, there were other reasons for engaging with spiritualism and mediums than communicating with the war dead. Mediums continued to engage in fortune-telling, and increasing numbers of mediums also acted as psychical healers.[15]

Public interest in psychical research grew concomitantly in France, Britain, and Germany. Across the Channel a new organizing body, the Institut Métapsychique International, was founded in 1919 with the central aim of scientifically investigating mediumship, and a new journal, the *Revue métapsychique*, commenced a year later. Popular interest was further spiked by the first French edition of Oliver Lodge's *Raymond*. There was a surge of interest in experimental parapsychology in Germany as well, along with a boom in occult periodicals. The famous laboratory of the psychical researcher Albert von Schrenck-Notzing (1862–1929) achieved more serious public interest after the war, in contrast with the 'amused incredulity' he attracted before it.[16] Meanwhile, in Britain, the Society for Psychical Research was riven between a sceptical 'scientific' wing and an increasingly influential 'spiritualist' faction that believed the society should dedicate itself to promoting the scientific validity of mediumship.[17] One consequence was that a recent member, Harry Price, decided to set up his own National Laboratory for Psychical Research in 1926 with the support of the University of London. With his love of publicity and shrewd engagement with the new medium of radio, Price would go on to become the most famous psychical researcher of the inter war years. While he was well known for exposing fraudulent mediums, Price also tantalized with the prospect that an amazing breakthrough in psychical science was just around the corner.

The Theosophical Society emerged from the war looking forward to the dawn of a great new spiritual world order, and it had a buoyant international membership of around 45,000 through the 1920s. But membership went into significant decline afterwards, partly due to splits in its leadership, and also due to disillusionment with Jiddu Krishnamurti's growing independence from the movement and dissolution of the Order of the Star. The Russian branch, along with other occult organizations, was dissolved by decree in Soviet Russia in 1923, and the society was banned in Nazi Germany during the mid-1930s along with other esoteric organizations such as the Anthroposophical Society.[18] But the expression of spiritual revelation and the hope in a new divine era continued to be channelled in traditional popular religious ways. In the realm of Catholic apparitions there were far more instances of Marian visions in Western Europe after than during the war, though, again, it needs to be noted that these were fairly regular events in the nineteenth century as well. Between 1932 and 1935 there was an epidemic of such apparitions in Belgium, along with claims of stigmata, bleeding crucifixes, and miraculous cures. The first outbreak occurred in the small Walloon town of Beauraing, near the French border, where children claimed to have seen over thirty appearances by the Virgin. It has been suggested that this wave of miracles was a popular response to growing anxieties over the rise of Hitler in light of the Walloon experience of German occupation and warfare during the First World War.[19] Similar tensions also help explain the succession of Marian apparitions in Germany between 1933 and 1940. Further visions were seen at the major shrine at Marpingen, but new visionary females reported the appearance of the Virgin in Westphalia, Lower Saxony, and Bavaria. Once the Nazi Party had consolidated power, the Gestapo were quick to arrest or suppress such visionaries. Four young girls who claimed to have been visited by the Virgin in Heede, Lower Saxony, for instance, were committed to a mental hospital.[20]

Moving on to the fate of divination in the post-war period, popular astrology really took off in France, particularly during the 1930s, with a rash of new guides and periodicals for a general readership. In 1926 the Paris newspaper *Le Petit Journal illustré* began to publish an astrological advice column, inviting readers to submit queries to their resident astrologer, Fakir Fhakya Khan. Its more successful rival, *Le Petit Parisien*, started to publish annual astrological predictions three years later regarding political, financial, and meteorological matters. In Germany an Astrologers' Congress was held in 1923 and the Academic Society for Astrological Research was founded the following year, while at least four hundred books and pamphlets were published in the inter war years.[21] The British folklorist A. R. Wright observed in 1928 that interest in astrology and horoscopes had also grown greatly in his country.[22] This is an exaggeration. Astrology in the form of almanacs, postal astrology, and adherence to traditional forms of natural astrology had considerable reach in popular culture back in the late nineteenth century. What changed was that the pre-war newspaper consensus that astrology was a pernicious 'superstition', to be condemned at every opportunity, broke down.

In Britain, as in France, the offer of horoscopes moved from the advertising columns to the main pages of the newspapers. The first British newspaper astrology column was commissioned by the *Sunday Express* in August 1930 and concerned the horoscope of the infant Princess Margaret. It proved very popular with readers, and was followed up the next week by a feature, 'Were you born in September?' The author of these and subsequent columns, astrologer R. H. Naylor, later remarked that his *Sunday Express* pieces 'entirely altered the orientation of the public mind towards astrology'.[23] Other newspapers jumped on the bandwagon. In 1932 several newspapers, including *The Sphere*, teamed up with mail-order astrologers to offer free horoscopes for their readers.[24] The *Sunday Express* went a step further the following year, when Naylor appeared in a cinema short that borrowed the title of his column, *What the Stars Foretell*. The advertisements punned that it contained an 'all star cast'. 'See the Film,' ran advertisements in the local press, 'then write to the "Sunday Express" for your Horoscope FREE.'[25] The Mass Observation Survey, set up in Britain in 1937 to explore the sociology of everyday life, took a considerable interest in the popularity of astrology. A survey it conducted in parts of London revealed that two-thirds of women believed or partly believed in horoscopes, although only 20 per cent of men were prepared to admit the same. In the survey's first major book of findings, published in 1939, its authors stated that the recent phenomenon of newspaper astrology 'is to be reckoned with as a very powerful force'. If all the horoscopic news from the previous year were analysed, it would, said the authors, reveal 'a whole ethic of contemporary England'.[26]

So, as the Second World War began, Europe was far from being disenchanted. On both the battlefields and the home fronts we find similar patterns of engagement with and reliance on the supernatural. The evidence is patchier than for the First World War, partly because there was less academic interest in war folklore at the time, partly because the authorities in Nazi Germany and Fascist Italy were more successful in suppressing some manifestations, or, at least, the reporting of them. In Britain a survey by the Mass Observation team in spring 1942 found that some 40 per cent of English men and just over half of women said they were, to varying degrees, disposed towards the reality of the supernatural, as defined by the belief in ghosts, prophecy, and fortune-telling. When asked about their personal experiences, ghosts and wraiths, omens, and prophetic experiences (including dreams) were the most commonly reported, followed by female premonitions.[27] But, as in the Great War, this popular experience did not translate into a great recourse to organized spiritualism in Britain. Indeed, membership of the SNU dropped to 10,250 by 1941 and its rival organization the British Spiritualists' Lyceum Union experienced financial difficulties. Spiritualist membership fluctuated only modestly during the rest of the war. Mediums once again became tangled up in the authorities' renewed concerns about the influence of wartime fortune tellers, exposing the same fault lines between spiritualism as a faith and the practices of bogus mediums and unscrupulous diviners. This culminated in the well-known prosecution of the medium Helen Duncan in 1944.[28]

Astrological almanacs came into vogue again despite the competition from the newspaper horoscopes. They sold in their millions, and the British local press continued to reproduce their annual pronouncements. In June 1941 the *Shipley Times* reported, for instance, on the predictions for 1942 in the latest edition of *Old Moore's Almanac* (no relation to Moore's *Vox Stellarum*). Its forecast for January was as follows: 'The troubles of the last few years are still with us. Frontiers have been crossed and recrossed. The whole of Europe is still one big question mark.' On more specific matters, for September 1942 *Old Moore's* predicted, 'tragic news is received of the serious loss of tonnage at sea. Our gallant seamen claim and receive more consideration.'[29] The Brighton astrologer P. J. Harwood published his *When the War Will End: An Astrological Almanac* in 1941, and gave a taste of his foresight at the Astrologists' Convention held in Harrogate that year. He predicted a massive invasion of German parachute troops that May as part of the blitzkrieg, but that the Allies would be victorious on 31 January the following year.[30] Omens continued to appear in the sky as well. In the autumn of 1940 a shepherd on the Sussex Downs near Lewes, England, while tending his sheep, saw a cloud vision form of Jesus on the cross and six angels with long white wings. An evacuee in Newhaven and her sister claimed to have seen the same, and told a reporter that 'the village is taking the vision as a sign for a British victory'. Later, in the spring of 1944, it was reported widely in the national and local press that a vision of the Crucifixion had appeared in the skies above East Anglia on 27 April. The Reverend Harold Godfrey Green, of St Nicholas, Ipswich, investigated and received hundreds of corroborating reports. He declared publicly that it was a good omen for Britain.[31]

The years between the Spanish Civil War and the end of the Second World War saw a raft of new prophetic literature about Armageddon and the fate of Europe.[32] The Nostradamian wars recommenced. An interpretation of his quatrains by a French medical doctor foretold the fall of Hitler. The book went through several editions in 1938–9 and was subsequently banned by the Vichy government.[33] The Saint Odile prophecy circulated widely once again in France as the war began. In 1940 the spring dedicated to the saint, which had been dry for a long time, began to flow once more, exactly as it supposedly did three months before the armistices of 1870 and 1918. Peace was in the air, or in the water to be more precise. Literary scholars have been intrigued by the importance the Jewish-American writer Gertrude Stein attached to the prophecy in making her own spiritual sense of the Second World War from her home in occupied France. She once wrote that she 'had to have the prophecies of Saint Odile' in order to have 'faith'.[34] In Germany the Pinsk prophecy attributed to Andrew Bobola received a new lease of life following the invasion of Poland. The familiar prophecies of early modern monks also resurfaced. One example was said to have been found in a bible in the town hall of Wismar. In an echo of the mayor of Eschweiler's public announcement on a similar matter in the previous war, the authorities in Wismar got so fed up with receiving enquiries about the prophecy that they had postcards printed that stated: 'The so-called testament of a fleeing clergyman is in all respects a complete invention. A document with such contents has neither been found here nor is it preserved in the City Hall. We request you to assist us in suppressing this falsehood.'[35]

New prophecies circulated. A prophetic legend known as 'The Corpse in the Car' spread across Europe, and particularly in France during 1938–40. It concerned a driver whose car stops or breaks down. A woman, sometimes described as a fortune teller or gypsy, passes by and foretells that Hitler will soon be dead. The proof will be that before the driver has reached his destination, a man will die in the back of his car. One of the more influential prophecies in Germany concerned a vision of a future cataclysmic European war where priests are imprisoned, but which ultimately ends in defeat for those who reject Christ. The vision was purportedly experienced by a wealthy Italian princess of Savoy, Franziska Maria Beliante, and she supposedly recorded it in a letter she sent to a cardinal in 1923. The Gestapo considered the prophecy to be a conspiracy against the state and the Nazi Party.[36]

New genres of lucky chain letters also circulated. For fifteen years, from around 1927, 'The Good Luck of Flanders' chain letter enjoyed considerable 'success' across the English-speaking world. One version ran as follows: 'The Good Luck of Flanders was sent to me and I am sending it out within twenty-four hours. This chain was started by an American officer in Flanders and is going around the world four times—and one who breaks it will have bad luck. Copy this letter and see what happens to you four days after mailing. It will bring you good luck.'[37] It disseminated widely across America in 1939 and 1940, and was so pervasive that the postmaster of Lincoln, Nebraska, complained that it was flooding the city's postal system, and urged people to 'use the waste basket instead'.[38] It then did the rounds in wartime Britain and Australia in 1940 and 1941. A resident of Chelmsford, England, wrote to his local newspaper in February 1940 enclosing a copy he had received, and suggested to the editor, 'you would be doing a public service by exposing this silly ramp, which is quite likely to play on the minds of some superstitious people'.[39]

German security service files for May 1942 include a report on the flood of good luck chain letters across the Reich. They had begun to circulate widely in early 1940, and to such an extent that communiqués were issued via the press, film, and radio pointing out their foolishness. This apparently proved effective, and the flow of such letters largely ceased—that is until February 1942, when they resurfaced once more. Police headquarters from twenty-two cities across the Reich reported unprecedented numbers. So many, indeed, that it was putting a burden on the Reichspost. The most popular was a new type called the 'Greetings from Lourdes' letter, which began, 'A mother passes it on, so that an armistice will come', and ended, 'Pray three Ave Marias, and within 177 hours you will experience unexpected good fortune.' It was reported from Innsbruck that the vogue for these chain letters had seized peasant women 'as if by a psychosis'. Memos from Graz and Oppeln said the chain letters were mostly copied by women to protect soldiers on the battlefield, and that the relatives of those in the army were urged by neighbours and friends to send them on to those at the fronts. In the town of Haslach im Kinzigtal police reported confiscating twenty copies of 'Greetings from Lourdes' in just one day. The Gestapo kept a close eye on the clergy and noted that while they were rarely active in disseminating the chain letters, they were doing little to stop the 'superstition' either. In one instance the Gestapo requested the bishop of Linz do something about the plague. He wrote to the clergy in his diocese instructing them that 'the Faithful are to be exhorted to destroy such chain letters'.[40]

The wearing of mascots, amulets, and talismans remained widespread in civilian society. In the 1920s a London East End doctor estimated that 40 per cent of the children he inspected in schools wore protective amulets under their clothes. The folklorist A. R. Wright was convinced that the First World War had 'undoubtedly caused a very great revival' in wearing charms, and remarked on the 'enormous outburst' of new types inspired by foreign influences, and on their promotion in public life. In 1922, for instance, the Great Western Railway Company handed out 50,000 small metal charms to staff to protect them from accidents.[41] They were also being sold widely in the high street. The Mass Observation team noted in July 1940 that Woolworths was selling good luck charms, Boots offered horseshoe amulets, and the Bolton jewellers Taylor's offered talismans for the RAF. A survey conducted in the

1950s indicated that one serving man or woman in three during the war 'had his or her private piece of solid magic'.[42] Familiar clerical concerns continued to be expressed in churches and chapels about the enthusiasm for such items. In January 1937 the archdeacon of Bradford bemoaned, 'How on earth can mascots help a football team to win?... There are still homes with horseshoes over the door. It is all bunkum and a return to paganism.'[43] But come the war and the press was once again forgiving. 'The ever-popular talisman is to the fore again,' observed one Scottish newspaper in December 1939. 'Men of our fighting forces are carrying the same selection of luck-bringers as were borne by our Tommies in the last war. That is, all except for the swastika.'[44]

The American military also embraced talismans, with several generals openly carrying their special lucky charms. In a study entitled *Psychology for the Armed Services*, published in 1945, it was considered a 'good thing' that soldiers heard of the rumour that General Eisenhower carried seven lucky coins in his pocket: 'Superstitions are psychologically unsound only if a man is more careful to make sure that his "rabbit's foot" is in his pocket than that his equipment is in good order.'[45] As was noted by the newspaper above, we do indeed find a familiar range of mascots and talismans worn by Allied military personnel in the Second World War, such as rabbit's feet, elephant amulets, golliwogs, cuddly toys, bones, lucky coins, black cats, four-leaf clovers, horseshoes, and playing cards. Similar lucky rituals were conducted as in the First World War, the usual jinxes and Jonahs were avoided, and triskaidekaphobia was quite common.[46]

With regard to religious protection, pocket bibles proved popular and a new American market opened up for 'bullet-proof' editions with steel covers. In July 1944 the Federal Trade Commission filed a suit against the manufacturer of the 'Shield of Faith Armored Bible' on the grounds that not only had it been tested and found not to offer any protection against rifles and police bullets, but that the bullets passing through them got distorted and could cause even worse wounds. Promises of divine protection were OK though. An American bible and card company promoted a miniature bible with the lines, 'As you march along in line your rifle by your side, your bayonet protects you, your officer's your guide. These things are all assurance but in moments of alarm, the word of Him is in this book, 'twill keep you safe from harm.'[47] Some pilots carried family pocket bibles that their fathers or relatives had carried for protection in the First World War trenches.

One B-17 gunner explained, 'My Dad, he carried it all the way through the Argonne in the last war and he came out okay.'[48] Rosaries, medals, and badges, including those dedicated to the Sacred Heart, were widely worn by Catholics and also non-Catholics, and the St Christopher medal became hugely popular.[49] *Schutzbriefe* and *Himmelsbriefe* continued to be kept by German soldiers, though perhaps to a lesser degree than in previous conflicts, due to surveillance. The German police reported that a version was circulating which stated that the 'letter' had been found in Jesus's grave, and had subsequently been carried and copied in medieval times by a knight named Count Felix of Flanders. American soldiers also continued to carry *Himmelsbriefe*. One Pennsylvanian soldier attributed his survival in the Omaha Beach landing to the copy he kept in his wallet.[50] Jewish-American veterans recalled decades later how their non-Jewish comrades expressed surprise that they did not wear lucky amulets, and that some Jewish soldiers felt embarrassed about it. But when the national Jewish Welfare Board took on the role of supporting the needs of the 550,000 Jews in the American armed forces it sent some 1,320,000 *mezuzot* that were enthusiastically received.[51]

Rumours of Hitler's 'superstitious' nature echoed those regarding the Kaiser thirty years earlier. It was claimed he visited seances and was deeply influenced by a fortune teller who told him, in 1923, that he would come to power in 1933. The enduring idea that he regularly consulted astrologers was well established in popular legend by the early years of the war. In December 1939 a Scottish newspaper reported that Hitler had condemned his once favourite astrologer, a 'Dr Huber', to a concentration camp. Then there was his supposed adherence to the significance of numbers. It was reported that seven was his lucky number and hence he only ordered large-scale attacks on Sundays. Then again, in October 1939 the British press reported that his lucky day was Friday, and that this was the day he always launched his major initiatives. Hitler was, indeed, aware of the influence of numerology on the public. 'I myself would never launch an attack on the thirteenth,' he once said in conversation, 'not because I myself am superstitious, but because others are.' In 1942 the press reported that Heinrich Himmler had a mania about the number three. He had to cut three apples or potatoes when eating, and when ordering executions, he required three people to be killed at a time.[52]

The academic study of wartime rumour and 'superstition' that had begun during the First World War developed further in the next, and the propaganda value of these expressions of popular belief was exploited more systematically this time.[53] In 1950 the US Air Force commissioned the Rand Corporation to assess the military value of supernatural ideas. The resulting report, 'The Exploitation of Superstitions for Purposes of Psychological Warfare', drew upon the recent experience of the war, including captured Nazi security service documents. As the report's author, Jean Hungerford, noted, sporadic attempts were made by the wartime propaganda departments 'to make use of the enemy's non-rational beliefs'.[54] The British 'weakness' for astrology was noted by Goebbels, for instance. He wrote in his diary for 28 April 1942: 'we shall take up our astrological propaganda again as soon as possible. I expect quite a little of it, especially in the United States and England.'[55] He also joined the Nostradamian wars. While, in November 1939, he banned fortune-telling and prophetic publications in the Reich, he ordered the production of a French-language pamphlet of Nostradamus's interpretations for dissemination. As the Battle for Britain began, he also put out English radio broadcasts explaining that Nostradamus had prophesied the destruction of London in 1940.[56] He renewed the strategy a couple of years later, writing in his diary for 19 May 1942, 'we are therefore pressing into our service all star witnesses for occult philosophy. Nostradamus must once again submit to being quoted.'[57]

In early 1942 the British War Cabinet Defence Committee considered the influence of newspaper astrology and astrologers on the public, and set up a subcommittee to investigate the matter. It reported that 'about four out of ten members of the public have some interest in, or belief in, astrology. It is extremely difficult to gauge the depth of this belief, but there is reason to believe that, in the great majority of cases, it is very superficial.'[58] There was no great concern about the influence on domestic morale, then, but the Colonial and Foreign Offices could see the potential propaganda value. They hatched a 'world-wide scheme' to seed the idea that experiments with the occult sciences had predicted Hitler's downfall that year. It was decided to fix on the rumour that a planchette message from a dead spirit had foretold as much. The Secretary of State agreed to the scheme on 1 May, and as the

Governor of Hong Kong, Geoffry Northcote, explained in a telegram to the Colonial Office:

> planchette message allegedly emanating from the Chinese Temple in Macao. Scheme will necessitate taking into confidence to some extent one Chinese gentleman whose complete loyalty and discretion was amply proved during 1925 boycott, and probably at later stage Reuters local correspondent who is very discreet. Matter will be set on foot May 18th unless I hear to the contrary. I have hopes of getting story to Germany via Tokyo possibly through Domei but suggest Embassy should not repeat not be apprised.[59]

Later in the war the American Office of Strategic Services (OSS), the forerunner of the CIA, also implemented a modest plan called Operation Hermit to undermine enemy morale in the Far East by spreading over the airwaves negative astrological, divinatory, and phrenological reports on Japanese puppet rulers in the region. One palmistry broadcast explained how the lines on the palms of the Japanese Prime Minister, Hideki Tōjō, confirmed that the empire's days were numbered. Another, on numerology, announced that a catastrophic disaster would befall Japan during the first week of August 1945. That certainly came true—an atomic bomb was dropped on Hiroshima on 6 August.[60]

Expressions of supernatural thought, belief, and imagination helped deal with the psychological consequences of war trauma and encapsulated new social norms. The expulsion of Germans from Czechoslovakia after 1945 led to reports of ghostly hauntings by both expelled Germans and those Czechs who occupied their former homes. Some claimed that departing Germans had bewitched or cursed their former properties. One reason proposed for an apparent spike in the number of witchcraft accusations in Germany during the 1950s is the influx of single women into rural communities as a result of the post-war displacements. Such was the concern regarding the continued popular belief in witchcraft and magic in the immediate post-war era that the German Society for Protection against Superstition was founded in 1954, and in Yugoslavia the Communist authorities launched a public campaign against folk magic and its practitioners. Meanwhile, in Britain, Parliament found itself debating the nature of fortune-telling, witchcraft, and spiritualism when it passed the Fraudulent Mediums Act in 1950 to protect bona fide adherents of the spiritualist faith.[61]

In surveying the continuities of supernatural belief during and between the two world wars the aim has not been to argue for the timelessness of such beliefs, or to conclude glibly with a weary, 'It was ever thus.' Beliefs and practices constantly ebbed and flowed, disappeared and emerged, in response to broader trends in social, cultural, and economic life. With respect to this continuum of supernatural beliefs and practices, the First World War was influential in the way it cemented the commercialization of talismans and amulets, helped incorporate mechanization into the realm of the magical, rendered mundane the notion of life after death, and psychologized the psychic realm. The wartime newspapers were important in reshaping the relevance of supernatural interventions in and interpretations of the contemporary world. New crises and social developments in the inter war period, most notably the Great Depression, played their part, but, in short, the First World War and its legacy confirmed that the supernatural was profoundly modern.

NOTES

Preface

1. See Roy MacLeod, 'The World of Science, the Great War and Beyond: Revisiting Max Weber's *Wissenschaft als Beruf*', in Marie-Eve Chagnon and Tomás Irish (eds), *The Academic World in the Era of the Great War* (Basingstoke, 2018), pp. 253–70. Philosophical debate over Weber's 'disenchantment' thesis is ongoing. See, for example, Jason A. Josephson-Storm, *The Myth of Disenchantment: Magic, Modernity, and the Birth of the Human Sciences* (Chicago, 2017), pp. 269–87; Anthony J. Carroll, 'Disenchantment, Rationality and the Modernity of Max Weber', *Forum Philosophicum* 16 (2011), 117–37.
2. Joachim Friedrich Baumhauer, *Johann Kruse und der 'neuzeitliche Hexenwahn'* (Neumünster, 1984), p. 25.
3. *Cambridge Independent Press*, 5 February 1915. Catherine E. Parsons, 'Notes on Cambridgeshire Witchcraft', *Proceedings of the Cambridgeshire Antiquarian Society* 19 (1915), 31–49.
4. *Aberdeen Press and Journal*, 5 October 1915; *Monmouth Guardian and Bargoed and Caerphilly Observer*, 10 November 1916.
5. *The Cambrian News and Merionethshire Standard*, 4 January 1918.

Chapter 1

1. Benito Mussolini, *Il mio diario di guerra* (Milan, 1923); quoted in *The Living Age* 317 (1923), 307.
2. Alexander Watson, *Enduring the Great War: Combat, Morale and Collapse in the German and British Armies, 1914–1918* (Cambridge, 2008), pp. 9, 98, 99.
3. James H. Capshew, *Psychologists on the March: Science, Practice, and Professional Identity in America, 1929–1969* (Cambridge, 1999), pp. 4–5, 16; Marianne Müller-Brettel, 'Psychologische Beiträge im Ersten Weltkrieg: Ausdruck von Kriegsbegeisterung und Patriotismus oder Ergebnis des Entwicklungsstandes psychologischer Teorie und Forschung', *Psychologie und Geschichte* 6 (1994), 27–47; Ben Shephard, 'Psychology and the Great War, 1914–1918', *The Psychologist* 28, 11 (2015), 944–6; Joanna Burke, 'Psychology at War, 1918–1945', in A. D. Lovie and G. D. Richards (eds), *Psychology in Britain: Historical Essays and Personal Reflections* (London, 2001), pp. 133–49.
4. George Crile, *A Mechanistic View of War and Peace* (New York, 1915), p. vii.
5. Fletcher Bascom Dresslar, *Superstition and Education* (Berkeley, CA, 1907), p. 2.

6. Edmund S. Conklin, 'Superstitious Belief and Practice among College Students', *American Journal of Psychiatry* 30 (1919), 83–102.
7. G. Stanley Hall, 'Psychological Notes on the War', *The Journal of Race Development* 6 (1916), 366.
8. J.C.B., 'War and Credulity', *Journal of Educational Psychology* 9 (1918), 299.
9. See George M. Johnson, *Dynamic Psychology in Modernist British Fiction* (Basingstoke, 2006), p. 91.
10. In English, see, for example, Charles Oman, *The Unfortunate Colonel Despard and Other Studies* (London, 1922), pp. 49–71; Tim Cook, 'Black-Hearted Traitors, Crucified Martyrs, and the Leaning Virgin: The Role of Rumor and the Great War Canadian Soldier', in Jennifer Keene and Michael Neiberg (eds), *Finding Common Ground: New Directions in First World War Studies* (Leiden, 2011), pp. 21–43. See also Christophe Prochasson and Anne Rasmussen (eds), *Vrai et faux dans la Grande Guerre* (Paris, 2004).
11. Lucien Graux, *Les Fausses Nouvelles de la Grande Guerre*, 3 vols (Paris, 1918).
12. Marc Bloch, 'Réflexions d'un historien sur les fausses nouvelles de la guerre', *Revue de synthèse historique* 33 (1921), 13–35. The article has been translated into English by James P. Holoka for the *Michigan War Studies Review* (2013), http://www.miwsr.com/2013-051.aspx.
13. See Graham Seal, '"We're Here Because We're Here": Trench Culture of the Great War', *Folklore* 124 (2013), 178–99.
14. On Dauzat, see François Cochet, 'Preface' to Albert Dauzat, *Légendes, prophéties et superstitions de la Grande Guerre* (Paris, [1918] 2012), pp. 5–21.
15. Cited in Reinhard Johler, 'Laboratory Conditions: German-Speaking *Volkskunde* and the Great War', in Reinhard Johler, Christian Marchetti, and Monique Scheer (eds), *Doing Anthropology in Wartime and War Zones: World War I and the Cultural Sciences in Europe* (Bielefeld, 2010), p. 130.
16. Ralph Linton, 'Totemism and the A.E.F', *American Anthropologist* 26 (1924), 294–300.
17. Eduard Hoffmann-Krayer, 'Folk-lore militaire', *Revue des Traditions Populaires* 30 (1915), 108–9.
18. Christoph Daxelmüller, 'Forward', in Hanns Bächtold-Stäubli and Eduard Hoffmann-Krayer (eds), *Handwörterbuch des deutschen Aberglaubens* (Berlin, [1927] 1987), pp. v–xxxiv.
19. Dauzat, *Légendes*, pp. 37–8; Johler, 'Laboratory Conditions: German-Speaking *Volkskunde*', pp. 133–4.
20. Fabio Dei and Paolo De Simonis, 'Folklore di guerra: l'antropologia italiana e il primo conflitto mondiale', *Lares* 78 (2012), 405–36.
21. Paolo De Simonis and Fabio Dei, 'Wartime Folklore: Italian Anthropology and the First World War', in Johler, Marchetti, and Scheer (eds), *Doing Anthropology in Wartime*, pp. 81–2. See also Henryk Misiak and Virginia M. Staudt, *Catholics in Psychology: A Historical Survey* (New York, 1954).
22. De Simonis and Dei, 'Wartime Folklore', pp. 90–1.

23. Dauzat, *Légendes*, p. 37.
24. R. R. Marett, 'War and Savagery', *Folklore* 26 (1915), 10.
25. R. R. Marett, 'The Transvaluation of Culture', *Folklore* 29 (1918), 31–2.
26. Henrika Kuklick, 'Continuity and Change in British Anthropology, 1914–1919', in Johler, Marchetti, and Scheer (eds), *Doing Anthropology in Wartime*, pp. 29–47; Henrika Kuklick, *The Savage Within: The Social History of British Anthropology, 1885–1945* (Cambridge, 1991), pp. 119–82.
27. *Tamworth Herald*, 9 December 1916. On Lovett's collection, see Jude Hill, 'The Story of the Amulet: Locating the Enchantment of Collections', *Journal of Material Culture* 12 (2007), 65–87.
28. Edward Lovett, *Magic in Modern London* (Croydon, 1925), pp. 13, 15, 18.
29. *The Times*, 20 November 1920.
30. F. C. S. Schiller, 'War Prophecies', *Journal of the Society for Psychical Research* 17 (1915–16), 185, 186.
31. Émile Durkheim, *'German above All': The German Mental Attitude and the War* (Paris, 1915), p. 44.
32. *L'Indépendance Belge*, 10 November 1914; *Light*, 21 November 1914, 560.
33. *Sunderland Daily Echo*, 24 October 1914.
34. Schiller, 'War Prophecies', 185.
35. Susanne Brandt, '*Nagelfiguren*: Nailing Patriotism in Germany 1914–18', in Nicholas J. Saunders (ed.), *Matters of Conflict: Material Culture, Memory and the First World War* (London, 2004), pp. 62–72; Gerhard Schneider, 'Über hannoversche Nagelfiguren im Ersten Weltkrieg', *Hannoversche Geschichtsblätter* 50 (1996), 207–58.
36. *Le Temps*, 30 October 1915.
37. René Verneau, 'Les Hindenburg en bois des Nègres du Loango', *L'Anthropologie* 27 (1916), 133.
38. W. Deonna, 'La Recrudescence des superstitions en temps de guerre et les statues à clous', *L'Anthropologie* 27 (1916), 267. For Deonna's views on the war, see Christina Theodosiou, 'A World in Collapse: How the Great War Shaped Waldemar Deonna's Theory on Europe's Decline', in Marie-Eve Chagnon and Tomás Irish (eds), *The Academic World in the Era of the Great War* (London, 2018), pp. 141–60.
39. Stephen Anthony Smith and Alan Knight (eds), *The Religion of Fools? Superstition Past and Present* (Oxford, 2008); Euan Cameron, *Enchanted Europe: Superstition, Reason, and Religion 1250–1750* (Oxford, 2010), pp. 4–14.
40. See Michael Roper, *The Secret Battle: Emotional Survival in the Great War* (Manchester, 2009), p. 63.
41. Vanda Wilcox, *Morale and the Italian Army during the First World War* (Cambridge, 2016), p. 16; Peter Gatrell, *Russia's First World War: A Social and Economic History* (London, 2005), p. 115; James E. Kitchen, *The British Imperial Army in the Middle East: Morale and Military Identity in the Sinai and Palestine Campaigns, 1916–1918* (London, 2014), p. 16.
42. IWM 25042, James Gough Cooper, reel 2.

Chapter 2

1. Arthur Edward Waite, 'Sainte Odile: The Growth of a Legend', *The Occult Review* 24 (1916), 207.

2. Maurice Maeterlinck, *The Wrack of the Storm*, trans. Alexander Teixeira de Mattos (London, 1916), p. 213.

3. See David G. Morgan-Owen, *The Fear of Invasion: Strategy, Politics, and British War Planning, 1880–1914* (Oxford, 2017); Catriona Pennell, *A Kingdom United: Popular Responses to the Outbreak of the First World War in Britain and Ireland* (Oxford, 2012), pp. 11–21; Ignatius Frederick Clarke, *Voices Prophesying War: Future Wars, 1763–3749*, 2nd edn (Oxford, 1992); Jean-Yves Le Naour, *Nostradamus s'en va-t-en guerre: 1914–1918* (Paris, 2008), pp. 19–39; Ignatius Frederick Clarke, *The Great War with Germany, 1890–1914: Fictions and Fantasies of the War-to-Come* (Liverpool, 1997).

4. Ian Foster, 'The Translation of William Le Queux's *The Invasion of 1910*: What Germany Made of Scaremongering in *The Daily Mail*', in Myriam Salama-Carr (ed.), *Translating and Interpreting Conflict* (New York, 2007), pp. 169–83.

5. Charles Oman, *The Unfortunate Colonel Despard and Other Studies* (London, 1922), p. 68.

6. Jean Vic, *La Littérature de la guerre* (Paris, 1918), pp. 129–31.

7. Maurice Maeterlinck, *Wrack of the Storm*, p. 213.

8. Giuseppe Ciuffa, *La guerra europea e le profezie* (Rome, 1915).

9. Jonathan Green, *The Strange and Terrible Visions of Wilhelm Friess: The Paths of Prophecy in Reformation Europe* (Ann Arbor, MI, 2014), p. 120; William Gregory, 'German Popular Prophecies', *Blackwood's Magazine* 67 (1850), 568; Margarete Rothbarth, 'Zur Völkerschlacht am Birkenbaum', *Zeitschrift des Vereins für Volkskunde*, 27/28 (1917–18), 245–7.

10. Wellesley Tudor Pole, *Some Deeper Aspects of the War* (Bristol, 1914), pp. 4, 5.

11. Adrian Gregory, 'Beliefs and Religion', in Jay Winter (ed.), *The Cambridge History of the First World War*, vol. 3: *Civil Society* (Cambridge, 2014), p. 426.

12. Edgar Leoni, *Nostradamus and his Prophecies* (New York, 1961), p. 70. The Franco-German Nostradamian tussle over the war continued in the years after 1918. See C. de Lamor, *La Guerre de 1914–18 vue en 1555 par Me Nostradamus* (La Roche-sur-Yon, 1922); C. L. Loog, *Die Weissagungen des Nostradamus: Erstmalige Auffindung des Chiffreschlüssels und Enthüllung der Prophezeiungen über Europas Zukunft und Frankreichs Glück und Niedergang, 1555–2200* (Pfullingen, 1921).

13. 'The Prophecies of Nostradamus from "Nostradamus" by A. Demar Latour', *The Occult Review* 24 (July 1916), 16–17, 21. Thanks to the International Association for the Preservation of Spiritualist and Occult Periodicals for making such historic periodicals open access: http://www.iapsop.com.

14. Albert Kniepf, *Die Weisagungen des altfranzösischen Sehers Michael Nostradamus und der jetzige Weltkrieg* (Hamburg, 1915), p. 43.

15. Reprinted in the *Liverpool Echo*, 24 February 1915.

16. *Birmingham Daily Gazette*, 30 November 1916; *The Scotsman*, 23 August 1916.

17. 'Joanna Southcott and the Year 1914', *Light*, 22 August 1914, 400; Alice Seymour, 'Joanna Southcott and the Year 1914', *Light*, 3 October 1914, 478.

18. *The Athenæum*, 10 October 1914, 357; 'Prophecy and the Press', *Light*, 16 January 1915, 31.

19. Reported in the *Liverpool Echo*, 25 July 1917.

20. *The People*, 5 August 1917.

21. George Stoffler, *La Prophétie de Sainte Odile et la fin de la guerre* (Paris, 1916).

22. Dauzat, '*Légendes*', p. 203. Waite, 'Sainte Odile: The Growth of a Legend', p. 212.

23. See, for example, *Église d'Albi: la semaine religieuse de l'archidiocèse d'Albi*, 12 August 1916, 410–13; *Bulletin religieux de l'archidiocèse de Rouen*, 29 July 1916, 692–3; *L'Indépendant du Berry*, 30 July 1916.

24. Vic, *La Littérature de la guerre*, p. 131.

25. Dauzat, *Légendes*, p. 206.

26. Stephan Bachter, 'Nostradamus und der Mühlhiasl: Transformation und Wiederkehr von Prophezeiungen', *Augsburger Volkskundliche Nachrichten* 5, 10 (1999), 30.

27. Bachter, 'Nostradamus und der Mühlhiasl', 31.

28. Gaudentius Rossi, *The Christian Trumpet; Or, Previsions and Predictions* (Boston, MA, 1873), pp. 187–8; *Le Devoir*, 29 August 1914; *La Croix*, 4 September 1914.

29. Margareta Rothbath, 'Zur Literatur der Kriegsprophezeiungen', *Zeitschrift des Vereins für Volkskunde*, 27/28 (1917–18), 247.

30. Raymond Gillespie, *Devoted People: Belief and Religion in Early Modern Ireland* (Manchester, 1997), p. 138.

31. *Irish Times*, 27 April 1918; Eleanor Hull, 'The Black Pig of Kiltrustan', *Folklore* 29 (1918), 226–37.

32. Maeterlinck, *Wrack of the Storm*, pp. 248–9.

33. Herbert Thurston, *The War and the Prophets* (London, 1915), p. 40.

34. For example, *Église d'Albi: la semaine religieuse de l'archidiocèse d'Albi*, 17 October 1914, 530; *New Zealand Tablet*, 14 January 1915.

35. *Occult Review* 20 (1914), 174.

36. Arthur Conan Doyle, *The History of Spiritualism* (Cambridge, 1926), vol. 2; 'A Scottish Seer', *Light*, 12 February 1916, 56.

37. Frederick Bligh Bond, *The Hill of Vision: A Forecast of the Great War* (Boston, MA, 1919), pp. 15, 16, 19.

38. Simone de Tervagne, *Madame Fraya m'a dit: les confidences de la plus grande voyante du siècle* (Paris, 1955).

39. Eugène Osty, *Lucidité et intuition: étude expérimentale* (Paris, 1913).

40. Gabriel Cabannes, *Galerie des Landais* (Hossegor, 1931), vol. 5, pp. 123–6; *Mècheroutiette* 26 (1912), 63; 18 (1911), 47; 13 (1910), 60; *Le Figaro*, 10 December 1914.

41. *La Revue hebdomadaire*, 10 January 1920, 7; *Le Petit Parisien*, 29 August 1931; *Écho de Bougie*, 16 December 1934.

42. Details of her early life were investigated by her contemporary the theatre journalist Louis Schneider. See his pieces in *Gil Blas*, 13 June 1906; *Le Petit Parisien*, 12 August 1932. See also *L'Ami de Ménilmontant: Organe de la paroisse Notre-Dame de la Croix* 104 (1919), 2–6.

43. *Le Figaro*, 31 March 1893.

44. *Le Gaulois*, 2 April 1893.

45. Chedomille Mijatovich, *The Memoirs of a Balkan Diplomat* (London, 1917), p. 195; Harry A. Franck, *Roaming through the West Indies* (New York, 1920), p. 163.

46. Nicole Edelman, *Histoire de la voyance et du paranormal du XVIIIe siècle à nos jours* (Paris, 2006), pp. 100–1.

47. '"Année sombre" dit le docteur Papus', *Mystéria* 1 (1913), 95–6.

48. J.-H. Lavaur, *Comment se réalise en ce moment même la fin de l'Empire allemand, annoncée par plusieurs prophéties célèbres, précises et concordantes* (Paris, 1915), p. 5. J.-H. Lavaur, *Cómo llega en los actuales momentos el fin del Imperio alemán*, trans. Juan García Valladolid (Madrid, 1915); J.-H. Lavaur, *Cum se îndeplineşte chiar in momentul acesta sfârşitul Imperiului german prevestit prin mai multe proorociri celebre, precise şi concordante*, trans. Scarlat Ion Ghica (Bucharest, 1919).

49. *Handwörterbuch des deutschen Aberglaubens*, vol. 9, p. 473.

50. Countess Zalinski, *Noted Prophecies, Predictions, Omens, and Legends Concerning the Great War* (Chicago, 1917), p. 83; F. L. Rawson, *How the War Will End* (London, 1917), p. 43.

51. Le Naour, *Nostradamus*, pp. 43–4.

52. See, for example, *Evening Post* (New Zealand), 12 December 1914.

53. *British Review* 8 (1914), 227.

54. *La Lanterne*, 29 October 1914.

55. *Wiener Journal*, 19 November 1915.

56. *Fortnightly Review*, 5 May 1916, 156.

57. See, for example, *The Argus* (Melbourne), 24 February 1917; *Boston Daily Globe*, 27 December 1917; *Der Tiroler*, 5 January 1917.

58. Dauzat, *Légendes*, p. 253; Nikola Marković, '"Od kopile kočicu i pobeg-zrno od kukuruz": Sujeverje u srpskoj vojsci tokom Prvog svetskog rata', *Godišnjak za društvenu istoriju* 13 (2006), 65; Le Naour, *Nostradamus*, pp. 53–4; *Huddersfield Daily Examiner*, 19 June 1918.

59. *Whitby Gazette*, 21 January 1916; Le Naour, *Nostradamus*, p. 44.

60. Edelman, *Histoire de la voyance*, p. 104; F. C. Barlet, *L'Astrologie et la guerre* (Paris, 1917).

61. Ellic Howe, *Urania's Children: The Strange World of the Astrologers* (London, 1967), pp. 77, 82–4; Kocku von Stuckrad, *Geschichte der Astrologie: von den Anfängen bis zur Gegenwart* (Munich, 2003), pp. 321–36.

62. *Devon and Exeter Gazette*, 24 February 1915; *Wells Journal*, 26 February 1915; *Dover Express*, 1 October 1915.

63. Patrick Curry, *Prophecy and Power: Astrology in Early Modern England* (Cambridge, 1989), pp. 101–2; Owen Davies, *Witchcraft, Magic and Culture, 1736–1951* (Manchester, 1999), pp. 153–7. In Ireland there was also *Old Moore's Almanac*, founded by the eighteenth-century Dublin astrologer Theophilus Moore.

64. Allan Haywood Bright, 'The Prophetic Literature of the War', *Proceedings of the Literary and Philosophical Society of Liverpool* 64 (1916), 88.

65. *500 of the Best Cockney War Stories* (London, 1921), pp. 114–15.

66. Nicholas Goodrick-Clarke, *The Occult Roots of Nazism: Secret Aryan Cults and their Influence on Nazi Ideology* (London, 1985), p. 103.

67. E. H. Bailey, 'The Armageddon of Nations', *Old Moore's Monthly Messenger* 7 (September 1914), 227–8.

68. Thurston, *The War and the Prophets*, pp. 108–9.

69. Bright, 'The Prophetic Literature of the War', 88.

70. *Newcastle Daily Journal*, 14 August 1917.

71. James Munson (ed.), *Echoes of the Great War: The Diary of the Reverend Andrew Clark 1914–1919* (Oxford, 1985), p. 211.

72. Sepharial, 'The End of the War: A Contest of Astrological Opinion', *The British Journal of Astrology* 8 (January 1915), 74–5; *Mittags-Zeitung*, 23 February 1916; 'Wann ist der Krieg zu Ende?', *Zentralblatt Okkultismus* 11 (1918), 473.

73. *Leamington Spa Courier*, 25 October 1918.

74. Alan Leo, *Mars: The War Lord* (London, 1915), p. 44.

75. 'Notes of the Month', *The Occult Review* 25 (1917), 9.

76. YRAM (Marcel Forhan), *La Guerre et le merveilleux. Prophéties connues et prédictions inédites. Apparitions célèbres. Les Nombres. Une Clef de l'histoire de France. Causes de la guerre* (Paris, 1915); Marcus Osterrieder, 'Der prophezeite Krieg', *Gegenwart. Zeitschrift für Kultur, Politik, Wirtschaft* 2 (2010), 25–34; Alex Owen, *The Place of Enchantment: British Occultism and the Culture of the Modern* (Chicago, 2004), pp. 221–3.

77. Marr Murray, *Bible Prophecies and the Present War* (London, 1915). See also, for example, Georg Greite, *Was bedeuten die Weissagungen d. Propheten Daniel* (Lorch, 1916); F. P. Argall, *The Prophet in War Time: Isaiah's Message for To-Day* (London, 1916).

78. Jay Winter, 'Painting Armageddon', in Hugh Cecil and Peter Liddle (eds), *Facing Armageddon: The First World War Experienced* (London, 1996), pp. 859–66.

79. Philip Jenkins, *The Great and Holy War: How World War I Changed Religion for Ever* (Oxford, 2014), pp. 143–4.

80. Matthew Avery Sutton, *American Apocalypse: A History of Modern Evangelicalism* (Cambridge, MA, 2014), p. 69.

81. D. W. Langelett, *Gog und seine Niederlage: Hesekiel 38 und 39; ein Nachweis, daß England der Gog ist, von welchem der Prophet geweissagt hat, und darum in diesem Kriege unterliegen muß* (Luzerne, IA, 1915); Langelett, *The World-War in the Light of Prophecy* (Luzerne, IA, 1915), pp. 3, 4.

82. Tony Wills, *A People for His Name: A History of Jehovah's Witnesses and an Evaluation* (New York, 1967), p. 52.

83. Albert Grundlingh, *War and Society: Participation and Remembrance: South African Black and Coloured Troops in the First World War, 1914–1918* (Stellenbosch, 2014), pp. 16–17.

84. Assa Okoth, *A History of Africa: African Societies and the Establishment of Colonial Rule, 1800–1915* (Nairobi, 2006), pp. 393–4; John McCracken, *A History of Malawi, 1859–1966* (Woodbridge, 2012), pp. 135–7.

85. W. F. T. Salt, *The Great War—in the Divine Light of Prophecy: Is it Armageddon?* (Bristol, 1915); Augusta Cook, *Is it Armageddon? The Present War in the Light of Divine Prophecy* (London, 1917).

86. Henry Sulley, *Is it Armageddon? Or Britain in Prophecy* (London, 1915), p. 5; Fernand Baldensperger, 'Prophesying in Time of War', *Columbia University Quarterly* 20 (1918), 108.

87. *Bucks Herald*, 3 November 1917.

88. Henry Charles Beeching, *Armageddon: A Sermon upon the War Preached in Norwich Cathedral* (London, 1914), p. 14.

89. *North Devon Journal*, 20 January 1916.

90. *Bucks Herald*, 3 November 1917.

91. *Belfast News-Letter*, 27 December 1915.

92. Maria Carlson, *No Religion Higher than Truth: A History of the Theosophical Movement in Russia, 1875–1922* (Princeton, NJ, 1993), p. 61; Herman A. O. de Tollenaere, *The Politics of Wisdom: Theosophy and Labour, National, and Women's Movements in Indonesia and South Asia 1875–1947* (Leiden, 1996), pp. 153, 156–60; Joy Dixon, *Divine Feminine: Theosophy and Feminism in England* (Baltimore, MD, 2001), p. 88.

93. Radha Rajagopal Sloss, *Lives in the Shadow with J. Krishnamurti* (London, 1991), p. 36.

94. A. P. Sinnett, *The Spiritual Powers and the War* (London, 1915), p. 23. For a theosophical critique of these views, see N. D. Khandalavala, 'The Great War and the Dark Powers', *The Theosophist* 37 (1916), 65–75.

95. *Theosophical Quarterly* 14 (1916), 84, 85, 90.

96. 'Some Spiritual Issues of the War', *Theosophical Quarterly* 14 (1916), 115.

97. F. Hallett, 'The Inner Side of the War', *The Theosophist* 36 (1915), 533–47. See also C. W. Leadbeater, 'The Great War', *The Theosophist* 37 (1916), 511–28.

98. 'On the Screen of Time', *Theosophical Quarterly* 13 (1915), 287.

99. Baldensperger, 'Prophesying in Time of War', 110.

100. Carlson, *No Religion Higher than Truth*, pp. 77–8.

101. Tudor Pole, *Some Deeper Aspects of the War*, p. 15.

102. 'The Karma of the Russians', *Theosophical Quarterly* 15 (1918), 201.

103. Ulrich Linse, *Geisterseher und Wunderwirker: Heilsuche im Industriezeitalter* (Frankfurt am Main, 1996), pp. 118–19; *The Irish Times*, 24 May 1929.

104. See Ulrich Linse, '"Universale Bruderschaft" oder nationaler Rassenkrieg: die deutschen Theosophen im Ersten Weltkrieg', in Heinz-Gerhard Haupt

and Dieter Langewiesche (eds), *Nation und Religion in der deutschen Geschichte* (Frankfurtam Main, 2001), pp. 602–45.

105. Goodrick-Clarke, *The Occult Roots of Nazism*, pp. 86–9, 90–104.
106. Quoted in Peter Staudenmaier, *Between Occultism and Nazism: Anthroposophy and the Politics of Race in the Fascist Era* (Leiden, 2014), p. 68.
107. Staudenmaier, *Between Occultism and Nazism*, pp. 65, 66. See also Peter Staudenmaier, 'Esoteric Alternatives in Imperial Germany: Science, Spirit, and the Modern Occult Revival', in Monica Black and Eric Kurlander (eds), *Revisiting the 'Nazi Occult': Histories, Realities, Legacies* (Rochester, NY, 2015), pp. 23–42; Markus Osterrieder, *Welt im Umbruch: Nationalitätenfrage, Ordnungspläne und Rudolf Steiners Haltung im Ersten Weltkrieg* (Stuttgart, 2014).
108. *Aberdeen Press and Journal*, 23 May 1916.
109. 'The Prophecy of Johannes', *Light*, 21 November 1914, 559.
110. *Le Figaro*, 10 September 1914.
111. Julien de Narfon, 'Prophéties de guerre', *La Guerre Mondiale*, 23 February 1916, 3658.
112. Thurston, *War and the Prophets*, pp. 47–68; Le Naour, *Nostradamus*, pp. 110–13.
113. *The People*, 6 December 1914; *West London Observer*, 30 October 1914.
114. *Light*, 24 October 1914, 506; 14 November 1914, 547; C. de Vesme, 'Petite Excursion critique à travers les prophéties de la guerre', *Annales des Sciences Psychiques* 25 (1915), 238.
115. Joanny Bricaud, *La Guerre et les prophéties célèbres: étude historique et critique* (Paris, 1916); Ralph Shirley, *Prophecies and Omens of the Great War* (London, 1914), p. 28. See also Ralph Shirley, 'The Kaiser and Antichrist', *Occult Review* 20 (1914), 354.
116. Arthur Trefusis, *The War in a New Light* (London, 1915), p. 41.
117. See, for example, *Taunton Courier*, 14 July 1915; *Evening Despatch*, 24 June 1915.
118. Dauzat, *Légendes*, p. 174.
119. *Western Gazette*, 29 December 1916.
120. Julian Symons, *Horatio Bottomley* (Looe, [1955] 2001), p. 140.
121. Henry J. Houston, *The Real Horatio Bottomley* (London, 1923), pp. 161–2.
122. *Sunday Pictorial*, 2 April 1916.
123. F. B. Naga, 'Deutschlands Krieg und die Zahlenmagie', *Zentralblatt für Okkultismus* 9 (1916), 4–6.
124. Cited in the *Belfast News-Letter*, 27 July 1915.
125. Sutton, *American Apocalypse: A History of Modern Evangelicalism*, p. 69.
126. 'Les Documents sur les prophéties de la guerre', *Annales des Sciences Psychiques* 25 (1915), 241.
127. Harold D. Lasswell, *Propaganda Technique in the World War* (New York, 1927), p. 201.
128. See, for example, Lesley Ann Coote, *Prophecy and Public Affairs in Later Medieval England* (Woodbridge, 2000); Ottavia Niccoli, *Prophecy and People in Renaissance*

Italy, trans. Lydia G. Cochrane (Princeton, NJ, 1990), ch. 1; Jürgen Beyer, *Lay Prophets in Lutheran Europe (c. 1550–1700)* (Leiden, 2016), ch. 6.

129. David Monger, *Patriotism and Propaganda in First World War Britain: The National War Aims Committee and Civilian Morale* (Liverpool, 2012), pp. 97–8.

Chapter 3

1. 'The Uncanny under Fire', *Globe*, 13 October 1914.
2. Jay Winter, *Sites of Memory, Sites of Mourning: The Great War in European Cultural History* (Cambridge, 1995), pp. 54–78. See Michael Snape's critique in his *God and the British Soldier: Religion and the British Army in the First and Second World Wars* (London, 2005), pp. 38, 39.
3. Cesare Caravaglios, *L'anima religiosa della guerra* (Milan, 1935), p. 129; Carlo Stiaccini, *L'anima religiosa della Grande Guerra* (Rome, 2009), pp. 166–76.
4. *Boston Guardian*, 3 June 1916; 'A Cross in the Sky in War-Time', *Confidence* (July 1916), 115.
5. *Derry Journal*, 21 October 1918.
6. F. Hadland Davis, 'Angels at Mons', *The Theosophist* 37 (1916), 211.
7. Cited in and discussed by Katherine Finlay, 'Angels in the Trenches: British Soldiers and Miracles in the First World War', in Kate Cooper and Jeremy Gregory (eds), *Signs, Wonders, Miracles: Representations of Divine Power in the Life of the Church* (Woodbridge, 2005), p. 447.
8. *Confidence*, March 1916, 43.
9. *Confidence*, January 1916, 7.
10. William Breckenridge, *From Vimy to Mons: A Historical Narrative* (Sherbrooke, 1919), pp. 92–3; cited in Tim Cook, 'Grave Beliefs: Stories of the Supernatural and the Uncanny among Canada's Great War Trench Soldiers', *The Journal of Military History* 77 (2013), 540.
11. *Lancashire Evening Post*, 18 September 1917; *Hull Daily Mail*, 5 January 1918.
12. *The Globe*, 15 October 1917.
13. For comprehensive accounts, see David Clarke, *The Angel of Mons: Phantom Soldiers and Ghostly Guardians* (Chichester, 2005); Richard J. Bleiler, *The Strange Case of 'The Angels of Mons': Arthur Machen's World War I Story, the Insistent Believers, and his Refutations* (Jefferson, NC, 2015).
14. Arthur Machen, *The Bowmen: And Other Legends of the War* (London, 1915), p. 7.
15. Machen, *The Bowmen*, p. 10.
16. Forbes Phillips and R. Thurston Hopkins, *War and the Weird* (London, 1916), p. 33.
17. *Confidence*, July–August 1917, 59.
18. *Manchester Evening News*, 6 September 1915.
19. *Light*, 4 September 1915, 422.
20. Herbert Hensley Henson, *War-Time Sermons* (London, 1915), p. 231.

21. *Light*, 11 September 1915, 440.
22. Quoted in Leo Ruickbie, 'Mrs Salter and the Angels: The 1915 Society for Psychical Research's Investigation of "Alleged Visions on the Battlefield" and the Angels of Mons', *Paranormal Review* 76 (2015), 9.
23. On the British propaganda machine, see Gary S. Messinger, *British Propaganda and the State in the First World War* (Manchester, 1992). On the Bureau and the Angel of Mons, see Clarke, *Angel of Mons*, p. 213.
24. *Daily Herald*, 17 July 1915.
25. Chris Maunder, *Our Lady of the Nations: Apparitions of Mary in 20th-Century Catholic Europe* (Oxford, 2016), pp. 18–21; David Blackbourn, *Marpingen: Apparitions of the Virgin Mary in Nineteenth-Century Germany* (New York, 1994), pp. 327–8.
26. Cesare Caravaglios, *L'anima religiosa della guerra* (Milan, 1935), figs 65–76.
27. *Irish Times*, 29 April 1918.
28. Michael P. Carroll, *Madonnas that Maim: Popular Catholicism in Italy since the Fifteenth Century* (Baltimore, MD, 1992), p. 55; Dauzat, *Légendes*, pp. 211–12.
29. Patrick J. Houlihan, *Catholicism and the Great War: Religion and Everyday Life in Germany and Austria-Hungary, 1914–1922* (Cambridge, 2015), pp. 175–6; Monique Scheer, 'Rettet Maria Deutschland? Die Diskussion um eine nationale Marienweihe nach dem Zweiten Weltkrieg', in Gottfried Korff (ed.), *Alliierte im Himmel: Populare Religiosität und Kriegserfahrung* (Tübingen, 2006), pp. 141–56.
30. *Le Courrier de la Manche*, 14 January 1917. Reprinted in Alain Denizot, *Le Sacré-Cœur et la Grande Guerre* (Paris, 1994), pp. 140, 143.
31. Raymond Jonas, *The Tragic Tale of Claire Ferchaud and the Great War* (Berkeley, CA, 2005), pp. 11–14; Annette Becker, *La Guerre et la foi: de la mort à la mémoire, 1914–années 1930* (Paris, 2015), pp. 93–7.
32. Théodore Delmont, *Pour la croisade du XXe siècle: sermons et conférences* (Paris, 1917), p. 274; Coubé cited in Becker, *La Guerre et la foi*, p. 95.
33. *Yorkshire Telegraph and Star*, 9 October 1914.
34. Karen Petrone, *The Great War in Russian Memory* (Bloomington, IN, 2011), pp. 35–6.
35. For details on the Fatima apparition, see Jeffrey S. Bennett, *When the Sun Danced: Myth, Miracles, and Modernity in Early Twentieth-Century Portugal* (Charlottesville, VA, 2012).
36. Bennett, *When the Sun Danced*, pp. 168, 189.
37. *Bath Chronicle and Weekly Gazette*, 24 July 1915.
38. Clarke, *The Angel of Mons*, pp. 177–83.
39. *Light*, 5 June 1915, 269.
40. *Portsmouth Evening News*, 16 June 1915.
41. *Benalla Standard*, 22 February 1916; *Shepparton News*, 28 February 1916; *The Yackandandah Times*, 29 June 1916.
42. W. H. Leathem, *The Comrade in White* (London, 1915), p. 2.

43. Clarke, *Angel of Mons*, pp. 179, 182.

44. Robert Haven Schauffler, *The White Comrade and Other Poems* (Boston, MA, 1920). See also Maud de Chantal Browne, 'Comrade in White', *Bulletin* 11 (1915), 378; Fred G. Bowles, 'The White Comrade', *Whitby Gazette*, 24 December 1915; Katherine Hale, *The White Comrade, and Other Poems, etc.* (Toronto, 1916).

45. Schauffler, *White Comrade*, p. 5.

46. *Manchester Courier and Lancashire General Advertiser*, 18 September 1915; *Cheltenham Looker-On*, 2 October 1915.

47. *Illustrated London News*, 2 October 1915; *Western Morning News*, 18 January 1916.

48. *Sunderland Daily Echo and Shipping Gazette*, 31 October 1916; *Grantham Journal*, 10 February 1917. On the growth of war shrines, see Mark Connelly, *The Great War, Memory and Ritual: Commemoration in the City and East London, 1916–1939* (Woodbridge, 2002), pp. 25–36.

49. *Light*, 17 November 1917, 364.

50. F. G. Gotwald, 'The White Comrade', *Lutheran Church Work and Observer*; reprinted in *The Lutheran Companion* 26 (1918), 301.

51. Robert Edward Crozier Long, *Colours of War* (New York, 1915), p. 278; *The Evening Telegraph and Post*, 6 August 1915; Tom Burnell, *Irishmen in the Great War: Reports from the Front 1915* (Barnsley, 2015), p. 161.

52. *Observer*, 16 January 1916; 'Armées, flottes et combats fantomatiques', *Annales des Sciences Psychiques* (February 1916), 26.

53. *Kilmore Free Press*, 24 June 1915.

54. Owen Davies, *The Haunted: A Social History of Ghosts* (Basingstoke, 2007), pp. 54–5; Owen Davies, 'Ghosts', in Christopher M. Moreman (ed.), *The Routledge Companion to Death and Dying* (London, 2018), p. 349; David Clarke, *A Natural History of Ghosts: 500 Years of Hunting for Proof* (New York, 2012).

55. Hereward Carrington, *Psychical Phenomena and the War* (New York, 1918), p. 175.

56. Carrington, *Psychical Phenomena and the War*, p. 175.

57. A. R. Wright, *English Folklore* (London, 1928), p. 59.

58. Frank Podmore, *Telepathic Hallucinations: The New View of Ghosts* (New York, 1910), p. 125.

59. Elliott O'Donnell, 'Hauntings in Belgium', *Occult Review* 21 (1915), 231; *Nottingham Evening Post*, 8 April 1915.

60. *Dublin Daily Express*, 13 August 1915.

61. Cook, 'Grave Beliefs: Stories of the Supernatural', 522.

62. *Liverpool Echo*, 21 November 1916.

63. George M. Johnson, *Mourning and Mysticism in First World War Literature and Beyond: Grappling with Ghosts* (Basingstoke, 2015). See also Randall Stevenson, *Literature and the Great War 1914–1918* (Oxford, 2013), pp. 80–4.

64. Quoted in David Williams, *Media, Memory, and the First World War* (Montreal, 2009), p. 141.

65. Robert Graves, *Goodbye to All That* (Oxford, 1995), p. 114.

66. David Williams, 'And We Go On, a Lost Classic of the Great War', Introduction to Will R. Bird, And We Go On (Montreal and Ontario, 2014), p. 1.

67. Johnson, Mourning and Mysticism, pp. 124–52; Winter, 'Spiritualism and the First World War', p. 194; M. Brady Brower, Unruly Spirits: The Science of Psychic Phenomena in Modern France (Chicago, 2010), p. 99.

68. René Nicolas, Campaign Diary of a French Officer, trans. K. Babbitt (Boston, MA, 1917), p. 56.

69. Coningsby Dawson, Khaki Courage: Letters in Wartime, 2nd ed. (New York, 1917), p. 96; cited in Cook, 'Grave Beliefs', 530.

70. Light, 24 November 1917, 376.

71. Joseph McCabe, Spiritualism: A Popular History from 1847 (London, 1920), p. 234.

72. For a more detailed overview of spiritualist membership, see Owen Davies, Ghosts: A Social History, vol. 5: Spiritualism during the Great War (London, 2010), pp. viii–x.

73. Robert Kugelmann, Psychology and Catholicism: Contested Boundaries (Cambridge, 2011), p. 142. See also Houlihan, Catholicism and the Great War, pp. 234–5; Francis Young, 'The Dangers of Spiritualism: The Roman Catholic Church's Campaign against Spiritualism during and after the First World War', Paranormal Review 71 (2014), 18–21.

74. Annales des Sciences Psychiques (January 1917), 15; Le Petit Journal, 12 March 1917.

75. Young, 'The Dangers of Spiritualism', 18–19.

76. Foreword, Elliot O'Donnell, The Menace of Spiritualism (New York, 1920), p. xii.

77. Davies, Ghosts: A Social History, vol. 5, p. 66; A. A. Boddy, 'Our Victory over Demons and Disease', Confidence (November 1916), 180.

78. Edward Clodd, The Question: 'If a Man Die, shall he Live again?' Job. XIV. 14: A Brief History and Examination of Modern Spiritualism, etc. (London, 1917).

79. Quoted in Dennis Taylor, 'Hardy and Hamlet', in Keith G. Wilson (ed.), Thomas Hardy Reappraised: Essays in Honour of Michael Millgate (Toronto, 2006), p. 49.

80. O'Donnell, Menace of Spiritualism, p. 96.

81. Stuart Cumberland, That Other World: Personal Experiences of Mystics and their Mysticism (London, 1918), p. 197.

82. Cumberland, That Other World, p. 200.

83. See, for example, Panikos Panayi, The Enemy in our Midst: Germans in Britain during the First World War (London, 2014), ch. 6; E. S. Turner, Dear Old Blighty (London, 1980), pp. 240–51.

84. Charles Gore, The Religion of the Church as Presented in the Church of England: A Manual of Membership (London, 1916), p. 85.

85. Georgina Byrne, Modern Spiritualism and the Church of England, 1850–1939 (Woodbridge, 2010), p. 182; Rene Kollar, Searching for Raymond: Anglicanism,

Spiritualism, and Bereavement between the Two World Wars (Lanham, MD, 2000), pp. 3–5.

86. Kollar, *Searching for Raymond*, pp. 22–3.

87. F. Fielding-Ould, *Is Spiritualism of the Devil?* (Beverley, 1917); reprinted in Davies, *Ghosts: A Social History*, vol. 5, p. 76.

88. Iris Van Der Knaap, '"War against the War!" Dutch Spiritualists during the First World War', *Paranormal Review* 76 (2015), 22.

89. There are eighteen spiritualists listed in Cyril Pearce's Conscientious Objector Register, http://www.1914.org/news/cos/, accessed 20 October 2017.

90. *Evening Despatch*, 28 April 1916.

91. *Preston Herald*, 29 July 1916.

92. Gerald O'Hara, *Dead Men's Embers* (York, 2006), p. 208; *Light*, 8 June 1918, 181.

93. *Birmingham Mail*, 22 February 1917.

94. 'The Story of the Motor Ambulances', *The Pioneer* 1, 3 (2014), 70–7.

95. Geoffrey K. Nelson, *Spiritualism and Society* (London, 1969), p. 154.

96. Arthur Conan Doyle, 'The Military Value of Spiritualism', *Light*, 11 May 1918, 147.

97. O'Hara, *Dead Men's Embers*, p. 202.

98. Lucy Harris, '"You Will Not See Me Again": Soldiers' Beliefs and Stories from the Front', *Paranormal Review*, 71 (2014), 17.

99. *Two Worlds*, 4 August 1916: *The Pioneer*, 1, 3 (2014), 76.

100. The point is well made in Snape, *God and the British Soldier*, p. 39; Harris, '"You Will Not See Me Again"', 14, 17.

101. *Two Worlds*, 26 February 1915; *The Pioneer*, 1, 3 (2014), 65.

102. *The Army and Religion: An Enquiry and its Bearing upon the Religious Life of the Nation* (London, 1919), pp. 19–20.

103. 'The Reality and Nearness of the Invisible World: A Soldier's Testimony', *Light*, 31 March 1917, 99; 'In a Pause of the Battle: A Soldier's Reflections at the Front', *Light*, 7 July 1917, 215; 'From a Soldier's Notebook', *Light*, 10 November 1917, 355.

104. 'Communication médianimique attribuée à Jeanne d'Arc', *Revue Spirite* 57 (1914), 410.

105. Léon Denis, *Le Monde invisible et la guerre* (Paris, 1919), pp. 8, 9. See also Le Naour, *Nostradamus*, pp. 125–6.

106. *Leeds Mercury*, 29 October 1915.

107. H.M.G. and M.M.H. (eds), *A Soldier Gone West: By a Soldier Doctor* (London, 1920); reprinted in Davies, *Ghosts: A Social History*, vol. 5, p. 45.

108. *Light*, 7 November 1914, 536.

109. *Dundee Evening Telegraph*, 24 June 1915; *Light*, 17 July 1915, 340.

110. Cited in *Light*, 30 November 1918, 381.

111. H. Pemberton, 'Mediums and the War', *The Occult Review*, 21, 2 (1915), 110–11.

112. Quoted in Clarke, *Angel of Mons*, p. 184.

113. 'Father John on the Battlefield', *Light*, 17 August, 1918, 262.
114. Van Der Knaap, '"War against the War!"', 22.
115. Winter, *Sites of Memory*, pp. 58–63; Kollar, *Searching for Raymond*, MD, pp. 9–14; Janet Oppenheim, *The Other World: Spiritualism and Psychical Research in England, 1850–1914* (Cambridge, 1985), pp. 371–90; Davies, *Ghosts: A Social History*, vol. 5, pp. x–xiii; Byrne, *Modern Spiritualism and the Church of England*, pp. 75–84; Johnson, *Mourning and Mysticism*, chs 2 and 3.
116. Arthur Conan Doyle, 'Where Is the Soul during Unconsciousness?', *Light*, 11 March 1916, 83.
117. Arthur Conan Doyle, *A History of Spiritualism*, vol. 2.
118. Winter, *Sites of Memory*, pp. 70–1; Cook, 'Grave Beliefs', 525.
119. *The Bookman* 51 (1920), 403.
120. Harris, '"You Will Not see Me Again"', 16.
121. Mrs Little, *Grenadier Rolf: By His Mother* (London, 1920), p. 33.
122. L. Kelway-Bamber (ed.), *Claude's Second Book* (London, 1919), p. xiv.
123. Hill, *Spiritualism*, p. 179.
124. *Hull Daily Mail*, 22 December 1917.
125. *New Metropolitan*, 46 (June 1917), 72. See also Mitch Horowitz, *Occult America* (New York, 2009), pp. 65–70.
126. J. Godfrey Raupert, 'The Truth about the Ouija Board', *American Ecclesiastical Review* 59 (1918), 463.
127. Carrington, *Psychical Phenomena*, p. 3. On Carrington, see Carlos S. Alvarado, 'Psychic Reach of the War: Comments on Psychical Phenomena and the War, by Hereward Carrington', *Paranormal Review* 76 (2015) 18–20.
128. Elliot O'Donnell, *The Menace of Spiritualism* (New York, 1920), preface.
129. *Journal of the Society for Psychical Research* 17 (1915–16), 20; *Journal of the Society for Psychical Research* 18 (1917–18), 13; *Journal of the Society for Psychical Research* 19 (1918–19), 18.
130. *Journal of the Society for Psychical Research* 17 (1915–16), 22; *Journal of the Society for Psychical Research* 17 (1915–16), 98.
131. *Journal of the Society for Psychical Research* 17 (1915–16), 154; *Journal of the Society for Psychical Research* 18 (1917–18), 15.
132. A. P. Sinnett, 'Super Physical Aspects of the War', *The Occult Review*, 20, 6 (1914), 352; Alison Butler, 'Conflict through an Occult Lens: The First World War in the Pages of the Occult Review', *Paranormal Review* 71 (2014), 12–13.
133. *Light*, 5 September 1914, 425; *Annales des Sciences Psychiques* (May 1916), 91.
134. 'Can We End the War by Thought?', *Herald of the Star* 5, 1 (1916), 101–7.
135. *Eastbourne Gazette*, 17 May 1916; *Barrier Miner* (NSW), 9 July 1916.
136. *The Northern Star* (Australia), 9 May 1916.
137. *Herald of the Star* 6, 1 (1917), 56.
138. *Light*, 5 September 1914, 427.

139. *Light*, 12 September 1914, 440.
140. Butler, 'Conflict through an Occult Lens', 12–13.
141. A. L. Ash, *Faith and Suggestion* (London, 1912); Dorothy Kerin, *The Living Touch* (London, 1914); James Robinson, *Divine Healing: The Years of Expansion, 1906–1930: Theological Variation in the Transatlantic World* (Eugene, OR, 2014), pp. 92–101.
142. *Sunderland Daily Echo*, 16 February 1915.
143. *Annales des Sciences Psychiques* (February 1916), 43.
144. M. L. Bardonnet, 'À propos de quelques séances de clairvoyance', *Annales des Sciences Psychiques* (October–November–December 1916), 173.
145. Émile Boirac, *L'Avenir des sciences psychiques* (Paris, 1917), p. 22.
146. *Evening Despatch*, 25 July 1917.
147. *Kent & Sussex Courier*, 20 August 1915.
148. *Yorkshire Evening Post*, 9 June 1916.
149. *Liverpool Echo*, 21 September 1915.
150. *Sunday Post*, 27 January 1918.
151. *Globe*, 3 July 1916.
152. Johnson, *Dynamic Psychology*, p. 134.
153. IWM, Documents.7822; Roper, *The Secret Battle*, p. 231.
154. Carrington, *Psychical Phenomena*, p. 159.
155. Philipp Witkop (ed.), *German Students' War Letters*, trans. A. F. Wedd (Philadelphia, PA, [1929] 2002), pp. 135–6; David Omissi (ed.), *Indian Voices of the Great War: Soldiers' Letters, 1914–18* (Basingstoke, 1999), p. 215.
156. Dauzat, *Légendes*, pp. 258–9.
157. *Surrey Advertiser*, 31 October 1914.
158. *Hull Daily Mail*, 21 October 1915.
159. Graham Shand, 'Anglo-French Psychical War Stories', *Light*, 23 March 1918, 94.
160. *Journal of the Society for Psychical Research* 16 (1913–14), 306–10.
161. Charles Richet, *Thirty Years of Psychical Research*, trans. Stanley De Brath (London, 1923), p. 269.
162. *Journal of the Society for Psychical Research* 17 (1916), 154.
163. *Journal of the Society for Psychical Research* 18 (1917–18), 15.
164. 'Coincidental Hallucination', *Journal of the Society for Psychical Research* 17 (1916), 204.
165. Cited in Cook, 'Grave Beliefs', 534; Baldensperger, 'Prophesying in Time of War', 101.
166. See Chris Woodyard, 'Our Lady of the Stereopticon', http://haunted ohiobooks.com/news/our-lady-of-the-stereopticon/, accessed 24 June 2018; Hereward Carrington, 'Occult Incidents of the Great War', *Psychical Research Review* 4 (February 1918), 3.
167. See, for example, Roper, *The Secret Battle*, pp. 260–3.

Chapter 4

1. *Evening Express*, 23 December 1914.
2. *Deutsches Volksblatt*, 26 January 1917; *Illustriertes Oesterreichisches Journal*, 1 January 1917.
3. On fortune-telling in the era, see Owen Davies, *Witchcraft, Magic, and Culture, 1736–1951* (Manchester, 1999), pp. 250–70.
4. *Sheffield Evening Telegraph*, 12 June 1915.
5. *Le Matin*, 1 April 1915.
6. *Luton Times*, 2 April 1915.
7. See S. C. Williams, *Religious Belief and Popular Culture in Southwark c. 1880–1939* (Oxford, 1999), p. 77.
8. Bonnie White, *The Women's Land Army in First World War Britain* (Basingstoke, 2014), p. 55.
9. *The People*, 31 December 1916.
10. *Sunderland Daily Echo*, 19 August 1916; *Birmingham Daily Gazette*, 6 June 1917. He was also prosecuted several times after the war. See, for example, *Lancashire Evening Post*, 3 October 1925.
11. Patrick Curry, *A Confusion of Prophets: Victorian and Edwardian Astrology* (London, 1992), pp. 136–7.
12. *Hastings and St Leonards Observer*, 19 February 1916.
13. *Belfast News-Letter*, 11 July 1917; *Northern Whig*, 8 May 1917.
14. *Glasgow Evening Post*, 5 January 1891.
15. *Logansport Pharos-Reporter*, 17 May 1919.
16. *Reichspost*, 30 June 1915; Cornelia Kemp and Ulrike Gierlinger (eds), *Wenn der Groschen fällt . . .: Münzautomaten—gestern und heute* (Munich, 1988), p. 87.
17. Faith Wigzell, *Reading Russian Fortunes: Print Culture, Gender and Divination in Russia from 1765* (Cambridge, 1998), pp. 161–2.
18. *La Cartomancie; ou, L'Avenir dévoilé par les cartes* (Paris, 1916); Elie Alta (G. Bouchet), *Cosmogonie humaine: essai de synthèse des sciences divinatoires* (Vichy, 1917).
19. *Dundee People's Journal*, 28 November 1914.
20. Ida Ellis, *A Catechism of Palmistry*, 3rd enlarged edn (London, 1917).
21. *The Courier*, 16 August 1915.
22. *The Courier*, 16 August 1915. See also Ellye Howell Glover, *'Dame Curtsey's' Book of Novel Entertainments for Every Day* (Chicago, 1916), p. 191.
23. *Manchester Evening News*, 7 May 1918.
24. Quoted in Frank Schumann (ed.), *'Zieh Dich warm an!' Soldatenpost und Heimatbriefe aus zwei Weltkriegen: Chronik einer Familie* (Berlin 1989), pp. 51–2; Patrick J. Houlihan, 'Religious Mobilization and Popular Belief', 1914–1918 Online: International Encyclopaedia of the First World War, http://encyclopedia.1914-1918-online.net/article/religious_mobilization_and_popular_belief, accessed 24 June 2018.
25. *Western Times*, 28 November 1917; *Western Morning News*, 28 September 1917.

26. *Birmingham Daily Post*, 3 October 1917.

27. Professor Dicksonn (pseudonym of A. de Saint Genois), *La Vérité sur le spiritisme et l'exploitation de la crédulité publique* (Arnouville-lès-Gonesse, 1917), p. 31; *Le Petit Parisien*, 4 September 1915; *L'Humanité*, 28 September 1915; David Allen Harvey, 'Fortune-Tellers in the French Courts: Antidivination Prosecutions in France in the Nineteenth and Twentieth Centuries', *French Historical Studies* 28 (2005), 149.

28. *Le Petit Parisien*, 9 January 1916; 14 May 1916; *Le Matin*, 11 June 1916; *Le Temps*, 18 August 1916.

29. Heather Wolffram, *The Stepchildren of Science: Psychical Research and Parapsychology in Germany, c. 1870–1939* (Amsterdam, 2009), p. 236; Corinna Treitel, *A Science for the Soul: Occultism and the Genesis of the German Modern* (Baltimore, MD, 2004), p. 201.

30. Harvey, 'Fortune-Tellers in the French Courts', 146–7. See also Le Naour, *Nostradamus*, pp. 79–80.

31. Chambers, 'Fighting Chance', 198–200.

32. Houlihan, *Catholicism and the Great War*, p. 149.

33. *Berliner Tageblatt*, 29 December 1915; *Berliner Volkszeitung*, 17 November 1916.

34. *Berliner Volkszeitung*, 27 March 1916.

35. *Brixener Chronik*, 29 September 1918.

36. *Luton Times*, 2 April 1915.

37. *Dundee Evening Telegraph*, 22 July 1918.

38. Charles à Court Repington, *The First World War: Personal Experiences* (Boston, MA, 1920), vol. 2, p. 14.

39. On charity fortune-telling, see Davies, *Witchcraft, Magic and Culture*, pp. 59–60.

40. *Liverpool Daily Post*, 25 November 1916.

41. *Sunderland Daily Echo*, 19 August 1916. Australian fortune tellers made the same defence: Alana Jayne Piper, '"A Menace and an Evil": Fortune-Telling in Australia, 1900–1918', *History Australia* 11 (2014), 71.

42. The National Archives HO 144/1806.

43. *Sheffield Independent*, 31 January 1923.

44. *The Pioneer*, 8 April 1916.

45. *The Cambrian News and Merionethshire Standard*, 3 May 1918.

46. Davies, *Witchcraft, Magic, and Culture*, pp. 58–9, 266–8.

47. *Daily Gazette for Middlesbrough*, 23 August 1915; *Sunday Mirror*, 18 February 1917.

48. *Justice of the Peace*, 21 April 1917.

49. *Burnley Express*, 20 June 1917.

50. Vanessa Chambers, 'A Shell with my Name on it: The Reliance on the Supernatural during the First World War', *Journal for the Academic Study of Magic* 2 (2004), 93; Piper, '"A Menace and an Evil"', 70–1; Alana Piper, 'Women's Work: The Professionalisation and Policing of Fortune-Telling in Australia', *Labour History* 108 (2015), 44.

51. Harvey, 'Fortune-Tellers in the French Courts', 146–7.
52. *Newcastle Daily Journal*, 28 May 1917.
53. *Western Times*, 3 December 1915.
54. *Gloucester Echo*, 29 April 1915.
55. *Dublin Daily Express*, 6 January 1915.
56. *Women Workers: Papers Read at the Conference Held in London October 4th to 7th, 1915* (London, 1915), p. 127.
57. *Yorkshire Evening Post*, 12 July 1917.
58. *Manchester Evening News*, 23 December 1916.
59. *Sheffield Evening Telegraph*, 8 June 1916.
60. *Belfast News-Letter*, 11 July 1917.
61. See Susan Grazel, 'The Enemy Within: The Problem of British Women's Sexuality during the First World War', in Nicole A. Dombrowski (ed.), *Women and War in the Twentieth Century: Enlisted with or without Consent* (Abingdon, 1999), pp. 72–92; Susan R. Grayzel, *Women and the First World War* (Harlow, 2002), pp. 62–79.
62. Williams, *Religious Belief and Popular Culture*, pp. 77–8.
63. *Preston Herald*, 11 September 1915.
64. *Jarrow Express*, 10 September 1915; *Coventry Evening Telegraph*, 7 December 1916; *Fulham Chronicle*, 3 November 1916.
65. Chambers, 'Fighting Chance', 238.
66. *Yorkshire Evening Post*, 12 July 1917.
67. *Liverpool Echo*, 30 October 1917.
68. *Dundee Evening Telegraph*, 26 December 1916.
69. *Hull Daily Mail*, 27 October 1915.
70. Alison Woodeson, 'The First Women Police: A Force for Equality or Infringement?', *Women's History Review* 2 (1993) 224; *Grantham Journal*, 3 March 1917.
71. Piper, 'Women's Work: The Professionalisation and Policing of Fortune-Telling', 50.
72. Treitel, *A Science for the Soul*, pp. 203–4.
73. 'Polizei und Wahrsager', *Zentralblatt für Okkultismus* 8 (15), 493–4.
74. On the status of phrenology in the late nineteenth century, see Roger Cooter, *The Cultural Meaning of Popular Science: Phrenology and the Organization of Consent in Nineteenth-Century Britain* (Cambridge, 1984).
75. *Liverpool Echo*, 11 November 1918; *Southern Reporter*, 14 November 1918.
76. *Hastings and St Leonards Observer*, 11 August 1917.
77. See the reports in the *Rushden Echo* compiled by the Rushden and District History Society Research Group: http://www.rushdenheritage.co.uk/war/prisonersWWIpart3.html, accessed 24 June 2018.
78. *Phrenology* 4, 17 (1932), 109; *Phrenology* 4, 16 (1932), 96.
79. *Bucks Herald*, 20 October 1917.
80. *Bath Chronicle and Weekly Gazette*, 9 February 1918; *Western Daily Press*, 8 February 1918.

81. *The Cambria Daily Leader*, 26 November 1915; *Western Mail*, 10 March 1917; *Illustrated Police News*, 4 July 1918.

82. Leo, *Mars: The War Lord*, p. v; Curry, *Confusion of Prophets*, p. 157.

83. *Evening Despatch*, 28 November 1917.

84. *The Cambrian News and Merionethshire Standard*, 3 May 1918.

85. *Derby Daily Telegraph*, 13 May 1918.

86. 'Psychic Science and the Vagrancy Act', *Light*, 11 May 1918, 149.

87. *Western Times*, 3 December 1915.

88. *Nantwich Guardian*, 4 June 1915.

89. *Western Daily Press*, 24 December 1915.

90. *Manchester Evening News*, 12 November 1915.

91. See, for example, *A History of the County of Stafford* (London, 1963), vol. 8; http://www.british-history.ac.uk/vch/staffs/vol8/pp54-64, accessed 24 June 2018.

92. Nelson, *Spiritualism and Society*, p. 163; *Arbroath Herald and Advertiser for the Montrose Burghs*, 8 March 1918.

93. Hereward Carrington, *Your Psychic Powers and How to Develop Them* (New York, 1920), p. 278.

94. Conan Doyle, *History of Spiritualism*, vol. 2, p. 199.

95. *Tamworth Herald*, 30 October 1915.

96. National Archives HO 144/1806 C622111.

97. National Archives HO 144/1806 C622111.

98. See Davies, *Witchcraft, Magic and Culture*, pp. 61–75; Owen Davies, 'Decriminalising the Witch: The Origin of and Response to the 1736 Witchcraft Act', in John Newton and J. Bath (eds), *Witchcraft and the Act of 1604* (Leiden, 2008), pp. 207–32.

99. *Justice of the Peace*, 20 January 1917; Chambers, 'Fighting Chance', 202.

100. *Two Worlds*, 10 November 1916. Reprinted in 'The S.N.U. Parliamentary Fund (Witchcraft Acts Amendment)', *Pioneer* 1, 3 (2014), 67.

101. *On the Side of the Angels: The Law v. Spiritualism* (Huddersfield, 1919); reprinted in Davies, *Ghosts: A Social History*, vol. 5, p. 179.

102. *Light*, 23 June 1917, 198.

103. *Light*, 2 June 1917, 174.

104. 'Psychic Science and the Vagrancy Act: Some Advice to Mediums', *Light*, 25 May 1918, 161.

105. O'Hara, *Dead Men's Embers*, p. 206.

106. *Liverpool Echo*, 23 July 1915; Le Naour, *Nostradamus*, p. 81; *Globe*, 17 March 1917.

107. *Coventry Evening Telegraph*, 3 February 1916.

108. *Aberdeen Evening Express*, 6 January 1917. For a similar case, see also *Sunday Mirror*, 18 February 1917.

109. *L'Heure*, 23 February 1917; Dicksonn, *La Vérité sur la spiritisme*, pp. 55–6.

110. *Globe*, 18 May 1917; *Nantwich Guardian*, 4 June 1915; *Evening Telegraph*, 7 March 1917.

111. *Manchester Evening News*, 8 December 1916.

112. *Manchester Evening News*, 7 May 1918; *Sheffield Independent*, 6 June 1917.
113. Jane Lewis, 'Marriage', in Ina Zweiniger-Bargielowska (ed.), *Women in Twentieth-Century Britain: Social, Cultural and Political Change* (London, [2001] 2014), p. 72.
114. *Evening Telegraph* (Scottish), 14 April 1916; *Birmingham Gazette*, 6 June 1915; *Lancashire Evening Post*, 20 July 1916.
115. *Yorkshire Post and Leeds Intelligencer*, 21 April 1917.
116. *Western Times*, 3 December 1915; *Luton Times*, 2 April 1915.
117. See James McDermott, *British Military Service Tribunals, 1916–18: A very much Abused Body of Men* (Manchester, 2011).
118. *The Cambrian News and Merionethshire Standard*, 3 May 1918; *Preston Herald*, 11 September 1915.
119. *Lincolnshire Echo*, 11 October 1917.
120. *The Cambrian News and Merionethshire Standard*, 3 May 1918.
121. *Tamworth Herald*, 30 October 1915.
122. *Hull Daily Mail*, 24 February 1917; *Birmingham Daily Post*, 3 October 1917.

Chapter 5

1. *500 of the Best Cockney War Stories*, p. 135.
2. See, for example, Benjamin Ziemann, *War Experiences in Rural Germany, 1914–1923*, trans. Alex Skinner (Oxford, 2007), p. 133; Snape, *God and the British Soldier*, pp. 28–38; Watson, *Enduring the Great War*, pp. 92–100.
3. Marković, '"Od kopile kočicu i pobeg-zrno od kukuruz"', p. 67; Gibbs, *Realities of War*, p. 117.
4. Cited in L. Macdonald, *1914–1918: Voices and Images of the Great War* (London, 1991), p. 186; Chambers, 'Fighting Chance', 46. See also William L. Gay, '"A Stout Heart Crushes Ill-Luck?": Materialism, British Masculinity, the Western Front, and the Changing Meaning of Luck in the Late-Nineteenth and Early-Twentieth Century', *Concept* 36 (2013), n.p.; Ross J. Wilson, *Landscapes of the Western Front: Materiality during the Great War* (New York, 2012), pp. 160–2.
5. See, for example, Nicholas Rescher, 'The Machinations of Luck', in Duncan Pritchard and Lee John Whittington (eds), *The Philosophy of Luck* (Chichester, 2015), pp. 169–77.
6. Jacques Mortanes, *Guynemer, the Ace of Aces*, trans. Clifton Harby Levy, together with transcripts from Guynemer's own note-book of flight (New York, 1918), pp. xxiii, xxiv, xxv.
7. Lucien Roure, 'Superstitions du front de guerre', *Études* 153 (1917) 719; Dauzat, *Légendes*, p. 261.
8. *Liverpool Daily Post*, 19 June 1915.
9. Edwin C. Parsons, *I Flew with the Lafayette Escadrille* (Indianapolis, IN, [1937] 1963), pp. 236–7. A wartime officers' dinner party experienced a similar problem of thirteen around the table. See Edward Madigan, *Faith under Fire: Anglican Army Chaplains and the Great War* (Basingstoke, 2011), p. 187.

10. *Leeds Mercury*, 28 August 1915. Named after the first black heavyweight champion of the world, 'Jack Johnson's' were the name of a German 15 cm shell that burst in a cloud of black smoke.

11. R. P. Thurston, *Month*, December 1914; Roure, 'Superstitions du front de guerre', 726; *Aberdeen Evening Express*, 1 April 1918; Guillaume Apollinaire, 'Contribution à l'étude des superstitions et du folklore du front', *Mercure de France*, 16 February 1917, 650; Newman Ivey White (ed.), *The Frank C. Brown Collection of North Carolina Folklore: Popular Beliefs and Superstitions from North Carolina* (Durham, NC, 1961), vol. 6, p. 393. For British oral history reminiscences of the belief, see IWM 10168, Donald Price, reel 5; IWM 24865 W. J. Brockman, reel 2.

12. P. J. Heather, 'Threefold Lights: The Origin of a Superstition', *Folklore* 37 (1926), 300.

13. H. W. Howes, 'Functional Aspects of European Folklore', *Folklore* 41 (1929), 256.

14. Charles Edward Peck, *Allen Peck's WW1 Letters Home 1917–1919: U.S. Army WW 1 Pilot Assigned to France* (Lincoln, NE, 2005), p. 93.

15. *Sheffield Independent*, 16 December 1914; *Aberdeen Evening Express*, 12 December 1914.

16. *Yorkshire Evening Post*, 7 October 1916; 8 November 1916.

17. *Liverpool Echo*, 2 February 1916.

18. See, for example, Major Charles J. Biddle, *The Way of the Eagle* (New York, 1919); Parsons, *I Flew*. More generally, see Bill Wallrich, 'Superstition and the Air Force', *Western Folklore* 19 (1960), 11–16.

19. See Orra L. Stone, *History of Massachusetts Industries: Their Inception, Growth and Success* (Boston, MA, 1930), vol. 4.

20. *Manchester Evening News*, 30 September 1915; Lovett, *Magic in Modern London*, p. 42; *Globe*, 6 November 1916.

21. *The Graphic*, 11 September 1915; Roure, 'Superstitions du front de guerre', 718.

22. *The Sphere*, 5 December 1914; *The Gentlewoman*, 22 April 1916. Thanks to Lucie Whitmore for the latter reference.

23. *Birmingham Gazette*, 26 November 1915.

24. Thomas Fliege, '"Mein Deutschland sei mein Engel Michael": Sankt Michael als nationalreligiöser Mythos', in Korff (ed.), *Alliierte im Himmel*, p. 188; Ernst Moritz Kronfeld, *Der Krieg im Aberglauben und Volksglauben* (Munich, 1915), p. 63. Thanks to James Wallis for a photo of examples in the Military History Museum in Dresden.

25. Norfolk Museum NWHRM 139, http://norfolkmuseumscollections.org/collections/objects/object-1494504413.html/#!/?q=zeppelin, accessed 24 June 2018. Thanks to Malcolm Gaskill for drawing my attention to the Norfolk charm. The Potters Bar example is in the author's collection.

26. Pat Tomczyszyn, 'A Material Link between War and Peace: First World War Silk Postcards', in Nicholas J. Saunders (ed.), *Matters of Conflict: Material Culture, Memory and the First World War* (London, 2004), pp. 126–7; Heidrun

Alzheimer (ed.), *Glaubenssache Krieg: Religiöse Motive auf Bildpostkarten des Ersten Weltkrieges* (Bad Windsheim, 2009).

27. 'Narratives from the War', *American Journal of Nursing* 16 (1916), 1212.

28. Philip Gibbs, *Realities of War* (London, 1920), p. 117.

29. IWM, EPH 4895, EPH 3464, EPH 4892.

30. IWM EPH 4894; A. R. Wright and Edward Lovett, 'Specimens of Modern Mascots and Ancient Amulets of the British Isles', *Folklore* 19 (1908), 290; Philip Gibbs, *Now It Can Be Told* (New York, 1920), p. 143.

31. IWM EPH 7455.

32. *Newcastle Daily Journal*, 14 August 1917; http://www.oucs.ox.ac.uk/ww1lit/gwa/item/5950, accessed 24 June 2018.

33. Lovett, *Magic in Modern London*, pp. 70–1.

34. Stiaccini, *L'anima religiosa*, pp. 107, 108.

35. Stiaccini, *L'anima religiosa*, p. 109.

36. *Welt-Blatt*, 31 October 1914.

37. Dauzat, *Légendes*, p. 276; Watson, *Enduring the Great War*, p. 98.

38. *Manchester Evening News*, 5 September 1914.

39. Apollinaire, 'Contribution à l'étude des superstitions et du folklore du front', 650.

40. Kronfeld, *Der Krieg*, p. 74. Devlin's wings and medals were auctioned in December 1916, https://www.the-saleroom.com/en-gb/auction-catalogues/laidlaw-auctioneers-and-valuers/catalogue-id-srlai10020/lot-52fc260d-6a34-4c43-9bda-a6d000e9effe, accessed 31 December 2016. See also Wilson, *Landscapes of the Western Front*, p. 161.

41. IWM EPH 4896.

42. http://www.bbc.com/news/magazine-15671943, accessed 24 June 2018.

43. See Bill Ellis, 'Why is a Lucky Rabbit's Foot Lucky? Body Parts as Fetishes', *Journal of Folklore Research* 39, 1 (2002), 58–9; Davies, *America Bewitched*, pp. 113–14.

44. *Winslow Dispatch*, 29 March 1916.

45. *Hutchinson News*, 5 July 1918; *Hammond Lake County Times*, 14 March 1929.

46. *Boston Sunday Globe*, 20 January 1918; *Lethbridge Daily Herald*, 19 September 1918.

47. *Aberdeen Evening Express*, 10 September 1915.

48. *Yorkshire Evening Post*, 8 November 1916; Benoît Clement, 'Auguste Salé mon grand père par alliance', Europeana 1914–1918, http://www.europeana.eu, accessed 19 June 2018.

49. Nicholas J. Saunders, *Trench Art: Materialities and Memories of War* (Oxford, 2003), pp. 99–100.

50. *The Hamilton Advertiser*, 26 October 1918.

51. *Newcastle Daily Journal*, 14 August 1917.

52. Lovett, *Magic in Modern London*, p. 34.

53. Lovett, *Magic in Modern London*, p. 72.

54. *Bristol Mercury*, 17 August 1850; *Liverpool Mercury*, 22 September 1854; *Liverpool Mercury*, 19 July 1866; Lovett, *Magic in Modern London*, p. 52.

55. *Liverpool Echo*, 4 March 1915.

56. *The Herald*, 9 December 1916; Lovett, *Magic in Modern London*, p. 53.

57. Matthew Stibbe, 'Germany's "Last Card": Wilhelm II and the Decision in Favour of Unrestricted Submarine Warfare in January 1917', in Annika Mombauer and Wilhelm Deist (eds), *The Kaiser: New Research on Wilhelm II's Role in Imperial Germany* (Cambridge, 2003), pp. 217–35; Gary S. Messinger, *British Propaganda and the State in the First World War* (Manchester, 1992), p. 144.

58. *Liverpool Daily Post*, 20 November 1917; *Western Gazette*, 1 March 1918; *Dover Express*, 16 November 1917; *Hastings and St Leonards Observer*, 28 September 1918.

59. *Dover Express*, 16 November 1917; *Western Times*, 22 December 1914.

60. *Irish Independent*, 20 September 1918.

61. Stiaccini, *L'anima religiosa*, p. 109; Dauzat, *Légendes*, p. 276.

62. *Leitrim Observer*, 30 September 1915; Ronnie Pigram, 'Benfleet's First WW1 Casualty', https://www.benfleethistory.org.uk/content/people/the_armed_forces/first_world_war/the_37_names_on_the_war_memorial/sapper_stanley_ellison_no_22421, accessed 24 June 2018.

63. http://www.kingsownmuseum.com/ko1181-194.htm, accessed 24 June 2018; *The Gentlewoman*, 22 April 1916, ii. Thanks to Lucie Whitmore for this reference.

64. https://www.europeana.eu/portal/en/record/2020601/contributions_13932.html?q=muguet+1915, accessed 24 June 2018.

65. *Irish Times*, 7 March 1916.

66. *Irish Independent*, 26 September 1914; 13 October 1914; 23 October 1914; *Irish Times*, 22 October 1914.

67. *Evening Express* (Aberdeen), 11 July 1916.

68. *Bucks Herald*, 28 October 1916; *Southern Reporter*, 22 August 1918.

69. Reprinted in *Evening Despatch* (Birmingham), 14 October 1914.

70. *Le Figaro*, 1 July 1915.

71. Susan Williams, *The People's King: The True Story of the Abdication* (London, 2004).

72. *War Letters of Edmond Genet* (New York, 1918), p. 66.

73. *Exeter and Plymouth Gazette*, 8 February 1915.

74. Robert Baden-Powell, *Scouting for Boys: A Handbook for Instruction in Good Citizenship* (London, [1908] 1915), p. 26; Ludvig S. Dale, 'With the Boy Scouts of Holland—II', *Boys' Life* (July 1913), 19.

75. Goodrick-Clarke, *Occult Roots of Nazism*, p. 129.

76. Greg VanWyngarden, *Albatros Aces of World War 1* (Oxford, 2007), pp. 23, 46, 89; Mike O'Connor, *Airfields and Airmen: Arras* (Barnsley, 2004), p. 131; Norman Franks, *Albatros Aces of World War 1* (Bloomington, IN, 2000), p. 37.

77. Dorothy T. Rainwater and Judy Redfield, *Encyclopedia of American Silver Manufacturers* (Atglen, PA, 1998), p. 244.

78. *Logansport Pharos*, 8 June 1907.

79. *Sheffield Evening Telegraph*, 10 December 1908; *Daily Mirror*, 14 February 1914.

80. *Daily Gazette* (Middlesbrough), 16 December 1916; *Western Mail*, 9 October 1917. See also *Liverpool Echo*, 30 April 1917.

81. *Sheffield Weekly Telegraph*, 9 December 1916; *Yorkshire Post*, 22 October 1917.

82. *Irish Times*, 26 August 1916; *Burnley News*, 29 May 1915.

83. The Pets of "Tommy" and "Jack"', *Sheffield Weekly Telegraph*, 28 August 1915; https://www.flickr.com/photos/nationallibrarynz_commons/21698112641/, accessed 24 June 2018. See also Neil R. Storey, *Animals in the First World War* (Oxford, 2014).

84. Mark Wilkins, 'Luck and Death: WW1 Pilots and their Superstitions', *Air & Space Magazine* (March 2014), https://www.airspacemag.com/multimedia/luck-and-death-wwi-pilots-and-their-superstitions-180950158/, accessed 24 June 2018.

85. Biddle, *The Way of the Eagle*, p. 41; *Birmingham Daily Mail*, 2 August 1915.

86. *The Reliquary* (1905), 22; *Cheltenham Chronicle*, 19 August 1916.

87. Ira Dye, 'The Tattoos of Early American Seafarers, 1796–1818', *Proceedings of the American Philosophical Society* 133 (1989), 547; Kevin J. Hayes, *Melville's Folk Roots* (Kent, OH, 1999), p. 4; *Daily Mirror*, 17 January 1914.

88. David Clark, *Between Pulpit and Pew: Folk Religion in a North Yorkshire Fishing Village* (Cambridge, 1982), pp. 152–4; *Aberdeen Daily Journal*, 29 May 1918.

89. *Manchester Courier*, 24 June 1913.

90. *Le Figaro*, 1 July 1915.

91. *Market Harborough Advertiser*, 25 October 1921; *Sporting Times*, 8 November 1924; Steve Roud, *The Penguin Guide to the Superstitions of Britain and Ireland* (London, 2003), p. 350; *Gloucester Echo*, 22 July 1933; *The Jewelers' Circular*, 2 February 1921, 193.

92. *Daily Mirror*, 22 September 1915.

93. Cited in Dauzat, *Légendes*, pp. 275–6.

94. See, for example, Roud, *Superstitions*, pp. 66–7.

95. *Daily Record*, 23 August 1917; *The People*, 3 September 1916.

96. Peck, *Allen Peck's WW1 Letters Home 1917–1919*, p. xv.

97. Parsons, *I Flew*, pp. 229, 232.

98. *Aberdeen Evening Express*, 10 October 1916.

99. *Shipley Times and Express*, 25 January 1918.

100. *Daily Mirror*, 26 May 1916.

101. Wright and Lovett, 'Modern Mascots and Ancient Amulets of the British Isles', 292; *Globe*, 18 November 1916.

102. *The Agricultural Economist and Horticultural Review* 47 (1914), 330. A billiken was a gnome-like mascot designed by an American art teacher from a figure in a dream. Billiken ornaments and trinkets were briefly a global sensation in the early twentieth century.

103. See, for example, *Sheffield Independent*, 19 October 1917.

104. *Birmingham Gazette*, 13 August 1917.

105. *Evening News*, 31 January 1914.

106. *The Standard*, 29 November 1913.

107. Phoenix, 'Touchwood', *Notes and Queries*, 9 May (1914), 370.

108. Jean Laporte, 'Les Petites Superstitions de nos contemporaines', *Femina* (May 1914), 245.

109. Tina Grant (ed.), *International Directory of Company Histories* (Detroit, MI, 2007), vol. 84, pp. 380–1.
110. *Evening News*, 10 September 1914.
111. *Printers' Ink*, 90 (1915), 87.
112. *Frederick Post*, 17 March 1915.
113. *Daily Mirror*, 24 March 1915; 22 April 1915; 8 May 1915; 30 July 1915.
114. *London Standard*, 16 August 1915; *The Times*, 14 August 1915.
115. Pathé, http://www.britishpathe.com/video/lucky-charms-presented/query/ mascots, accessed 24 June 2018; *The Times*, 20 August 1915.
116. Sandy Turton, 'Fumsup and Touch Wood Charms', https:// www.sandysvintagecharms.com/pages/fumsup-and-touch-wood-charms, accessed 24 June 2018.
117. *Hull Daily Mail*, 26 November 1915.
118. See, for example, *Aberdeen Evening Express*, 23 December 1915.
119. *Daily Mirror*, 13 December 1915.
120. *The Daily Colonist*, 17 March 1916; *The Advertiser* (Adelaide), 5 December 1916; *La Lettura: Rivista-mensile Corriere della Sera* 17 (1917), 744.
121. *Sheffield Independent*, 20 December 1916.
122. *Birmingham Gazette*, 4 December 1916.
123. Jacques Boulenger, *En escadrille* (Paris, 1918), p. 63.
124. RAF Museum, Hendon, gallery exhibit X001-2591; Chambers, 'Fighting Chance', 43.
125. 'Fums Up! 1-2-3-4! A Tale of Four Camels from 204 Squadron, RAF', *Cross & Cockade* 14, 4 (1973), 371–3.
126. *Yorkshire Evening Post*, 2 July 1919.
127. http://www.horniman.ac.uk/collections/browse-our-collections/object/ 71843, accessed 24 June 2018; see Bristol Museum's online collection search.
128. *Le Figaro*, 15 December 1916; *Le Temps*, 8 December 1916.
129. 'What Jewels Women Wear in Paris: Touch Wood and Wish', *Jewelers' Circular* 74 (1917), 45.
130. Apollinaire, *Œuvres en prose complètes*, edited by P. Caizergues and M. Décaudin (Paris, 1993), vol. 3, p. 557.
131. Adolphe E. Smylie, *The Marines, and Other War Verse* (New York, 1919), pp. 54–5.
132. Caroline Frevert, 'Nenette and Rintintin', *St Nicholas: An Illustrated Magazine for Boys and Girls* 46 (1918–19); 120; M. É. Delabarre, 'Nénettes et Rintintins', *Précis analytique des travaux de L'Académie des Sciences, Belles-Lettres et Art de Rouen* (Rouen, 1919), p. 698.
133. *Le Carnet de la Semaine*, 2 June 1918, 4; Dauzat, *Légendes*, pp. 271, 273.
134. On *La Baïonnette*, see Allen Douglas, *War, Memory, and the Politics of Humor: The Canard Enchaîné and World War I* (Berkeley, CA, 2002).
135. *On Duty and Off: Letters of Elizabeth Cabot Putnam* (Cambridge, 1919), p. 203.
136. Parsons, *I Flew*, p. 228; Marquise de Ravenel, 'French Fashions: The Spirit of Nenette and Rintintin Help [*sic*] Parisians to Hold Out for Victory en

Route', *La France: An American Magazine* 2 (1918–19), 172; *Twin Falls Daily Times*, 18 July 1918.

137. Le Naour, *Nostradamus*, pp. 101–3.

138. *Pester Lloyd*, 23 July 1918; *Neues Wiener Journal*, 18 June 1918; *Prager Tagblatt*, 1 June 1918.

139. *Western Times*, 17 July 1918.

140. http://www.britishpathe.com/video/latest-mascots/query/mascots, accessed 24 June 2018.

141. De Ravenel, 'French Fashions', 172.

142. Frevert, 'Nenette and Rintintin', 120.

143. *The Activities of the Mayor's Committee of Women on National Defense* (New York, 1918–19), p. 28.

144. De Ravenel, 'French Fashions', 172.

145. *Kansas City Star*, 15 October 1918.

146. *American Cloak and Suit Review* 17 (1919), 167, 189.

147. Susan Orlean, *Rin Tin Tin: The Life and the Legend* (New York, 2011), pp. 30, 81.

148. Christopher Fischer, 'Of Occupied Territories and Lost Provinces: German and Entente Propaganda in the West during World War 1', in Troy R. E. Paddock (ed.), *World War 1 and Propaganda* (Leiden, 2014), pp. 217–18.

149. *Les Annales politiques et littéraires*, 8 September 1918, 200.

150. *Illustrated Sporting and Dramatic News*, 2 November 1918; *Tatler*, 2 October 1918.

151. *Le Temps*, 1 September 1918; Charles Delacommune, *L'Escadrille des éperviers: impressions vécues de guerre aérienne* (Paris, 1918), pp. 304–5.

152. *Chester Chronicle*, 1 December 1917; *Yorkshire Post*, 23 July 1917.

153. *The Times*, 19 August 1915.

154. *The Times*, 20 August 1915.

155. *Western Mail*, 26 August 1915.

156. *Daily Mirror*, 27 December 1915; *Hamilton Advertiser*, 26 October 1918.

157. Ernest Jones, 'The Theory of Symbolism', *British Journal of Psychology* 9 (1918), 215.

158. Parsons, *I Flew*, p. 237; Howes, 'Functional Aspects of European Folklore', 255.

159. Richard Wiseman and Caroline Watt, 'Measuring Superstitious Belief: Why Lucky Charms Matter', *Proceedings of the 47th Annual Convention of the Parapsychological Association, Vienna, Austria* (2004), pp. 171–7.

Chapter 6

1. See, for example, Philip Jenkins, *The Great and Holy War: How World War 1 Became a Religious Crusade* (New York, 2014); Gordon L. Heath (ed.), *American Churches and the First World War* (Eugene, OR, 2016); Stiaccini, *L'anima religiosa*, pp. 31–9; Annette Becker, *War and Faith: The Religious Imagination in France, 1914–1930* (Oxford, 1998), pp. 11–18; Xavier Boniface, *Histoire religieuse de la Grande Guerre* (Paris, 2014), pp. 223–32.

2. Stefan Goebel, *The Great War and Medieval Memory: War, Remembrance and Medievalism in Britain and Germany, 1914–1940* (Cambridge, 2007), p. 85.
3. Boniface, *Histoire religieuse*, pp. 223–32, 348–51; Mehmet Beşikçi, *The Ottoman Mobilization of Manpower in the First World War* (Leiden, 2012), p. 73.
4. *The Army and Religion*, p. 19.
5. Cited in Richard Sykes, 'Popular Religion in Decline: A Study from the Black Country', *Journal of Ecclesiastical History* 56 (2005), 294.
6. Snape, *God and the British Soldier*, pp. 178–86; Madigan, *Faith under Fire*, pp. 90–3; Adrian Gregory, *The Last Great War: British Society and the First World War* (Cambridge, 2008), ch. 5; Stuart Bell, '"Soldiers of Christ Arise": Religious Nationalism in the East Midlands during World War I', *Midland History* 39 (2014), 219–35; Clive Field, 'Keeping the Spiritual Home Fires Burning: Religious Belonging in Britain during the First World War', *War & Society* 33 (2014), 244–68; Becker, *La Guerre et la foi*, pp. 125–34; Boniface, *Histoire religieuse*, pp. 87–97; Ziemann, *War Experiences in Rural Germany*, pp. 134–5, 222–3. The extent of religiosity amongst British soldiers is an ongoing debate. As well as publications cited above, see also Richard Schweitzer, *The Cross and the Trenches: Religious Faith and Doubt among British and American Great War Soldiers* (Westport, CT, 2003).
7. Boniface, *Histoire religieuse*, p. 91; Neil Allison, 'Free Church Revivalism in the British Army during the First World War', in Michael Snape and Edward Madigan (eds), *The Clergy in Khaki: New Perspectives on British Army Chaplaincy in the First World War* (Abingdon, 2016), pp. 43–55.
8. Snape, *God and the British Soldier*, pp. 24–6; Madigan, *Faith under Fire*, pp. 184–5; Stephen Parker, *Faith on the Home Front* (Berne, 2005).
9. See, for example, Williams, *Religious Belief in Popular Culture*, pp. 1–23; Marion Bowman and Ülo Valk (eds), *Vernacular Religion in Everyday Life: Expressions of Belief* (New York, 2012); Per D. Smith, 'Vernacular Religion: Because You'll Find More than the Devil in the Details', Religious Studies Project, 2012, http://www.religiousstudiesproject.com/2012/06/27/vernacular-religion-because-youll-find-more-than-the-devil-in-the-details-by-per-smith/, accessed 24 June 2018.
10. Wilkinson, *The Church of England and the First World War*, p. 153; Snape, *God and the British Soldier*, pp. 232–3; Shafquat Towheed and Edmund King, 'Introduction', in Shafquat Towheed and Edmund King (eds), *Reading and the First World War: Readers, Texts, Archives* (Basingstoke, 2015), p. 13; *Emporia Gazette*, 22 January 1918; *The Cornishman*, 24 May 1917.
11. John William Tebbel, *A History of Book Publishers in the United States: The Expansion in Industry, 1865–1919* (New York, 1975) p. 544; Schweitzer, *The Cross and the Trenches*, p. 31.
12. *Bible Society Record* 62 (1917), 194.
13. Williams, *Religious Belief and Popular Culture in Southwark*, p. 66; Hayes, *Folklore and Book Culture*, pp. 33–6.
14. *Liverpool Echo*, 25 May 1918.
15. See, for example, http://www.walesonline.co.uk/news/wales-news/bible-saved-wwi-soldiers-life-1885194, accessed 24 June 2018; http://www.express.co.uk/

news/world-war-1/467542/Hand-of-God-Bible-that-saved-my-WWI-soldier-father-from-being-shot-dead, accessed 24 June 2018.

16. *Birmingham Gazette*, 23 October 1915.
17. *Bloomington Evening World*, 28 May 1918; *Syracuse Herald*, 29 May 1918.
18. Hayes, *Folklore and Book Culture*, pp. 35–6; David Cressy, 'Books as Totems in Seventeenth-Century England and New England', *Journal of Library History* 21 (1986), 99; George C. Rable, *God's Almost Chosen Peoples: A Religious History of the American Civil War* (Chapel Hill, NC, 2010), p. 166.
19. *Bible Society Record* 61 (1916), 149. On Holden during the war, see, Ian M. Randall, 'Spiritual Renewal and Social Reform: Attempts to Develop Social Awareness in the Early Keswick Movement', *Vox Evangelica* 23 (1993), 78.
20. *The Courier*, 18 August 1915.
21. *Manchester Evening News*, 21 October 1915.
22. *Yorkshire Evening Post*, 4 August 1915.
23. *Evening Telegraph*, 26 March 1915.
24. *Bible Society Record* 62 (1917), 197.
25. Hector Macquarrie, *How to Live at the Front: Tips for American Soldiers* (Philadelphia, PA, 1917), pp. 254–5. On Macquarrie's life, see http://press.anu.edu.au/apps/bookworm/view/Watriama+and+Co%3A+Further+Pacific+Islands+Portraits/10821/ch13.xhtml, accessed 24 June 2018.
26. Cited in Watson, *Enduring the Great War*, p. 98, n. 77.
27. See Robert Priebsch, *Letter from Heaven on the Observance of the Lord's Day* (Oxford, 1936); Hippolyte Delahaye, 'Note sur la légende de la lettre du Christ tombée du ciel', *Bulletins de l'Académie Royale de Belgique* 2 (1899), 171–213.
28. See Davies, *Witchcraft, Magic and Culture*, pp. 126–30; W. R. Halliday, 'A Note upon the Sunday Epistle and the Letter of Pope Leo', *Speculum* 2 (1927), 73–8; Paul Suter, 'Himmels- und Schutzbriefe im Baselbiet', *Schweizerisches Archiv für Volkskunde* 85 (1989), 271–8; Martyn Lyons, 'Celestial Letters: Morals and Magic in Nineteenth-Century France', *French History* 27 (2013), 496–514.
29. Steve Smith, 'Heavenly Letters and Tales of the Forest: "Superstition" against Bolshevism', *Forum for Anthropology and Culture* 2 (2006), 322; *Tennessee Folklore Society Bulletin* 29 (1963), 9; A. Monroe Aurand, *The Pow-Wow Book* (Harrisburg, PA, 1929), pp. 68–9.
30. Hermann Sökeland, 'Zwei Himmelsbriefe von 1815 und 1915', *Zeitschrift des Vereins für Volkskunde* 25 (1915), 244.
31. My thanks to Sylvie Magerstadt for this translation.
32. Albrecht Dietrich, *Kleine Schriften* (Leipzig, 1911), pp. 240, 249, 234; Dr Olbrich, 'Über Waffensegen', *Mitteilungen der Schlesischen Gesellschaft für Volkskunde* 2 (1897), 90; Hanns Bächtold-Stäubli, *Deutsche Soldatenbrauch und Soldatenglaube* (Strasburg, 1917), pp. 17–25; Sabine Wienker-Piepho, *'Je gelehrter, desto verkehrster'? Volkskundlich-kulturgeschichtliches zur Schriftbeherrschung* (Münster, 2000), pp. 317–30.
33. Oskar Ebermann, 'Le Médecin des pauvres', *Zeitschrift des Vereins für Volkskunde* 24 (1914), 134–62; *Zeitschrift des Vereins für Volkskunde* 27 (1917), 280.

34. *Le Temps*, 4 November 1914; *Le Temps*, 9 January 1915.
35. Paul Tillich, *Frühe Predigten (1909–1918)* (Berlin, 1993), p. 374; Karl Schwarzlose, *Krieg und Aberglaube: Predigt gehalten in der St Katharinen-Kirche zu Frankfurt a. M.* (Berlin, 1915), p. 9.
36. Ziemann, *War Experiences in Rural Germany*, p. 133; LkA EKvW 4.53 (Archiv der Ev. Kg. Hiddenhausen), Nr. 958; https://archiveowl.wordpress.com/1914/10/15/meyersieck03/, accessed 24 June 2018.
37. *La Cloche: écho paroissial de Guémené*, 4 October 1914, 6; *Le Courrier de Saint-Gervais*, 1 October 1914, 157; *Bulletin paroissial lorrain* [Diocèse de Nancy] (September 1915), 5.
38. Roure, 'Superstitions du front de guerre', 711.
39. *The Cornishman*, 5 November 1914.
40. *Irish Times*, 8 February 1917.
41. *The Daily Republican* (Rushville, IN), 15 November 1917.
42. *The Jewelers' Circular* 76 (1918), 97.
43. Eleanor Johnson, *Ladies Dress Accessories*, new edn (Princes Risborough, 2004), p. 22; Nina Edward, *Dressed for War: Uniform, Civilian Clothing and Trappings 1914–1918* (London, 2015), p. 98; http://artofmourning.com/2011/05/08/symbolism-sunday-mizpah/, accessed 24 June 2018.
44. *Bridgeport Telegram*, 26 August 1918.
45. *Le Temps*, 2 November 1915.
46. Reprinted in Roure, 'Superstitions du front de guerre', 709–10.
47. Owen Davies, *Grimoires: A History of Magic Books* (Oxford, 2009), pp. 191–7, 206–7.
48. Christoph Daxelmüller, 'Forward', Bächtold-Stäubli and Hoffmann-Krayer (eds), *Handwörterbuch des deutschen Aberglaubens*, p. xviii; Hanns Bächtold-Stäubli, *Leben und Sprache Schweizer Soldaten* (Basle, 1916), p. 25.
49. Gisela Griepentrog, 'Himmelsbrief und Kugelsegen. Aberglauben im Krieg', in *Der Erste Weltkrieg in und um Fürstenwalde 1914–1918* (Jacobsdorf, 2004), p. 96.
50. *Weekly Freeman's Journal*, 1 May 1915.
51. Cited in Becker, *War and Faith*, p. 93.
52. Snape, *God and the British Soldier*, p. 234.
53. *Liverpool Daily Post*, 1 December 1914; *Chelmsford Chronicle*, 29 January 1915; Michael MacDonagh, *The Irish on the Somme* (London, 1917), p. 99.
54. *Harrogate Herald*, 21 March 1917.
55. *Sheffield Evening Telegraph*, 27 May 1915. See also Snape, *God and the British Soldier*, pp. 42–3.
56. *Burnley News*, 8 September 1915.
57. *Grantham Journal*, 22 January 1916.
58. Roure, 'Superstitions du front de guerre', 725.
59. Saunders, *Trench Art*, pp. 100–2; Nicholas Saunders, 'Kruzifix, Kalvarienberg und Kreuz: Materialität und Spiritualität in den Landschaften des Ersten Weltkrieges', in Korff (ed.), *Alliierte im Himmel*, pp. 291–311.

60. *The Scotsman*, 19 August 1916.

61. MacDonagh, *Irish on the Somme*, p. 100; Ziemann, *War Experiences in Rural Germany*, p. 131.

62. Stiaccini, *L'anima religiosa*, p. 109; MacDonagh, *Irish on the Somme*, p. 97; *Yorkshire Evening Post*, 8 November 1916.

63. MacDonagh, *Irish on the Somme*, pp. 90, 95.

64. MacDonagh, *Irish on the Somme*, p. 90.

65. Parsons, *I Flew*, p. 228.

66. MacDonagh, *Irish on the Somme*, p. 102.

67. Caravaglios, *L'anima religiosa della guerra*, p. 110.

68. *The Jewelers' Circular*, 28 August 1918.

69. See, for example, Paul Fussell, *Wartime: Understanding and Behavior in the Second World War* (Oxford, 1989), p. 49; Michael Snape, *God and Uncle Sam: Religion and America's Armed Forces in World War II* (Woodbridge, 2015), p. 358; Snape, *God and the British Soldier*, p. 35; Chambers, 'Fighting Chance', p. 254.

70. Caravaglios, *L'anima religiosa della guerra*, p. 124; MacDonagh, *Irish on the Somme*, p. 90.

71. *The Tablet*, 7 January 1911.

72. *The Tablet*, 17 October 1914.

73. *Dundalk Examiner and Louth Advertiser*, 11 September 1915.

74. MacDonagh, *Irish on the Somme*, p. 101; *Globe*, 19 April 1918; *Motherwell Times*, 7 June 1918; *Liverpool Echo*, 16 May 1918.

75. MacDonagh, *Irish on the Somme*, pp. 99, 100.

76. *Weekly Freeman's Journal*, 4 November 1917.

77. Charles Calippe, *La Guerre en Picardie* (Paris, 1916), p. 46.

78. MacDonagh, *Irish on the Somme*, p. 100.

79. Becker, *War and Faith*, pp. 75–85; Caravaglios, *L'anima religiosa della guerra*, pp. 161–92; Houlihan, *Catholicism and the Great War*, p. 127.

80. Stiaccini, *L'anima religiosa*, p. 137.

81. Stiaccini, *L'anima religiosa*, p. 138.

82. *Pluie de roses: interventions de Sr Thérèse de l'Enfant-Jésus pendant la guerre* (Bayeux, 1920). For context on its publication, see Antoinette Guise, 'Les Miracles de Sœur Thérèse de l'Enfant-Jésus entre 1898 et 1926: genèse d'un culte', Mémoire de D. E. A., École pratique des Hautes Études, 2000; Thomas R. Nevin, *The Last Years of Saint Thérèse: Doubt and Darkness, 1895–1897* (Oxford, 2013), p. 265.

83. *Interventions*, pp. 12, 21–2, 42–3, 74.

84. *Interventions*, pp. 9, 16–17.

85. Raymond Jonas, *France and the Cult of the Sacred Heart: An Epic Tale for Modern Times* (Berkeley, CA, 2000).

86. Ziemann, *War Experiences in Rural Germany*, p. 26.

87. *Le Temps*, 4 November 1914.

88. Claudia Schlager, *Kult und Krieg: Herz Jesu-Sacré Cœur-Christus Rex im deutsch-französischen Vergleich 1914–1925* (Tübingen, 2011), p. 74.

89. See Raymond Jonas, *The Tragic Tale of Claire Ferchaud and the Great War* (Berkeley, CA, 2005); Becker, *War and Faith*, pp. 85–96.

90. MacDonagh, *Irish on the Somme*, p. 94.

91. *Skibbereen Eagle*, 7 August 1915.

92. MacDonagh, *Irish on the Somme*, pp. 95, 91; see also, Becker, *War and Faith*, p. 96.

93. *Le Petit Écho du 21ᵉ Régiment d'infanterie* (September 1917), 8.

94. *Freemans Journal*, 9 July 1915.

95. *Freemans Journal*, 19 July 1918.

96. W. S. Leake, *How to Protect our Soldiers* (San Francisco, 1917), pp. 22, 23.

97. Bryan R. Wilson, *Sects and Society: A Sociological Study of the Elim Tabernacle, Christian Science, and Christadelphians* (Berkeley, CA, 1961), p. 149.

98. Wilson, *Sects and Society*, p. 153; Callum G. Brown, *Religion and Society in Twentieth-Century Britain* (London, 2006), p. 103.

99. *Christian Science War Time Activities: A Report to the Board of Directors of the Mother Church by the Christian Science War Relief Committee* (Boston, MA, 1922), pp. 133–43.

100. *Christian Science Sentinel*, 24 November 1917, 254.

101. *Christian Science Sentinel*, 6 July 1918, 894.

102. Michael Lucas, *The Journey's End Battalion: The 9th East Surrey in the Great War* (Barnsley, 2012); CWGC: http://www.cwgc.org/find-war-dead/casualty/ 541128/ERICSON,%20ERIC%20CHARLES, accessed 24 June 2018.

103. *Christian Science Sentinel*, 22 November 1919, 234.

104. *Christian Science Sentinel*, 31 August 1918, 1054.

105. Braden, *Spirits in Rebellion*, pp. 233–64; Roy M. Anker, *Self-Help and Popular Religion in Early American Culture: An Interpretive Guide* (Westport, CT, 1999), pp. 213–21; Catherine L. Albanese, *A Republic of Mind and Spirit: A Cultural History of American Metaphysical Religion* (New Haven, CT, 2007), pp. 327–9, 430–6.

106. *Unity* 41 (1914) 258–9.

107. *Unity* 42 (1915) 160–1.

108. *Unity* 49 (1918) n.p.

109. *Boston Sunday Post*, 24 December 1916.

110. F. L. Rawson, *Man's Powers and Work, etc.* (London, 1914), pp. 30–2.

111. *The Pittsburgh Press*, 3 September 1905. Hearst's holiday is described in Ben Procter, *William Randolph Hearst: The Early Years, 1863–1910* (Oxford, 1998), p. 204.

112. *Manchester Courier*, 2 August 1905.

113. Charles S. Braden, *Spirits in Rebellion: The Rise and Development of New Thought* (Dallas, TX, 1963), pp. 431–40; Claire F. Gartrell-Mills, 'Christian Science: An American Religion in Britain, 1895–1940', DPhil thesis, Oxford University, 1991, 72, 314–17.

114. John K. Simmons, 'Charisma and Covenant: The Christian Science Movement in its Initial Postcharismatic Phase', in Timothy Miller (ed.), *When*

Prophets Die: The Postcharismatic Fate of New Religious Movements (Albany, NY, 1991), p. 116. On malicious animal magnetism, see Owen Davies, *America Bewitched: The Story of Witchcraft after Salem* (Oxford, 2013), pp. 95–9.

115. E. S. Turner, *Dear Old Blighty* (London, 1980), p. 140.

116. *Bullet-Proof Soldiers*, p. 6.

117. *Bullet-Proof Soldiers*, pp. 7–8.

118. Gibbs, *Now It Can Be Told*, p. 399.

119. *Kent and Sussex Courier*, 12 January 1917.

120. *Birmingham Daily Post*, 20 November 1917.

121. *The Daily Clintonian*, 18 March 1920; *Anaconda Standard*, 16 November 1923; *The Daily News* (Frederick), 14 November 1923; *The Times*, 13 November 1923; *Western Daily Press*, 13 November 1923.

122. *Mind and Memory* (New York, 1920), p. 10.

123. Graham Seal, *The Soldiers' Press: Trench Journals in the First World War* (Basingstoke, 2013), p. 31.

124. *The Tablet*, 20 July 1918.

125. See Callum G. Brown, *Religion and Society in Twentieth-Century Britain* (London, 2006), p. 103. See also Rhodri Hayward, *The Transformation of the Psyche in British Primary Care, 1870–1970* (London, 2014), pp. 22, 99.

126. *Stars and Stripes*, 19 April 1918.

127. *The Jewish Veteran* 7–9 (1938), 10–14.

128. Ekkehart P. Guth, 'Ottoman Empire', in Spencer C. Tucker (ed.), *The European Powers in the First World War: An Encyclopedia* (New York, 2013), p. 527; Santanu Das, 'Introduction', in Santanu Das (ed.), *Race, Empire and First World War Writing* (Cambridge, 2011); Christian Koller, 'Colonial Military Participation in Europe (Africa)', http://encyclopedia.1914-1918-online.net/article/colonial_military_participation_in_europe_africa, accessed 24 June 2018.

129. Joshua Trachtenberg, *Jewish Magic and Superstition: A Study in Folk Religion* (New York, 1939), p. 147; Leah Rachel Yoffie, 'Popular Beliefs and Customs among the Yiddish-Speaking Jews of St. Louis, MO', *Journal of American Folklore* 38 (1925), 376; Pierre Hirsch, *De Moïse à Jésus: confession d'un juif* (Paris, 1933), p. 193; Becker, *War and Faith*, p. 61. On Jewish religion at the front, see, for example, David J. Fine, *Jewish Integration in the German Army in the First World War* (Berlin, 2012), pp. 19–71.

130. Jonathan Fishburn, *The Jewish Experience* (London, 2007), p. 14.

131. T. E. Lawrence, *Seven Pillars of Wisdom*, Introduction by Angus Calder (Ware, 1997), p. 295.

132. Jan Knappert, *Swahili Islamic Poetry* (Leiden, 1971), vol. 1, p. 75.

133. See Richard S. Fogarty, 'Islam in the French Army during the Great War: Between Accommodation and Suspicion', in Eric Storm and Ali Al Tuma (eds), *Colonial Soldiers in Europe, 1914–1945: 'Aliens in Uniform' in Wartime Societies* (New York, 2016), pp. 23–41.

134. *Le Temps*, 16 March 1915.
135. See, for example, Jaffur Shurreef, *Islam in India* (London [1832], 1999), p. 260.
136. Omissi, *Indian Voices of the Great War*, pp. 342–3.
137. Edmund Dane, *British Campaigns in Africa and the Pacific, 1914–1918* (London, 1919), p. 82.
138. Karen Petrone, *The Great War in Russian Memory* (Bloomington, IN, 2011), p. 47; Bakary Diallo, *Force-Bonté* (Paris, 1926), pp. 112–13; Le Naour, *Nostradamus*, p. 90; János Riesz and Aija Bjornson, 'The *Tirailleur Sénégalais* Who Did Not Want to Be a "Grand Enfant": Bakary Diallo's *Force Bonté* (1926) Reconsidered', *Research in African Literatures* 27 (1996), 157–79.
139. Caravaglios, *L'anima religiosa della guerra*, p. 128; Hirsch, *De Moïse à Jésus*, p. 193; 'Narratives from the War', *American Journal of Nursing* 16 (1916), 1212.

Chapter 7

1. Charles Madge and Tom Harrisson, *Britain by Mass Observation* (London, 1939), pp. 19, 21, 22.
2. Winter, *Sites of Memory, Sites of Mourning*, p. 178; Paul Fussell, *The Great War and Modern Memory* (London, 1975), p. 115.
3. For recent revisionist assessments of European 'disenchantment' in terms of supernatural belief, see Alexandra Walsham, 'The Reformation and "the Disenchantment of the World"', *Historical Journal* 51 (2008), 497–528; Peter Marshall, 'Disenchantment and Re-Enchantment in Europe, 1250–1920', *Historical Journal* 54, 2 (2011), 599–606; Karl Bell, 'Breaking Modernity's Spell: Magic and Modern History', *Cultural & Social History* 4 (2007), 115–23; Wouter J. Hanegraaff, 'How Magic Survived the Disenchantment of the World', *Religion* 33 (2003), 357–80; Michael D. Bailey, 'The Disenchantment of Magic: Spells, Charms, and Superstition in Early European Witchcraft Literature', *American Historical Review* 111 (2006), 383–404.
4. Peter N. Sterns, 'Periodization in Social History', in Peter N. Stearns (ed.), *Encyclopaedia of European Social History, 1350–2000* (New York, 2001), pp. 125–30; Béla Tomka, *A Social History of Twentieth-Century Europe* (London, 2013), pp. 424–7. See also Ludmilla Jordanova, *History in Practice* (London, 2000), pp. 114–40.
5. See Davies, *Witchcraft, Magic and Culture*, pp. 278–94.
6. Johann Kruse, *Hexen unter uns? Magie und Zauberglauben in unserer Zeit* (Hamburg, 1951), pp. 76–7, 80.
7. *Lincolnshire Standard and Boston Guardian*, 8 July 1922; *Yorkshire Post and Leeds Intelligencer*, 24 April 1928.
8. *Daily Herald*, 10 April 1929. For American examples, see Davies, *America Bewitched*.

9. See, for example, Willem de Blécourt, 'The Witch, her Victim, the Un-witcher and the Researcher: The Continued Existence of Traditional Witch-craft', in Willem de Blécourt, Ronald Hutton, and Jean La Fontaine, *Witchcraft and Magic in Europe: The Twentieth Century* (London, 1999), pp. 141–220; Owen Davies, 'Witchcraft Accusations in France, 1850–1990', in Willem de Blécourt and Owen Davies (eds), *Witchcraft Continued: Popular Magic in Modern Europe* (Manchester, 2003), pp. 107–33; Thomas Waters, 'Maleficent Witchcraft in Britain since 1900', *Historical Workshop Journal* 80 (2015), 101–6.

10. Marion Gibson, *Rediscovering Renaissance Witchcraft* (Abingdon, 2018), pp. 58–76.

11. Gibson, *Rediscovering Renaissance Witchcraft*, p. 73.

12. Nelson, *Spiritualism and Society*, pp. 157–64.

13. Jenny Hazelgrove, *Spiritualism and British Society between the Wars* (Manchester, 2000), p. 15.

14. Madge and Harrisson, *Britain by Mass Observation*, p. 22.

15. Hazelgrove, *Spiritualism*, pp. 36–7.

16. Brady Brower, *Unruly Spirits*, pp. 93–112; Sofie Lachapelle, *Investigating the Supernatural: From Spiritism and Occultism to Psychical Research and Metapsychics in France, 1853–1931* (Baltimore, MD, 2011), pp. 113–17; Eric Kurlander, *Hitler's Monsters: A Supernatural History of the Third Reich* (New Haven, CT, and London, 2017), pp. 66–7; Wolffram, *The Stepchildren of Science*, p. 142.

17. For a recent provocative reading of the cultural consequences, see Beth A. Robertson, *Science of the Seance: Transnational Networks and Gendered Bodies in the Study of Psychic Phenomena, 1918–1940* (Vancouver, 2016).

18. Carlson, *No Religion Higher than Truth*, p. 176; Staudenmaier, *Between Occultism and Nazism*, pp. 111–12.

19. Maunder, *Our Lady of the Nations*, pp. 84–99; Tine Van Osselaer, 'A Question of Competence and Authority: Lay Views on the Medical Examinations of the Marian Apparition Series in 1930s Belgium', in Tine Van Osselaer, Henk de Smaele, and Kaat Wils (eds), *Sign or Symptom? Exceptional Corporeal Phenomena in Religion and Medicine in the Nineteenth and Twentieth Centuries* (Leuven, 2017), pp. 163–87.

20. Maunder, *Our Lady of the Nations*, pp. 99–108.

21. Edelman, *Histoire de la voyance*, pp. 158–70; Howe, *Urania's Children*, pp. 77, 87–103.

22. Wright, *English Folklore*, p. 63.

23. Nicholas Campion, *Astrology and Popular Religion in the Modern West: Prophecy, Cosmology and the New Age Movement* (London, 2012), pp. 77–8.

24. *The Sphere*, 23 January 1932.

25. For example, *Nelson Leader*, 7 July 1933.

26. Madge and Harrisson, *Britain by Mass Observation*, pp. 19, 20.

27. M.O.A., 'Belief in the Supernatural', 15/5/1942; M.O.A., 'Report on Death and the Supernatural', 18/6/42, p. 4.
28. Malcolm Gaskill, *Hellish Nell: Last of Britain's Witches* (London, 2001), pp. 181–223; Nelson, *Spiritualism and Society*, p. 164.
29. *Shipley Times and Express*, 18 June 1941.
30. *Western Morning News*, 14 April 1941.
31. *Sunderland Daily Echo and Shipping Gazette*, 7 November 1940; *Daily Mirror*, 5 May 1944.
32. See, for example, Reginald T. Naish, *Is it Peace or War? On Biblical Prophecy in Relation to Contemporary Events* (London, 1937); R. S. Newcomb, *The War in the Light of Prophecy: Is This Armageddon?* (Auckland, 1940); Georges Anquetil, *L'Anti-Nostradamus ou vrais et faux prophètes* (Paris, 1940).
33. Max de Fontbrune [Max Pigeard de Gurbert], *Les Prophéties de Maistre Michel Nostradamus, expliquées et commentées* (Sarlat 1939); Edelman, *Histoire de la voyance*, p. 167. See also Le Naour, *Nostradamus*, pp. 152–5.
34. Judith Devlin, *The Superstitious Mind: French Peasants and the Supernatural in the Nineteenth Century* (New Haven, CT, 1987), p. 149; Marie Bonaparte, *Myths of War*, trans. John Rodker (London, 1947), p. 72; Barbara Will, *Unlikely Collaboration: Gertrude Stein, Bernard Faÿ, and the Vichy Dilemma* (New York, 2011), p. 120.
35. P. Ellerhorst, *Prophezeiungen über das Schicksal Europas* (Munich, 1951), p. 38; Peter Fritzsche, *An Iron Wind: Europe under Hitler* (New York, 2016).
36. Bonaparte, *Myths of War*, pp. 13–41; Gottfried Gansinger, *Nationalsozialismus im Bezirk Ried im Innkreis: Widerstand und Verfolgung 1938–1945* (Innsbruck, 2016); Ellerhorst, *Prophezeiungen*, p. 37.
37. Gary Alan Fine and Jacqueline Boles, 'Chain Letters', in Simon J. Bronner (ed.), *Encyclopedia of American Folklife* (New York, 2015), p. 167.
38. *Nebraska State Journal*, 14 March 1939.
39. *Sunday Mail* (Brisbane), 22 September 1940; *Chelmsford Chronicle*, 23 February 1940.
40. Jean Hungerford, 'The Exploitation of Superstitions for Purposes of Psychological Warfare', Rand Corporation report (1950), Appendix A.
41. Wright, *English Folklore*, pp. 71–2.
42. M.O.A., 'Astrology and Spiritualism, 1938–1947', 25/7/1940; Geoffrey Gorer, *Exploring English Character* (London, 1955), p. 265.
43. *Leeds Mercury*, 4 January 1937. See also Snape, *God and the British Soldier*, p. 31; Parker, *Faith on the Home Front*, p. 87.
44. *Dundee Evening Telegraph*, 5 December 1939.
45. Edwin G. Boring (ed.), *Psychology for the Armed Services* (Washington DC, 1945), p. 423.
46. S. P. MacKenzie, *Flying against Fate: Superstition and Allied Aircrews in World War II* (Lawrence, KS, 2017); Fussell, *Wartime: Understanding and Behavior*, pp. 48–51; Michael Snape, *God and Uncle Sam: Religion and America's Armed Forces in World War II* (Woodbridge, 2015), pp. 356–61; Chambers, 'Fighting Chance', 74–84;

Kevin L. Walters, 'Beyond the Battlefield: Religion and American Troops in World War II', PhD thesis, University of Kentucky, 2013, 105–31.

47. *Federal Trade Commission Decisions* 40 (1947), 29–34; Walters, 'Beyond the Battlefield', 111.

48. Mackenzie, *Flying against Fate*, p. 29.

49. Snape, *God and Uncle Sam*, p. 359; Snape, *God and the British Soldier*, p. 35.

50. Friedbert Ficker '"Wer diesen Brief bei sich hat . . .": Anmerkungen zu einem "Haus- und Schutzbrief"', *Traditiones* 36 (2007), 191–5; Hungerford, 'The Exploitation of Superstitions', Appendix A; David W. Kriebel, *Powwowing among the Pennsylvania Dutch: A Traditional Medical Practice in the Modern World* (University Park, PA, 2007), p. 20.

51. 'NJWB and the Chaplains', *Heritage: Newsletter of the American Jewish Historical Society* 1, 2 (2003), 19; *Jewish Language Review* 7 (1987), 417.

52. *Linlithgowshire Gazette*, 22 December 1939; Johann Chapoutot, *Greeks, Romans, Germans: How the Nazis Usurped Europe's Classical Past*, trans. Richard R. Nybakken (Oakland, CA, 2016), p. 234; Hungerford, 'The Exploitation of Superstitions', p. 5; *Sheffield Evening Telegraph*, 11 October 1939; *Birmingham Daily Gazette*, 6 October 1942.

53. Robert Henry Knapp, 'A Psychology of Rumor', *Public Opinion Quarterly* 8 (1944), 22–37; C. Faye, 'Governing the Grapevine: The Study of Rumor during World War II', *History of Psychology* 10 (2007), 1–21.

54. Hungerford, 'The Exploitation of Superstitions', p. 3.

55. Louis P. Lochner, *The Goebbels Diaries, 1942–1943* (New York, 1948), p. 193.

56. Willi A. Boelcke and Ewald Osers, *The Secret Conferences of Dr Goebbels, October 1939–March 1943* (London, 1970), p. 6; Howe, *Urania's Children*, pp. 164–6; Kurlander, *Hitler's Monsters*, p. 218.

57. Lochner, *The Goebbels Diaries*, p. 220.

58. Chambers, 'Fighting Chance', pp. 177–8.

59. Chambers, 'Fighting Chance', p. 189.

60. Elizabeth P. MacDonald, *Undercover Girl* (New York, 1947), pp. 200–1.

61. Monica Black, 'The Ghosts of War', in Michael Geyer and Adam Tooze (eds), *The Cambridge History of the Second World War*, vol. 3: *Total War: Economy, Society and Culture* (Cambridge, 2015); H. J. Pinstschovius, '"Heute wie zu allen Zeiten . . .": Hexerei vor deutschen Gerichten', in D. Harmening and D. Bauer (eds), *Hexen heute: Magische Traditionen und neue Zutaten* (Wurzburg, 1991), pp. 79–85; de Blécourt, 'The Witch, her Victim', p. 214; Davies, *Grimoires*, p. 254; Monica Black, 'Miracles in the Shadow of the Economic Miracle: The "Supernatural '50s" in West Germany', *Journal of Modern History* 84 (2012), 833–60; Owen Davies, 'Magic in Common and Legal Perspectives', in David J. Collins (ed.), *The Cambridge History of Magic and Witchcraft in the West: From Antiquity to the Present* (Cambridge, 2015), p. 542; Davies, *Witchcraft, Magic and Culture*, pp. 73–5.

PICTURE ACKNOWLEDGEMENTS

1.1, 2.1, 3.1, 3.2, 5.1, 5.2, 5.3, 5.4, 5.5, 5.6, 5.7, 5.8, 5.9, 6.1, 6.2, 6.3, 6.4: Author's collection; 2.2: Madame de Thèbes/Agence Meurisse. 1913. Photo courtesy Bibliothèque nationale de France; 2.3: *Wiener Caricaturen*, 8 October 1916. Photo courtesy Austrian National Library; 5.10: *La Baïonnette*, 4 July 2018. Photo courtesy Bibliothèque nationale de France

INDEX

Note: Italicized page numbers indicate illustrations.